W9-BTG-177

Roads Taken

Roads Taken

The Professorial Life,
Scholarship in Place,
and the Public Good

Edited by

Roger Epp and
Bill Spellman

Truman State University Press
Kirksville, Missouri

Copyright © 2014 Truman State University Press, Kirksville, Missouri 63501
All rights reserved
tsup.truman.edu

Cover photograph by Milton Schlosser.

Cover design: Teresa Wheeler

Library of Congress Cataloging-in-Publication Data
Roads taken (2014)
 Roads taken : the professorial life, scholarship in place, and the public good / edited by Roger Epp and Bill Spellman.
        pages cm
Includes bibliographical references.
ISBN 978-1-61248-104-3 (pbk. : alk. paper) — ISBN 978-1-61248-105-0 (e-book)
1. College teachers—Attitudes. 2. College teaching. 3. Learning and scholarship. 4. Common good. 5. Education, Higher—Aims and objectives. I. Epp, Roger, editor of compilation. II. Spellman, W. M., editor of compilation. III. Title.
LB1778.R63 2014
378.1'25—dc23
                                                                    2013045537

No part of this work may be reproduced or transmitted in any format by any means without written permission from the publisher.

The paper in this publication meets or exceeds the minimum requirements of the American National Standard for Information Sciences—Permanence of Paper for Printed Library Materials, ANSI Z39.48–1992.

Contents

Acknowledgments

The editors wish to acknowledge the COPLAC board for its affirmation of this project from the start and its financial support in bringing the contributors together in June 2013 to share drafts and workshop the manuscript. Senior administrators at each of the participating campuses also provided travel assistance to their faculty colleagues. Sarah Olivo at COPLAC provided invaluable support to the workshop. We are grateful to the anonymous reviewer who provided timely criticism and guidance on each of the essays, together with solid suggestions for the thematic organization of the essays. The professionals at Truman State University Press worked skillfully under tight deadlines and were always available when expert advice was needed. In particular, we wish to thank Nancy Rediger, Director and Editor-in-Chief at Truman State University Press, who oversaw the early stages of production, and copy editor Barbara Smith-Mandell, who gently and efficiently advanced the typescript through to final publication. Finally, we wish to thank each of the contributors to the volume for their timely submissions and revisions, their patience, and their collegial support for the editorial team and for each other in the development of chapters from first to final drafts. We've come to know them as outstanding people as well as scholars. They've made our work on this volume a matter of pleasure.

Introduction
Roads Taken

Roger Epp and Bill Spellman

Liberal arts colleges are home to professors who, sometimes to their own surprise, find themselves teaching on campuses unlike the larger research universities at which they earned PhDs, and who then, not always easily, find their place *as scholars* and flourish in ways that also enlarge the public missions of their institutions. Such stories are, in fact, hardly uncommon. They speak to the promise of what Sam Schuman in *Old Main: Small Colleges in Twenty-First Century America* called the integrated life—one in which the work of teaching, scholarship, and citizenship is joined in ways that mirror a holistic undergraduate education in intimate campus settings.[1] But the same stories are reminders that the cultural gaps within higher education are real; that the advantages of liberal arts colleges are not for everyone, and not always so obvious at the start; that there are no guarantees of successful adaptation; and that for all those reasons the task of faculty orientation and renewal must be a matter of sustained institutional attention. In every generation it requires pathfinders, exemplars, personal stories.

This is a book of such stories, told by professors who represent a range of career stages and disciplines across the arts and sciences. Though they are drawn from North American campuses within a particular sector of higher education—that of public liberal arts colleges[2]—we expect that their accounts will resonate with colleagues in other kinds of institutions as well; for the transitions from PhD to professorship, the rhythms of academic careers, the enlistment into the civic cultures and collegial governance of campuses, and the commitment to teach well in the face of serious workplace challenges are broadly similar across the academy. At the same time, they are too rarely the subject of serious self-reflection.[3]

1

This book rests on three central premises. The first is that the future of liberal education, public and private, rests with professors—especially the next generation of them—who will live out its aspirations in intelligent, creative, and sustainable ways. Their work, in other words, is more fundamental than savvy marketing, new funding sources, or articulate, dynamic leadership, important as those things are; and it is integral to renewed curricula, the right mix of learning technologies, community engagement, and most other proposed cures. The second premise is that personal stories will be more compelling than social-scientific data in inviting new faculty to imagine meaningful career trajectories and integrated scholarly lives for themselves. The third premise provides the framework for this book project: that such careers will often require *multiple* adaptations—among them, to undergraduate teaching on small campuses, to living in places outside the continent's intellectual-cultural capitals, and, increasingly, to the public mission that connects colleges to the well-being of regional communities.

A generation ago, the anthropologist Clifford Geertz described the peculiar patterns of academic careers in terms of an "exile from Eden syndrome." By that he meant that inductees into the profession typically are trained at "the center of things," at a small number of elite doctoral programs, and then, for the most part, must move "toward the edges," to some "region lower down, further out," to take up a professorial appointment.[4] Few make their way back. Some, alas, never get over it. Geertz's spatial metaphors, horizontal and vertical, are telling. They suggest both the real separation of distance from clusters of disciplinary colleagues, experienced as a kind of loneliness, as well as the power of reputational hierarchies in higher education. A generation later, the academic job market is, if anything, even tighter, even if it now includes a growing stratum of community colleges. The prestige factor meanwhile is as strong as ever.[5] The preeminence of the major research universities and the desire for respectability, both institutional and individual, measured by the standards they set have been identified as among the significant threats to liberal arts colleges and the distinctive educational option they have represented for students.[6]

While Geertz may have exaggerated or simplified the career motivations of doctoral candidates to make a point—some of them, after all, will have earned baccalaureate degrees at liberal arts colleges and want to return to teach in such a setting—the patterns to which he pointed have implications that still bear consideration. There *are* cultural divides in higher education. Liberal arts colleges *are* different from major research and regional comprehensive universities. Whether public or private, they generally are smaller in scale. Their missions are more likely to stress undergraduate teaching, a common curriculum, and a holistic student experience, including on-campus residences.[7] Not least, liberal arts colleges are more likely to be found in smaller centers, where their founders might once have imagined idyllic or else ascetic havens, fit for learning, away from the clamor and temptations associated with big cities. None of these differences, of course, is absolute. The goals and the language of liberal education have their champions in large research universities. Land-grant institutions can be larger than the towns adjacent to them. Liberal arts colleges, for their part, can include small graduate programs, often in professional fields, often to serve regional vocational needs. In recent years they have embraced and touted the relative advantages of size in providing one-on-one undergraduate research opportunities to students. Moreover, given the economic, technological, cultural, and political challenges facing all sectors, the defense of quality in higher education is, at some level, a shared enterprise.

In one important structural respect, though, the difference between liberal arts colleges and research universities is definitive: the former are not self-generative. They do not produce their own next generations of faculty. Instead, they hire PhDs trained in elite research universities, which serve to orient students to disciplines, the academy, and the expectations that attend a scholarly career.[8] By design or default, that orientation is essentially a matter of self-replication—however poorly it may match the changing employment realities in higher education. As David Kirp, a professor of public policy at the University of California, Berkeley, puts it, disapprovingly, professors "discourage [their] best students from considering careers in liberal arts colleges, instead preparing them for positions in research universities—that is, after all, where academic reputations are made."[9]

Our purpose here is not to denigrate research universities. One of us now teaches at one. It is rather to underline the importance of adaptation and reorientation to the different contexts, cultures, and expectations that PhD graduates invariably encounter when they take positions at liberal arts colleges. It is also to revalue such positions as much more than consolation prizes or second-best outcomes—the kind that need to be explained apologetically to peers and disappointed supervisors. The stories in this collection suggest otherwise. We count our own among them.

Bill

I disregarded the sober advice of my undergraduate mentor. He and his department colleagues cautioned me against graduate training in history in light of the difficult job market awaiting newly minted PhDs in the mid-1980s. They were right, of course. I completed my dissertation in 1986 and published it with Oxford University Press the following year. As soon as the typescript was accepted, I began applying for positions across the United States, hoping that the book would put me over the top. And while I would have preferred the research-intensive professional lifestyle of my dissertation advisor, if necessary I was prepared to begin my career at either a regional comprehensive or a small liberal arts college.

But beginning was not easy. After two years, no campus interviews, and 151 rejection letters, I was invited to fly out of the urban northeast and compete for a post at a small public liberal arts institution in southern Appalachia. By this point in my non-career I had lots of adjunct teaching experience, the book had received generally positive reviews, and I was well into a second research project. I wanted this interview and thought I could beat the odds in the on-campus competition.

After the hiring miracle took place in the spring of 1988, I began my first semester with three preparations and four classes, served as faculty advisor to the department's student organization, and joined a search committee for a new department colleague. It was a demanding but exhilarating semester, even if my scholarly output was reduced to one book review. I found myself amidst supportive and hard working colleagues who invested themselves in my success. Most importantly my students, the majority of whom were, like me, first in family to attend college, were generally dedicated and eager to learn. Some were balancing multiple obligations: living at home with parents, supporting children of their own, and working part-time to achieve their dream of a college degree. I saw a bit of myself in these students, and over the course of that first year I gradually let go the paradigm for professional success that had been inculcated at graduate school.

Over the next few years I found myself developing and teaching interdisciplinary courses with colleagues from across campus. I continued to teach four classes, but each was small enough (18–22 students) to facilitate community building. I engaged with student affairs professionals on service projects, served on multiple university committees and ad hoc planning groups, and yes, continued to write, albeit at a

modest pace. My writing increasingly reflected my broad teaching interests, and no one on the tenure committee called the question when the
historian of early modern England started publishing monographs on the
recent history of international migration and freshman-level textbooks
on Western civilization. I was now teaching and writing in a manner that
encouraged work across disciplinary boundaries—the very approach to
learning that we tell our students is necessary to their success as citizens and professionals in the twenty-first century. Over the years my
colleagues generously allowed me to chair a department, direct an
all-college core program, and serve as a divisional dean. One quarter
century after that flood of rejection letters, the small public liberal arts
setting still comes to the rescue, still offers opportunities to engage pro-
ductively with others, especially with undergraduates, and always in a
learning environment on a human scale.

Of the three adaptations identified above, the adaptation of new professors
to a campus context in which undergraduate teaching is the highest priority for their time and tenure dossiers will be the most familiar—though
it is no easier to accomplish for all that. On arrival, those new professors
will quickly become generalists in small departments. Rather than being
assigned to teach in a narrow subject range, one that is tied to and reinforces their research specialization, they will stretch across the subfields of
their discipline. They may also be asked to contribute to a core-curricular
or general education course. They may experience all this as either liber-
ating or intimidating—or both. They will have more freedom to introduce
courses of interest and propose changes to the requirements for majors.
But they will also simply spend more time in the classroom than their
graduate-school peers who have landed at research universities. In addition, they may be asked to mentor students and take on other "service"
obligations—committees, clubs, coaching, conferences—often without
compensatory adjustments to their teaching assignment. They get to know
students outside the classroom, and show other sides of themselves. If they
are fortunate, they will have senior colleagues who do this happily, who
seem to regard their work on a small campus as "a lifestyle, even a passion,"
"not a job,"[10] who attend concerts and home games, and who have grown
accustomed to the lack of anonymity on campus.

In this context, the advice of former supervisors about how to achieve tenure may not always be helpful for new professors at liberal arts colleges, who will not be assessed primarily on the basis of publications and grants, and who will need to take local guidance about expectations given a different teaching-research balance. They may hear conflicting messages. They know they will not have the equipment, travel funds, or, in the sciences, the cadre of graduate students to sustain the kind of research program around which they were once encouraged to imagine an academic career. The time for them to be single-minded scholars may be limited to a fraction of the summer. Sabbaticals may or may not be available. In any event these new professors must find, and sometimes will struggle to find, a more modest scholarship program that fits their circumstances. It might have a local connection. It might involve undergraduates in ways that join teaching and research, not put them in tension.

In addition to the adjustments required in the standard categories of professorial work, faculty at liberal arts colleges live closer to a deeper existential challenge, a crisis of identity. While higher education generally is now the site of much restructuring and creative disruption, few doubt that the major research and regional comprehensive universities will continue to exist in some recognizable form well into the future, albeit likely with a diminished humanities presence. They are, as the saying goes, too big to fail. They are tightly integrated into regional economies; government-industry agendas for science, technology, and commercialization; and the professional labor market needs of health-care systems for North America's aging populations. Liberal arts colleges as a sector face a more precarious future. They live with periodic predictions of their demise and the sober reality that peer institutions have disappeared or abandoned their mission in recent decades.[11] On one hand, they still have eloquent champions in high places who value their role in shaping well-rounded citizens, leaders, and multiskilled employees.[12] Indeed, the model has been transplanted of late into the emerging economies of China, Brazil, and central Europe. On the other hand, though, liberal arts colleges on the traditional four-year residential model are particularly vulnerable to political and societal expectations with respect to online learning, student transfer mobility, vocational preparation ("a major that leads to a job!"), and the availability of degree-completion options close enough to enable not just adult students but also the children of the shrinking middle class to live at home while taking courses. For understandable reasons, credentialing and accessibility have moved to the forefront of the public policy agenda for higher education. The qualitative advantages of a liberal arts college and the holistic experience it offers are sometimes most apparent years after graduation.

Liberal arts colleges do not all fit equally into the crisis scenario we have painted. We have reason to think, in particular, that the public institutions we know are relatively well placed to balance affordability and educational experience for students.[13] But even in the best cases, there is no settled consensus about the meaning and value and future viability of a liberal arts education, or about how much the model should or should not be changed, at its peril, or whether the signifier "liberal" ought to be soft-pedaled for the sake of regional political sensitivities. That lack of consensus, whenever it arises, may be as bewildering to new professors as the sedimented faculty cultures and the self-referential appeals to some golden age that flavor the local conversation.[14] Adaptation in such situations may mean finding a stake in the conversation. It may mean learning an unfamiliar language, using it to help students understand what they are learning, and becoming an advocate, not so much for a discipline as for liberal education itself. Needless to say, there is no preparation in graduate school for such work.

The adaptation to place is closely linked to the adaptation to an undergraduate teaching campus. Though it typically receives far less attention, it may represent the greater challenge. For historic reasons, public liberal arts colleges are often located in relatively small, rural communities—"backwaters"—where the local Main Street is unlikely to feature the full array of microbreweries, fusion restaurants, and art-house film theaters typical of larger cities or research university towns. Diversity is less obvious. In such communities, the relatively high numbers of first-generation students from the surrounding region experience higher education less as a late-adolescent rite of passage or a matter of expectation and more as a risk, a divide, sometimes a matter of liberation and self-discovery. Many of them will not have a passport when they get to college. In such places, local politics and pieties sometimes clash with prevailing campus cultures; they may even shock new professors hired on the basis of national searches. The corresponding temptation to approach the parochial as the opposite of educated flows naturally enough from the universalism and principled indifference to place that are deeply embedded in the academy's disciplinary guilds.[15]

We want to beware of caricaturing either small towns or professors. As several chapters in this book make clear, neither is necessarily what each might seem to be when judged from the outside. From our own experience, though, we know that location—and with it, opportunities for domestic partners—can be a real barrier to faculty recruitment and retention. Settling in requires real adaptation. North Americans now live primarily in urban places; their cultural prejudices reflect that reality. Popular writers like Richard Florida and Richard Longworth describe the clustering of the "creative classes" in smart, tolerant, diverse cities—typically university cities—and the hollowing out of the heartland, which most people encounter only from a height of 35,000 feet.[16] When a columnist in the *Chronicle of Higher Education* advised academic job-seekers in a saturated job market to be prepared to "embrace your inner North Dakotan," readers surely got the point.[17] The same can be said of the recent declaration of one Ivy League president: "When you picture a global university"—presumably a good thing—"you picture urban."[18]

The stories in this volume suggest the discovery of a different ethos in places like Morris, Minnesota, or Geneseo, New York, or Montevallo, Alabama, or Kirksville, Missouri—the kinds of places small enough that your realtor may have heard of your positive tenure decision before you do, the cashier at the grocery store will want to know about your next piano recital, and the class differences that are sequestered in big cities by good planning coexist on the same street. To *settle* in places like this as a scholar does not mean lowering ambitions, accepting defeat, or making excuses. To settle is to take up residence. It is to find a place in a community, a region, a watershed, a history; to accept the responsibilities of membership and offer relevant skills; to cultivate a critical affection rather than condescension. Depending on discipline and opportunity, to settle as a scholar is to treat the local as a valid subject for rigorous, respectful inquiry and hands-on pedagogy that reframes the familiar for students as an entry point into big questions around climate change, ecological sustainability, the global economy, patterns of immigration, poverty, and homelessness, or into forgotten histories, traditional knowledges, and the unfinished business of colonialism. In many ways, the local, the peripheral, affords a clearer perspective on those questions. Consequently, a critical scholarship and pedagogy of place has much to teach the entire academy at a time when it is reinvesting much of its energies in global collaborations and the latest versions of online learning.[19] But that critical alternative requires professors to be someplace rather than no place—to think, teach, and write out of a lived sense of the complexity and context of real communities.

Roger

If I had not been so desperate at the time, I would say that I applied on a dare—or perhaps in a fit of regional chauvinism, a familiar reflex in Canada, when a PhD colleague told me that the graduate chair in our department had advised him against taking an advertised position at what was then a small church-owned college in the west, in Alberta. He could do better, he was told. I had scarcely heard of the place. When I interviewed and was offered the position late in the winter, it came as a relief. I had a young family. There were virtually no other tenure-track positions in the country that year for which I might be qualified. On the positive side, the college was located in a small city where we could afford a house on a modest salary. We were back within driving distance of grandparents. The college was expanding. I was reassured by the presence of impressive colleagues, many of them recently hired, who in better times would have gone elsewhere too. The college offered the chance to shape a new program in political science. And it prized teaching in ways I found attractive—having watched professors scramble for offices that would isolate them from the disruptions of student traffic.

At the start I taught four different courses each term to small classes, none of them anywhere near my dissertation research. I said yes to local requests: organizing a conference; co-editing an ambitious journal dedicated to interdisciplinary dialogue around the liberal arts; serving as president of the faculty association—untenured!—with budget troubles and a grievance suddenly on the agenda. Each May I was exhausted. I never did turn the dissertation into a book, despite a favorable response from a good university press. There was no encouragement to do so. There were no senior colleagues on campus who were teachers and researchers in the way I wanted to be. On the contrary, the word through the grapevine was that at least one of my elders was suspicious of all those who aspired to do research. It was a sure sign, he said, that we were looking to leave. Over the next decade, I published enough articles and book chapters to achieve a modest scholarly profile particularly in Britain. But there was no money for transatlantic conferences, no graduate teaching to keep me reading the journals. When I was congratulated on receiving tenure, I had the distinct feeling that a heavy door had closed behind me. A colleague later admitted the same.[20]

Two things saved me. The first was my students—bright, teachable. Invariably I taught some of them in multiple courses, from first to graduating years. I continue to connect with some of them long after graduation. A handful of them are now successful scholars. Some are lawyers: prosecuting notorious crimes, arguing a Supreme Court case, working at international war crimes tribunals. Others are journalists, writers, teachers, photographers, woodworkers, legislative aides, political activists, public servants, and community leaders. I'm honored to have been part of their formation. At their invitation I have attended weddings, christenings, farm auctions, a national rodeo final, a book launch.

The second thing that saved me was a renewed sense of my own rootedness in the prairie region of western Canada. It grew out of experiences with Cree people, including students, my proximity to the working countryside, and my awareness that the kind of farm-based rural communities in which I and many of my students had grown up had been abandoned to the relentless crush of the global economy. The creative result took many forms. I developed a one-of-a-kind course. I began to write—everything from literary non-fiction to political economy. I was invited to speak to dozens of rural audiences and once to a parliamentary committee. I took my students to a hog farm. I co-edited a book, *Writing Off the Rural West*, that was read by farmers, politicians, and scholars alike, coproduced a national radio documentary on the contemporary "clearances" in the Canadian countryside, and collected my own prairie essays into another volume, *We Are All Treaty People*—evidence of how far I had traveled as a public scholar. I did regular media interviews on rural issues. All of this would have been beyond my imagination as a PhD student.

In 2004, after a decade of acute financial stress, the college was incorporated into the University of Alberta, the province's flagship, as a distinctive, small-campus setting for undergraduate teaching, the liberal arts, and rural access. I was appointed to lead it—another role that would have been unthinkable in graduate school. At that point my regional connections and my experience with public audiences in every kind of venue served me well. So did the commitments I had formed about the importance of the university learning to be at home, unapologetically, in the rural. During my tenure, I took particular satisfaction in the initiation of a local-food procurement policy, a center for sustainable rural communities, and a collaborative relationship with city and county governments that created hands-on opportunities for students. My faculty colleagues worked on wildlife biodiversity projects and imagined an ecological field station. They put talented student musicians and athletes into local schools. They taught history through the prism of a restored vaudeville-era theater on Main Street. Together, they gave a powerful answer to a question that was once all too real: if the campus disappeared, would the community notice?

The third adaptation that frames this book is one in which professors start to prod and shape the public missions of their institutions. They move beyond the campus. They learn to think with, not just for, the communities they engage. They sometimes bring their students with them. They discover what Wendell Berry calls a "beloved country"—a point of reference and accountability beyond the academy alone.[21] In doing so, they erode the old ivory-tower perceptions of higher education. They make a fresh case for public investment in budget-straitened times. They demonstrate that the value of a college to its region extends beyond access and economic-impact multipliers. Above all, they point in the direction of a transformed academy.

Historically, the mandate to serve the public good has rested most explicitly with land-grant institutions in the United States and their equivalents especially in western Canada. The public good was broadly synonymous with the development of agrarian-settler societies. The first president of the University of Alberta, for example, expressed that mandate in inspiring, democratic-populist terms: "The modern state university has sprung from a demand on the part of the people themselves for intellectual recognition, a recognition that only a century ago was denied them. . . . The people demand that knowledge shall not be the concern of scholars alone. The uplifting of the whole people shall be its final goal."[22] Our interest is not to judge whether and how large public universities have lived up to that standard in subsequent generations. Rather it is to acknowledge that, during the same historical period, liberal arts colleges, typically private, with supporting constituencies defined by wealth or denomination, imagined themselves as something more like an oasis, set apart for shaping mind and character in young people of their particular kind. If service to humanity was the purpose of education, that purpose was to be met *after* graduation and in other places. Tellingly, Ernest Boyer's influential book *Scholarship Reconsidered*, which helped open the door to what is now well developed as a scholarship of community engagement, proposed that a regional mission was a good thing for doctoral-comprehensive universities, but it was silent about liberal arts colleges.[23]

While public liberal arts colleges often have different origins than private colleges, it is fair to say that they too are latecomers to some of the conversation about higher education and the public good. The focus on undergraduate teaching comes with an inherent inwardness—so it should not be surprising that some of the first steps off campus, such as service learning, have been about new, high-impact learning experiences for students. Typically the institutional case for the public good has been made on shared ground with other public and, increasingly, private colleges and universities. The foremost public good is accessibility and its near twin, affordability.[24] For critics, no amount of university-sponsored civic engagement or contribution to economic development in general can make up for the simple fact that, as access to higher education erodes, social-economic inequality increases—so that skeptical taxpayers in the future will need to be convinced to support a costly system for the benefit of the few.[25] Our point is not to diminish the case for accessibility or the concerns it raises. Indeed, we share them. But we do not think that greater accessibility for students exhausts the public good that colleges and universities might do, any more than it ensures that, once in the door, those students will necessarily participate in a high-quality educational experience.

The emerging reality is already much more promising. Public liberal arts colleges in particular have begun to take seriously the roles of neighbor and citizen. They share facilities. They open their doors for concerts, exhibits, and lectures. They make available "protected spaces"—a common realm—for "informed public discussion of the fault lines within society, local and global."[26] They partner with local municipalities, schools, and cultural and social-service agencies in projects that match their resources, expertise, and faculty and student energies with community needs. In smaller centers, they often are able to accomplish a great deal together, first, because the campus is not big enough to be a world unto itself, and second, because informal personal relationships built in the community help to overcome mutual suspicions and create the trust that is needed to do something new.[27] Campus leaders can signal intent and sign agreements, but it usually takes committed professors to make things happen on the ground. At least some of the essays in this book reflect the emerging model of what is called public scholarship or community-engaged research, undertaken with non-university partners.[28] They show that it is hard, meaningful work, that it does integrate teaching and research with everyday life, and that it is rooted in place.

The professorial lives represented in the following chapters do not follow a single template. By their own accounts, their authors came to positions in public liberal arts colleges as a result of accidental meetings and careful consideration, desperate applications, and, in at least one case, a long-held dream. They arrived on campuses direct from PhD programs, from private colleges, or sometimes with tenure-track histories in Research I universities. To greater and lesser degrees, they do report a lingering sense of deprivation—some of it material, some intellectual, some the result of engrained status hierarchies. Like professors everywhere, they worry about tenure and promotion. They tell honest stories, as they were asked, about struggles, successes, and adaptations. But the word adaptation is perhaps insufficient, perhaps too inflected with connotations of "settling for" or "making do," to capture fully the kinds of energy, the ambition, the innovation, the creative intellect, and the scholarly rigor exemplified in these stories. They are about adaptation, to be sure, but only in the strongest sense. They are as much about surprises—about discoveries and self-discoveries made in unlikely places. First among them is a recurring sense of either having become *who one really is* or having been able to reclaim a purpose that might have first formed in college and been abandoned in graduate school, precisely because of where in the world the author has made a scholarly life. As if the road taken, to paraphrase Robert Frost, had made all the difference.

Second, there is a freedom on the presumed periphery to be teacher-scholars in relatively unfettered, unhurried, and undisciplined ways. In this volume, for example, a mathematician cultivates a parallel interest in Dante. A musician transcends the rigidities of the classical canon and the scholar-performer divide. An ecologist and a sociologist are drawn out of the classroom by student enthusiasm into the complexities of forests, post-genocide societies, and a new model of research. Professors of literature and biology learn to collaborate to make environmental sustainability a curricular and operational objective.

Third, these chapters reflect a realization that the noblest traditions of higher education, in fact, might be lived out most meaningfully in our times on small, public liberal arts campuses. From experience they describe campuses where disciplinary boundaries are crossed every day; where the mutual isolations of specialist knowledge do not prevail; where faculty collectively do still shape curricula and institutional identity through sustained action; where connections with surrounding communities are close; and where the presence of high percentages of first-generation students is an ongoing reminder both of what is at stake and what should not be taken for granted as a matter of public mission. This realization is not framed in defensive tones. But it is particularly sensitive to the importance of academic leadership that is grounded in an understanding of public liberal arts colleges and can articulate their aspirations—not the kind marked by personal ambition that regards such campuses as stepping stones on a fast-track to more prestigious positions elsewhere. These chapters are clearly the work of teacher-scholars, of whom only a very few admit to reluctant turns as department chairs. But they show an appreciation for leadership that fosters and supports faculty creativity, establishes fairness around promotion and tenure decisions, and draws members of the professoriate into broader institutional roles. For the professoriate is necessarily more enduring in place than any president, provost, or dean; its development is also the work of leadership.

When this volume was first conceived, one of its purposes was to support the recruitment and orientation of new faculty at liberal arts colleges, especially on the public side. That purpose still stands. What is clear from these diverse stories of professorial lives, however, is that they have much to say to faculty at all ranks and to higher education in general. Together, the stories serve to delineate, validate, and raise the profile of an important, emerging sector of higher education. They use some of the tools of the academy to look inward. They identify cultural strengths, peculiarities, and vulnerabilities of their institutions. They do not assume either that the contemporary threats to liberal arts colleges come only from the outside—from budget-cutting legislators, ill-fitting corporate models, know-nothing voters—or that professors are mere passive spectators in the shaping of their campus futures and their working lives. These stories do not indulge in nostalgia for a golden age; they do not reject new pedagogies and technologies on principle. Rather, they are shaped by the adaptive, high-minded realism of careers at public institutions with more humble histories and less insulation to protect against the prevailing winds. At bottom, they suggest that the fragile promise of liberal arts colleges like the ones they describe must be renewed in every generation by hard, intentional, often countercultural work.

As the reader will quickly experience, these stories deploy a wide range of faculty voices. They are playful and measured, surprised and experienced, fearful and hopeful, sometimes all at once. They are not necessarily meant to be read from first to last. If there is a rough ordering principle at work, it is that the earlier chapters tend to put greater emphasis on campus, on students, teaching, undergraduate research mentorship, curriculum, scholarship—in short, on the different balances of a professorial life at a public liberal arts college. The middle chapters might be said to engage place more directly, while the latter chapters and the afterword, like the outer ripples in a pond, give more attention to issues of public mission. But all hard divisions are artificial.

When most of the contributors came together for a workshop in the spring of 2013 from across the archipelago of COPLAC campuses, as one put it, their meeting was marked by two striking features. One was their instant recognition of what they held in common. The other was the impressive, respectful collegiality they offered to each other. The result is a more refined, more reflexive volume than we had imagined as editors. We were well aware that in soliciting the personal stories of exemplary professorial lives, we were asking individuals to violate well-worn academic conventions about using the first-person pronoun and to take the considerable risks of self-disclosure. We encouraged a posture of critical affection. We assured contributors, in case it helped, that they were writing as individual scholars, not as emissaries for their home campuses. In the end, we think that they speak for all of us who care about the liberal arts and public education in human-scale settings. They are among our best faces, our best guides, our best hope.

Works Cited

Austin, Ann. "The Socialization of Future Faculty in a Changing Context." In *The American Academic Profession: Transformation in Contemporary Higher Education*, edited by Joseph Hermanowicz, 145–67. Baltimore: Johns Hopkins University Press, 2011.

Baker, Vicki L., Roger G. Baldwin, and Sumedha Makker. "Where Are They Now? Revisiting Breneman's Study of Liberal Arts Colleges." *Liberal Education* 98, no. 3 (Summer 2012). Accessed at http://www.aacu.org/liberaleducation/le-su12/baker_baldwin_makker.cfm.

Berry, Wendell. *What Are People For?* New York: Farrar, Straus and Giroux, 1990.

Bérubé, Michael. *What's Liberal about the Liberal Arts: Classroom Politics and "Bias" in Higher Education*. New York: W. W. Norton, 2006.

Blanchard, Kathryn. "I've Got Tenure. I'm Depressed." *Chronicle of Higher Education*, January 31, 2012. Accessed at http://chronicle.com/article/Ive-Got-Tenure-How/130490/.

Boice, Robert. *The New Faculty Member*. San Francisco: Jossey-Bass, 1992.

Boice, Robert, et al. *Faculty in New Jobs: A Guide to Settling in, Becoming Established and Building Institutional Support*. San Francisco: Jossey-Bass, 1999.

Boyer, Ernest. *Scholarship Reconsidered: Priorities of the Professoriate*. San Francisco: Jossey-Bass and the Carnegie Foundation for the Advancement of Teaching, 1990.

Burgan, Mary. *Whatever Happened to the Faculty?* Baltimore: Johns Hopkins University Press, 2006.

Campus Compact. *New Times Demand New Scholarship: Research Universities and Civic Engagement*. Conference Report 2007. Los Angeles: University of California, Los Angeles, 2007. Accessed at http://www.compact.org/wp-content/uploads/initiatives/research_universities/Civic_Engagement.pdf.

Carlson, Scott. "Oberlin, Ohio: Laboratory for a New Way of Life." *Chronicle of Higher Education*, November 6, 2011. Accessed at http://chronicle.com/article/A-College-Town-Imagines-a-New/129650/.

Carnegie Commission on Higher Education. *The Campus and the City*. New York: McGraw-Hill, 1972.

Corbett, E. A. *Henry Marshall Tory: A Biography*. Edmonton: University of Alberta Press, 1954. Reprint, 1992.

Correcting Course: How We Can Restore the Ideals of Public Higher Education in a Market-Driven Era. Report of The Futures Project: Policy for Higher Education in a Changing World, February 2005. Accessed at http://www.nerche.org/futuresproject/publications/Correcting_Course.pdf.

Cronon, William. "'Only Connect . . . ': The Goals of a Liberal Education." *American Scholar* 67 (Autumn 1998): 73–80.

Curris, Constantine. "The Public Purposes of Public Colleges." *Chronicle of Higher Education*, April 7, 2006. Accessed at http://chronicle.com/article/The-Public-Purposes-of-Public/20104/.

Delbanco, Andrew. *College: What It Was, Is, and Could Be*. Princeton: Princeton University Press, 2012.

Ehrenberg, Ronald, ed. *What's Happening to Public Education?* Westport, CT: Praeger, 2006.

Ellison, Julie, and Timothy Eatman. *Scholarship in Public: Knowledge Creation and Tenure*

Policy in the Engaged University. Syracuse, NY: Imagining America, 2008. Accessed at http://imaginingamerica.org/wp-content/uploads/2011/05/TTI_FINAL.pdf.

Epp, Roger. *We Are All Treaty People: Prairie Essays*. Edmonton: University of Alberta Press, 2008.

Finder, Alan. "Rural Colleges Seek New Edge and Urbanize." *New York Times*, February 7, 2007.

Florida, Richard. *The Rise of the Creative Class, Revisited*. New York: Basic Books, 2011.

Gappa, Judith, Ann Austin, and Andrea Trice, eds. *Rethinking Faculty Work: Higher Education's Strategic Imperative*. San Francisco: Jossey-Bass, 2006.

Geertz, Clifford. *Local Knowledge: Further Essays in Interpretive Anthropology*. New York: Basic Books, 1983.

Glenn, David. "After the Crash, Scholars Say, Higher Education Must Refocus on Its Public Mission." *Chronicle of Higher Education*, April 6, 2009. Accessed at http://chronicle.com/article/Scholars-Call-for-Higher/47161/.

Gruenewald, David. "The Best of Both Worlds: A Critical Pedagogy of Place." *Educational Researcher* 32, no. 4 (2003): 3–12.

Hebel, Sara. "Private Colleges Peddle Their Public Mission." *Chronicle of Higher Education*, November 19, 2004. Accessed at http://chronicle.com/article/Private-Colleges-Peddle-Their/16539/.

Hersch, Richard, and John Merrow, eds. *Declining by Degrees: Higher Education at Risk*. New York: Palgrave Macmillan, 2005.

Holmwood, John, ed. *A Manifesto for the Public University*. London: Bloomsbury, 2011.

Jack, Zachary Michael, ed. *Black Earth and Ivory Tower: New American Essays from Farm and Classroom*. Columbia: University of South Carolina Press, 2005.

Kalivoda, Trish, ed. *The Research University Civic Engagement Network*. Special issue of *Journal of Higher Education Outreach and Engagement* 16, no. 4 (2012).

Keohane, Nannerl O. "The Liberal Arts as Guideposts in the 21st Century." *Chronicle of Higher Education*, January 29, 2012.

Kirp, David. "This Little Student Went to Market." In Hersch and Merrow, *Declining by Degrees*, 113–29.

Kozar, Adrianna J., Tony C. Chambers, and John C. Burkhardt, eds. *Higher Education for the Public Good: Emerging Voices from a National Movement*. San Francisco: Jossey-Bass, 2005.

Longworth, Richard. *Caught in the Middle: America's Heartland in the Age of Globalism*. New York: Bloomsbury, 2008.

Lord, Alexandra. "Location, Location, Location." *Chronicle of Higher Education*, September 12, 2012. Accessed at http://chronicle.com/article/Location-Location-Location/134264.

Morphew, Christopher, and Matthew Hartley. "Mission Statements: A Thematic Analysis of Rhetoric Across Institutional Type." *Journal of Higher Education* 77 (2006): 456–71.

Newfield, Christopher. *Unmaking the Public University: The Forty-Year Assault on the Middle Class*. Cambridge, MA: Harvard University Press, 2008.

Newson, Janice, and Claire Polster, eds. *Academic Callings: The University We Have Had, Now Have, and Could Have*. Toronto: Canadian Scholars' Press, 2010.

Nussbaum, Martha. *Not for Profit: Why Democracy Needs the Humanities*. Princeton:

Princeton University Press, 2012.

Orr, David. *Hope Is an Imperative: The Essential David Orr*. Washington, DC: Island Press, 2010.

Perlmutter, David. "Embrace Your Inner North Dakotan." *Chronicle of Higher Education,* August 12, 2012. Accessed at http://chronicle.com/article/Embrace-Your-Inner-North/133493.

Perlmutter, David. *Promotion and Tenure Confidential*. Cambridge, MA: Harvard University Press, 2010.

Rhode, Deborah. *In Pursuit of Knowledge: Scholars, Status and Academic Culture*. Stanford, CA: Stanford University Press, 2006.

Schuman, Samuel. *Old Main: Small Colleges in Twenty-First Century America*. Baltimore: Johns Hopkins University Press, 2005.

Snider, William. *Light on the Hill: A History of the University of North Carolina at Chapel Hill*. Chapel Hill: University of North Carolina Press, 1992.

Spellman, Bill. "The Resilient Liberal Arts College." *Inside Higher Education*, July 30, 2009. Accessed at http://www.insidehighered.com/views/2009/07/30/spellman.

Stein, Janice Gross. "The University as Citizen." *Academic Matters: The Journal of Higher Education*, October 2007, 7.

Tannock, Stuart. "Higher Education, Inequality and the Public Good." *Dissent* 53, no. 2 (Spring 2006): 45–51.

Wadsworth, Deborah. "Ready or Not? Where the Public Stands on Higher Education Reform." In Hersh and Merrow, *Declining by Degrees*, 23–38.

Zencey, Eric. "The Rootless Professors." *Chronicle of Higher Education*, June 12, 1985. Reprinted in William Vitek and Wes Jackson, eds., *Rooted in the Land: Essays on Community and Place* (New Haven: Yale University Press, 1996).

Notes

1. Schuman, *Old Main*, chap. 6.

2. The Council of Public Liberal Arts Colleges is an association of twenty-seven small- to medium-sized campuses located across North America. For further information see http://coplac.org.

3. One thoughtful exception is Boice et al., *Faculty in New Jobs*. See also Boice, *New Faculty Member*; and, in the context of a changing academy, Gappa, Austin, and Trice, *Rethinking Faculty Work*; Burgan, *Whatever Happened to the Faculty?* A recent collection of essays that links personal narratives with critical perspectives, though it is not directly primarily to new faculty members, is Newson and Polster, *Academic Callings*.

4. Geertz, *Local Knowledge*, 158–59.

5. Deborah Rhode, a former senior academic administrator, highlights both reputation and status as the (unhappy) currency of the contemporary university in her book, *In Pursuit of Knowledge: Scholars, Status and Academic Culture*.

6. See, e.g., Baker, Baldwin, and Makker, "Where Are They Now? Revisiting Breneman's Study of Liberal Arts Colleges."

7. See, e.g., Schuman, *Old Main*; Morphew and Hartley, "Mission Statements."

8. Austin, "Socialization of Future Faculty in a Changing Context." See also Perlmutter,

Promotion and Tenure Confidential. Perlmutter observes that, in general, PhD programs "adequately train graduate students in conducting research and do a fair job in tutoring them how to teach but do a poor job in inculcating in them the skills and ethos to become satisfied and successful tenured professors" (10)—in other words, to be full university citizens. This is an adaptation challenge that is not specific to liberal arts colleges.

9. Kirp, "This Little Student Went to Market," 123.

10. Interviewee quoted in Schuman, *Old Main*, 79.

11. Baker, Baldwin, and Makker, "Where Are They Now?"

12. Andrew Delbanco's book *College: What It Was, Is, and Could Be* is the most recent, spirited, and high-profile defense of the four-year liberal arts college experience. On the broader subject of liberal education, see Keohane, "Liberal Arts as Guideposts in the 21st Century"; Nussbaum, *Not for Profit: Why Democracy Needs the Humanities*; Bérubé, *What's Liberal about the Liberal Arts*; and Cronon, "'Only Connect . . . ': The Goals of a Liberal Education."

13. Spellman, "Resilient Liberal Arts College."

14. Schuman observes that small colleges, normally nimble and responsive, can find conversations about change and identity especially difficult because of their self-referential, self-protective tendencies; *Old Main*, chap. 5.

15. This minority position was argued forcefully by Eric Zencey in an essay, "The Rootless Professors," first published in the *Chronicle of Higher Education*, June 12, 1985, and reprinted in Vitek and Jackson, *Rooted in the Land: Essays on Community and Place*. It is developed in several essays in Jack, *Black Earth and Ivory Tower*, and in Epp, "The University at Home in the Rural," in *We Are All Treaty People*.

16. Florida, *The Rise of the Creative Class, Revisited*; Longworth, *Caught in the Middle: America's Heartland in the Age of Globalism*.

17. Perlmutter, "Embrace Your Inner North Dakotan." Equally telling is the response, Lord, "Location, Location, Location."

18. Amy Gutmann, quoted in Finder, "Rural Colleges Seek New Edge and Urbanize," *New York Times*, February 7, 2007.

19. David Orr is an important pioneer in thinking about ecology, place, pedagogy, and the liberal arts. His best-known essays on these subjects are collected in *Hope Is an Imperative: The Essential David Orr*. See also Gruenewald, "The Best of Both Worlds: A Critical Pedagogy of Place."

20. Apparently post-tenure depression is a familiar phrase. It turned up numerous references in a search of the *Chronicle of Higher Education*, including Blanchard, "I've Got Tenure. I'm Depressed."

21. Berry, *What Are People For?*, 117.

22. Quoted in Corbett, *Henry Marshall Tory*, 100. The words are from Tory's first convocation speech. Tory had his rhetorical equal in Frank Porter Graham, president of the University of North Carolina from 1930 to 1949, who in his inaugural speech referred to the "great teachers on this hill" who muster the "intellectual and spiritual resources of the race for the development of the whole personality of the poorest boy" and "kindle the fires that burn for him and light up the heavens of the commonwealth"; Snider, *Light on the Hill*, 1.

23. Boyer, *Scholarship Reconsidered*, 59–60. Interestingly, in a 1972 report, *The Campus and the City*, the Carnegie Commission on Higher Education encouraged urban universities to make a commitment to their cities akin to that of the land-grant universities to rural life.

24. See, e.g., Curris, "Public Purposes of Public Colleges"; Glenn, "After the Crash, Scholars Say, Higher Education Must Refocus on Its Public Mission"; *Correcting Course: How We Can Restore the Ideals of Public Higher Education in a Market-Driven Era.* Accessibility is the primary theme in such studies as Newfield, *Unmaking the Public University*; Ehrenberg, *What's Happening to Public Education?*; Holmwood, *A Manifesto for the Public University*; and, from the perspective of public opinion, Wadsworth, "Ready or Not? Where the Public Stands on Higher Education Reform." Private colleges have joined the pitch for accessibility and the government funding attached to it. See, e.g., Hebel, "Private Colleges Peddle Their Public Mission."

25. Tannock, "Higher Education, Inequality and the Public Good."

26. Stein, "The University as Citizen," 7.

27. One particularly ambitious example of college-civic collaboration is the Oberlin Project in Oberlin, Ohio, where ecologist-professor David Orr has taken the lead in a large-scale, long-range plan to make the town and college a prototype for sustainability. See Carlson, "Laboratory for a New Way of Life."

28. An important 2008 study undertaken under the auspices of the consortium Imagining America: Artists and Scholars in Public Life is Ellison and Eatman, *Scholarship in Public: Knowledge Creation and Tenure Policy in the Engaged University.* On various related issues, see also Campus Compact, *New Times Demand New Scholarship: Research Universities and Civic Engagement*; and Kalivoda, *The Research University Civic Engagement Network*, a special issue of *Journal of Higher Education Outreach and Engagement.* Particularly in the latter two cases, the articles and authors are drawn almost entirely from larger research universities, which may reflect the greater challenge of making the case for the legitimacy of community-engaged scholarship in contexts where research matters more for tenure and promotion. Another useful volume is Kozar, Chambers, and Burkhardt, *Higher Education for the Public Good: Emerging Voices from a National Movement.*

1

A Place Where Ideas Matter

Joel M. Sipress

History, University of Wisconsin–Superior

As I recall, I was a sophomore in college. I was having a conversation with my TA in an undergraduate political theory class. (For the life of me, I can't remember her name.) She had a rather cynical attitude toward academic culture and was explaining why she was nonetheless pursuing an academic career. "Colleges and universities," she said, "are among the only places where ideas are taken seriously." Little could I imagine then that I—born, raised, and educated in the state of New Jersey—would myself find such a place at a small state school on the western tip of Lake Superior.

I attended college at Princeton University, an institution that emphasized undergraduate education while also hosting highly competitive and high-powered graduate programs. As an undergraduate, I experienced the joy and personal growth that comes from being someplace where ideas were taken seriously. But I also got a glimpse into the dominant academic culture. I came to know many graduate students—both as teaching assistants and, in some cases, as friends. I observed how difficult their lives were, both financially and emotionally. I saw the ways that the dominant values of the academy could be at odds with the things that made my college experience so meaningful.

I embarked upon graduate school knowing exactly what I was after. I was not looking for a continuation of college. I was not looking for personal affirmation. And I was not hoping to become the next "great historian." I had one simple goal—to be able to earn a living in a place where ideas truly matter, and to do that I needed a PhD. Even my choice of discipline was somewhat a matter of happenstance. History's freewheeling culture, which involves borrowing (some would say abusing) theories and methods from

21

other disciplines, certainly had its appeal. And the discipline's emphasis on lived human experience was important to me. In the end, however, it was the culture of my undergraduate department that drew me in. To put it simply, the history department was where the intellectual action was.

Unlike many of my peers, I arrived in graduate school with a very clear understanding of my professional goals and my academic values. While I certainly valued the scholarly world of the discipline, my priority was finding a professional home (a place) with a rich and lively intellectual life. It would need to be a place that put a premium on undergraduate education. After all, no matter where I ended up, I would spend my days surrounded by undergraduates and it was vital that I be able to make meaningful intellectual connections with them. Ideally, it would be a place with an economically diverse student body—I was not particularly interested in spending all my time with children of privilege. And it would need to be a good place to work. That meant having colleagues with broad and diverse interests who respected each other and were genuinely interested in each other's perspectives. The status of the institution, the opportunity to train graduate students, the time and resources available for scholarship and publication—all these items mattered far less to me.

At the time, I did not have the words to describe such a place, but I now understand that my goal was to work at a public liberal arts college. Upon completing my PhD, I was fortunate to be hired at the University of Wisconsin–Superior, a small undergraduate-oriented state institution. A few years later, we were designated Wisconsin's public liberal arts college. Two decades after my arrival, I remain employed at UW–Superior and have never seriously considered working elsewhere. In that time, I have discovered that public liberal arts colleges do not simply provide an alternative environment for teaching and scholarship, they actually embody an alternative set of academic values.[1]

If I had to choose one word to describe UW–Superior and its surrounding community, that word would be "gritty." Located at the western tip of Lake Superior, the greatest of the Great Lakes, the city of Superior was built upon railroads and shipping. While transportation industries employ just a fraction of what they did in the city's heyday, Superior remains a blue-collar town. Superior and neighboring Duluth, Minnesota, together comprise the Twin Ports, a metropolitan area of about 135,000 people.

Unlike Duluth, which has a more urban feel, Superior (with a population of just under 30,000) is a big small town. Most Superiorites were born and raised there, went to school together (there is a single high school), and frequent the same eateries and taverns. While Superior and Duluth have had some significant success in diversifying into new industries, such as tourism, health care, light manufacturing, and aerospace, the Twin Ports and the surrounding region face many of the same challenges as the rest of the midwestern rust belt. Yet, despite limited economic opportunities, many young people want to stay, attracted by the strong sense of community and spectacular scenic beauty.

The Twin Ports are home to the University of Minnesota–Duluth, the College of St. Scholastica (a Catholic institution), and UW–Superior. Of the three campuses, UW–Superior has long had the reputation of being the most working class. The campus attracts large numbers of first-generation and non-traditionally aged students, and it has the highest percentage of Pell Grant–eligible students in the University of Wisconsin System. While the majority of our students come from northwestern Wisconsin and northeastern Minnesota (Minnesota and Wisconsin have a tuition reciprocity agreement), the campus has made a concerted effort to reach out to other parts of Wisconsin and to the Minneapolis–Saint Paul metropolitan area. We have also had considerable success in recruiting international students and have among the highest percentage of such students in the UW System. UW–Superior's chief attraction to prospective students has traditionally been the opportunity for personal attention on a campus whose size (about three thousand students) allows for meaningful interaction with faculty.

To many in higher education, UW–Superior would seem an academic backwater. At twelve credits per semester, the teaching load is heavy (though, due to our small class sizes, it is rare to have more than ninety to one hundred students in total per semester). With roughly one hundred tenured and tenure-track faculty, individuals are responsible for teaching a dizzying array of courses. (I am personally responsible for virtually all coursework in United States history plus some limited Latin American history offerings.) UW–Superior is also service heavy. There are certain things that simply must get done for a campus, regardless of size, to function, and at UW–Superior this work is divvied up among a relatively small total faculty. The demands of teaching and service limit the time available for disciplinary scholarship, except in the summers, which is when faculty are able to give priority to research and writing.

While many UW–Superior faculty are engaged in important and innovative scholarship, by necessity that work must proceed at a slower pace that results in fewer finished products than on campuses with a greater research orientation and lighter teaching loads.

Many of my graduate faculty would have told me that UW–Superior was fine for a first job, but that after paying dues for a few years I should begin to look for greener pastures—someplace that would afford more time and resources to pursue "my work," by which they would mean my scholarship. And yet, most of the faculty hired into my department (the interdisciplinary Department of Social Inquiry) have stayed and built careers at UW–Superior. The reason for this is simple. While other institutions provide more time and resources to support the type of individual scholarship that the academy prizes most highly, few other institutions provide an environment in which one can make as meaningful a daily difference in the lives of others and do so in collaboration with colleagues who share a sense of common purpose and mission.

The dominant values of the academy encourage faculty to see national and international disciplinary peer groups as the primary source of professional identity and intellectual community. For many faculty, the home campus and department serve simply as a base of operation from which one engages that broader disciplinary peer group. On a public liberal arts campus, by contrast, one finds meaning and community primarily from the students, faculty, and staff one encounters every day.

Among the most memorable of my students arrived in my introductory course on historical research and writing frighteningly underprepared. I wasn't even sure how to respond to his first "paper." Obviously he had worked very hard on it, but it bore virtually no resemblance to a coherent piece of writing, let alone a research paper. After a little bit of soul-searching, I assigned a grade of D+ (the plus was for effort), provided some encouraging comments, and asked him to go over the paper with me. Fortunately, course enrollment was capped at twenty, which allowed considerable time for student consultations within the scheduled class period. By the end of the semester, his work was among the best in the class. Two years later, I served as his senior thesis advisor. The thesis, among the strongest I have seen, explored the influence of East Asia on the political thought of W. E. B. DuBois and the Black Panther Party. While not graduate-level work, the thesis nevertheless gave me a deepened appreciation for the role of anti-colonial internationalism in African American political thought and practice. After graduating, this student spent a year teaching English in rural Japan as part of the highly acclaimed JET [Japan Exchange and Teaching] Program.

To thrive at a public liberal arts college, one must find intellectual engagement through one's relationships with undergraduate students, and this requires one to adopt the role of a mentor whose job it is to incorporate novice thinkers into a community of higher-order learners. This stands at odds with an approach to undergraduate education that casts the professor as the producer of scholarly knowledge, with students (apart from the exceptional few) relegated to the status of consumers whose task is to absorb and reproduce such knowledge. For faculty and students to see each other as members of a common community of learners, we must ask students to engage the central issues of our various disciplines in meaningful ways and help them develop the tools to do so. Of course, some students will embrace the intellectual life of the campus with greater passion and facility than others. Some will struggle to understand why they are in college at all, and others will simply depart. Nevertheless, to find meaning at a public liberal arts college, we must see each of our students as creative individuals who have both the ability and the right to be part of a shared learning community, and we must view ourselves as mentors to such students.

To be successful in the role of mentor to undergraduates as a whole (as opposed to mentor to the talented few), the classroom itself must become an object of intellectual inquiry. From my first semester as a graduate teaching assistant, I wanted my classroom to be an intellectually engaged space, much as it was for me as undergraduate. For that reason, my approach to teaching has always placed a heavy emphasis on historical argument. I want students to think deeply about major issues in the discipline and come to their own conclusions on the basis of their analysis and interpretation of historical evidence. I quickly discovered, however, that relatively few of my students arrived at college prepared, either academically or personally, to participate in a question-driven historical discourse. I thus began experimenting with different teaching methods, such as cooperative learning groups and ungraded reading responses designed to help students develop the academic skills necessary to participate in argument. I gradually purged from my courses those exercises and activities, such as short identification exam questions, that did not promote meaningful student engagement.

Over time, through trial and error, I became a good intuitive teacher. And then I discovered the Scholarship of Teaching and Learning (SoTL) movement. It was during my fourth or fifth year at UW–Superior. I was at a statewide teaching and learning conference sponsored by the UW System's Office of Professional and Instructional Development (OPID) when I attended a session on the subject of teaching for understanding presented by Bill Cerbin, a psychology professor at the University of Wisconsin–LaCrosse. Bill's main point—that just because we teach something doesn't mean students understand it—should have been obvious. The main value of the workshop, though, was that it gave me the words to articulate things with which I had been struggling for years. Bill shared a study of elementary math students who were asked to determine how many buses were needed to transport a certain number of students to an event. Most of the students were able to use division to perform the appropriate calculation, but then reported their answers in the form of a whole number plus a remainder, rather than reporting the actual number of buses needed. While the students had learned to perform the necessary algorithm, they did not understand the underlying meaning. We then viewed *A Private Universe*, a film that documents the failure of a single high school class, including its most academically successful members, to grasp a basic scientific concept they had just been taught.[2] The teacher's confusion and disappointment when she discovered that her star pupil did not truly understand what she had just learned had a profound impact on me.

I returned to campus with an almost obsessive drive to get inside my students' heads, identify their preconceptions, and uncover the barriers to the type of engaged learning I wished to promote. As part of the Wisconsin Teaching Fellows Program (sponsored by OPID) I had the opportunity to redesign one of my general education courses from scratch with a focus on historical argument. As I evaluated student work, I made a remarkable discovery: on the final exam (which asked a single interpretative question tied to the central theme of the course) almost none of my students provided meaningful evidence for the positions they had taken. This was my "private universe" moment. I realized that most of my students (including those I considered strong students) had failed to understand the relationship between assertions and evidence in historical argumentation, which meant they lacked a basic understanding of discipline.

I had a mystery on my hands—why don't students understand evidence and its role in historical argument? When confronted with such a mystery, historians are trained to seek out detailed and relevant empirical evidence and to attempt to make sense of that evidence using whatever methods and models appear most useful. As a historian, I thus made careful empirical observations of my students' behaviors (as manifested in assignments and class participation) and then searched for models of student learning that might explain what I had observed. It was at that moment that I became a practitioner of the Scholarship of Teaching and Learning, a scholarly movement that asks us to engage in systematic investigation of student learning using methods that are appropriate to our disciplines. At the UW System's annual Faculty College professional development gathering, I was introduced to William Perry's classic 1960s study of the cognitive development of college students and in it discovered my answer. Perry found that most students enter college assuming that truth is clear-cut and revealed by authority. Relatively early in their college careers, he determined, students come to accept that knowledge is often subject to rival truth claims, but they tend to view such disagreements as matters of mere opinion. Perry found his subjects quite resistant to abandoning this view and to embracing the need for truth claims to be justified on the basis of disciplinary criteria of judgment. In fact, Perry found that most of his sample (made up mostly of male Harvard students) graduated from college comfortably viewing truth claims and expressions of opinion as essentially the same thing.[3]

Apparently, my argument-based course had empowered my students to find their own voices. What it had failed to do, however, was to help my students distinguish an evidence-based position from a mere expression of opinion. This insight led to a radical restructuring of how I organized my courses, especially at the introductory level. I began to take a developmental approach to teaching history that explicitly asked students to make judgments among rival scholarly positions and to use concrete historical evidence as the criteria by which they would make these judgments. Throughout the semester, students repeatedly engage in exercises and activities where they practice making such judgments. Through assessing students' written work, I was able to document an almost immediate improvement in student use of evidence in making historical arguments. These findings formed the basis for my first SoTL publication, "Why Students Don't Get Evidence and What We Can Do About It."[4]

Since that first excursion into the Scholarship of Teaching and Learning, my primary scholarly agenda has been to critique the "coverage" model, which has dominated the teaching of history at the introductory college level and to make the case for an argument-based approach. The coverage model emphasizes the transfer of expert knowledge from professor to student. In the argument-based model, by contrast, students are asked to be novice practitioners of the discipline.[5] While I continue to engage in traditional scholarship in my graduate field of southern history, my work on the argument-based model has received far more recognition and has had a far greater scholarly impact. The response to my work has been particularly enthusiastic among history faculty who work at institutions that emphasize undergraduate teaching. The reason for this is simple. For them, as for me, our students are central to our intellectual world, and the challenge of fostering deep engagement among our students is the central intellectual problem we face in our daily professional lives.

If the world of the research university encourages faculty to find academic community primarily in national and international disciplinary peer groups, it also leads faculty to define themselves largely through the mastery of specialized knowledge. In the current academic landscape, even disciplinary knowledge is insufficient for self-identity, as fields such as history increasingly splinter into ever more specialized subdisciplines that rarely even speak to each other. At a public liberal arts college, faculty have their fields of expertise, but these specialized fields do not define them professionally. At UW–Superior, I am an academic first and a historian second. Only when I leave campus to attend specialized conferences do I become primarily a scholar of the late nineteenth-century American South. As a member of an interdisciplinary department, some of my most important academic relationships are with colleagues in such fields as sociology, philosophy, political science, and anthropology. This everyday crossing of disciplinary boundaries and subdisciplinary specializations encourages faculty at public liberal arts colleges to remain engaged with the type of "big questions" that have traditionally animated liberal education.[6]

When I interviewed for my position at UW–Superior, I was informed that as the only U.S. historian in a four-person history program, I would be responsible for developing a broad array of courses in U.S. history. Although that prospect was daunting, it was also exciting. It was the big questions of history that had first attracted me to the discipline, and throughout graduate school I had maintained a wide range of interests within the field. During my first two years on the job, I spent an extraordinary amount of time designing and preparing upper-division courses on such diverse topics as the Civil War and Reconstruction, U.S. labor history, the social upheavals of the 1960s, and the construction of gender in the United States. Within just a few years of my arrival, two of my three colleagues in the history program had retired. My remaining colleague and I realized that if we replaced one of those positions with an Asian historian, we would have the ability (with just four faculty) to offer a truly globalized history curriculum. To achieve this goal, I would need to develop some courses in Latin American history, which had been my PhD minor field. As I explain to sometimes-stunned colleagues from larger campuses, within our history curriculum I am responsible for the Western Hemisphere.

Interestingly, I have found that some of my most rewarding teaching experiences have been in courses that lie outside my primary areas of expertise. My upper-division course on modern Mexico is a case in point. Given my limited specialized expertise in Mexican history, it would simply be impossible for me to take a comprehensive coverage approach to the course. Instead, I looked for a conceptual framework that would allow students to engage deeply with major historical questions using Mexico as a case study. At the time I developed the course, issues of nationalism loomed large in my mind. For that reason, I turned the course into an exploration of the relationship between the nation and the state, a topic for which modern Mexican history is ideally suited. In designing and teaching the course, I was able to pursue a topic of deep personal concern while providing students a learning experience whose significance transcended the particular course content. More recently, I taught a special onetime seminar entitled The Causes and Consequences of Financial Crashes. Following the crash of 2008, I realized that my understanding of financial history was woefully inadequate, particularly given the importance of financial instability to the contemporary world. What better way to give myself a crash course on the workings of modern financial systems than to design an upper-level course on the topic? To prepare for the course, I spent six months intensively reading both theoretical and narrative works focused on financial instability. I then constructed a course that asked students first to read historical and journalistic accounts of four financial panics (1873, 1929, 1997, and 2008) and then to explore a body of theoretical work that ranged from authors such as Milton Friedman on the right to Hyman Minsky on the left. In the end, it was the challenge of rendering a set of theoretical concepts comprehensible to a group of undergraduates through which I gained a basic working mastery of the field.

For me, this crossing of intellectual boundaries has extended beyond the field of history. Early in my career at UW–Superior I had the opportunity to team-teach a class on the construction of race and nation with a departmental colleague in sociology. I had not formally studied sociology since I was a senior in high school, and my knowledge of the field was extremely limited. Despite our different disciplinary backgrounds, however, my colleague and I shared a passionate interest in the construction of ethnic, racial, and national identities. Together, we designed a truly interdisciplinary course in which students engaged texts and employed methods drawn from diverse disciplines. Team-teaching this class for over a decade provided me with a much deeper and sophisticated understanding of race and nation, but also gave me a new appreciation for the discipline of sociology. While still drawn to the methodologically freewheeling (some would say chaotic) culture of history, I came to see the value of those disciplines, such as sociology, that place a premium on methodological consistency and rigor. Serving on departmental search committees for faculty positions in anthropology and political science gave me a deeper understanding of and appreciation for those fields as well.

My most fully interdisciplinary experience at UW–Superior was participation in a working group that spent several years developing and piloting an innovative first-year seminar model. This team included faculty and staff colleagues in such fields as English, mathematics, sociology, and First Nations studies. Inspired by scholarship on the first-year transition, which stresses the importance of students' making a strong connection to the academic mission of the university, we began with a shared commitment to providing new students an academic experience that would help integrate them into a community of higher-order learners.[7] In 2003, the first year of the pilot, we pursued this goal by offering seven experimental academic seminars whose topics were specifically designed to engage the interest and imagination of first-year students. During the initial pilot, however, we became acutely aware that many students bring to college a set of dispositions that militate against their integration into a community defined by academic learning. (A member of our team who had taught first-year writing for many years found our amazement at this "discovery" most amusing.) Before launching a second pilot, we therefore adopted an explicitly developmental approach designed to reshape student dispositions toward learning. Recognizing that no single course could be fully transformative, the team spent the better part of a year identifying those dispositions that seemed most amenable to an early intervention. Through intensive study, reflection, and discussion, we arrived at the following learning goals for the first-year seminar pilot program:

- Students will be more disposed to value learning in its own right and see themselves as having the ability and the right to invest themselves in this learning.
- Students will be more disposed to pursue learning collaboratively, both in formal academic settings and elsewhere.
- Students will be more disposed to actively question previous knowledge and examine new ideas and multiple perspectives.

A decade later, UW–Superior has a required first-year seminar whose defining feature is the set of learning goals developed by the pilot group. While I am pleased by the team's practical accomplishments, for me the most rewarding aspect of the project was the opportunity to work intensively on issues of student learning with engaged colleagues from multiple disciplines. Working together to identify student-learning goals that transcend particular fields deepened my own thinking about the ultimate purposes and goals of a liberal education, and about the methods required to achieve these goals. I had already come to see the teaching and learning of history in developmental terms. I now came to see the undergraduate curriculum as a whole in that way. This has influenced how I think about curricular issues and how I approach my own courses. I am now acutely aware that my introductory history courses are general education courses in history rather than history courses that fulfill a general education requirement.

At a public liberal arts college, the commitment to place finds perhaps its highest form in service. If a campus is simply a home base from which one engages national and international disciplinary peer groups, then service obligations truly are a distraction from one's "work." If, by contrast, one finds meaning and community primarily from the students, faculty, and staff that one encounters every day, then campus service becomes vital and meaningful work. Uniquely among state universities, the administrative code of the UW System by law grants faculty "primary responsibility" for academic and educational matters. Within this long-standing legal context, UW campuses, including UW–Superior, have developed a culture of strong faculty governance. Faculty at UW–Superior take seriously their responsibility to exercise academic leadership, and by doing so gain significant influence over broader campus affairs. And, at a small public liberal arts campus like UW–Superior, an individual faculty member, working in collaboration with others, can make a significant institutional impact.

Having been active in the civic life of the communities where I have lived, university governance had immediate appeal to me. The demographics of UW–Superior provided opportunities to quickly take on governance roles. A serious fiscal crisis in the late 1970s had prevented the campus from engaging in much hiring during the 1980s. When I was hired in 1994, UW–Superior had an absent faculty generation, which allowed younger faculty to take leadership roles much sooner than is typical. In my second year on campus, I began serving as my department's representative on UW–Superior's Undergraduate Academic Affairs Council. A year later I was elected to the council's subcommittee on general education and served as subcommittee chair for three years. After two terms on the Undergraduate Academic Affairs Council I began service on the Faculty Senate and, two years later, was elected as senate president. Since that time, I have served in a variety of governance positions, including a second term as senate president following a hiatus of four years.

For me, the main attraction of governance service is the ability to work collaboratively with others to achieve goals that make a real difference in the academic lives of students, faculty, and staff. During my initial term as Faculty Senate president, our regional accrediting body raised significant questions about our public liberal arts mission. The campus had only recently gained membership in COPLAC through a process that had been somewhat divisive on campus. Many faculty and staff were unclear about the implications of our public liberal arts designation and its impact on particular program areas and majors. Others questioned the fit between the new mission and our traditional student constituencies. While many saw UW–Superior's size, student-centered culture, and traditional strength in the arts and sciences to be a solid foundation for the public liberal arts college designation, the campus had yet to come to a common understanding of and vision for the public liberal arts mission. During our first reaccreditation visit following our admission to COPLAC, our team of visitors pressed us to identify how the mission was expressed in institutional practice. When neither administration nor faculty were able to provide a clear answer, the site team challenged the campus to address this deficiency. In particular, they challenged the faculty (who under the principles of shared governance have primary responsibility for the academic mission) to take leadership on this issue. (I have a vivid memory of the meeting at which a site team member issued this challenge personally and quite directly to faculty governance leadership.)

Over the next several years, the campus (under the leadership of faculty governance) successfully met this challenge. We began by appointing a special faculty committee to foster an inclusive campus discussion regarding concrete initiatives that could be pursued to further UW–Superior's public liberal arts mission and to recommend a finite number of such initiatives to pursue. After a year of discussion, analysis, research, and study, the committee recommended five concrete initiatives: (1) academic service-learning; (2) first-year experience; (3) global awareness; (4) senior experience; and (5) writing across the curriculum. By emphasizing student experiences that cut across traditional disciplinary lines, the recommended initiatives allowed all departments and programs to feel a sense of ownership over the public liberal arts mission. Once governance and administration approved the recommendations, the task of planning and implementation began. For two years, I received a part-time administrative assignment to oversee the development of detailed implementation plans. Today the five initiatives are integrated in the institutional fabric of UW–Superior in what we call our liberal arts high-impact practices. These practices have not only improved the quality of the student experience at UW–Superior, but have also allowed faculty and staff to arrive at a shared and unifying understanding of our public liberal arts mission.

On a larger campus, it would be difficult for an individual faculty member, even working in collaboration with others, to have this type of impact. Where high levels of scholarly productivity are an expectation, such deep involvement with academic initiatives at the institutional level might require a shift into an administrative career. On a public liberal arts campus, by contrast, one can remain full-time faculty and exercise academic leadership through shared governance. As faculty increasingly withdraw into their own individual pursuits, often at the expense of the collective academic enterprise, public liberal arts colleges are ideally positioned to maintain the tradition of faculty responsibility for the academic mission of the university.

At a public liberal arts college, those immediately around you provide the primary intellectual community and the work of teaching provides the chief intellectual challenge. What then is the role of disciplinary scholarship at a public liberal arts college? Without conscious attention to scholarly pursuits, the heavy time demands of teaching and service might squeeze out research and writing entirely. And yet, both the personnel rules of my campus and my department require faculty to engage in scholarly activities that are public and peer-reviewed. While our departmental rules emphasize the process of scholarship rather than arbitrary time lines and quotas, there is a shared expectation that we each lead an active scholarly life. This expectation reflects our commitment to the ideal of the scholar-teacher and our belief that faculty cannot encourage students to become novice disciplinary practitioners unless faculty remain engaged disciplinary scholars themselves. In a sense, we serve as a bridge between the non-academic world that our students inhabit and the world of the academic disciplines.

A career at a public liberal arts college is not for everyone. Those whose central driving passion is the production of traditional disciplinary scholarship would find the daily demands of teaching and service to be a frustrating distraction from their calling, which would be a disservice both to the individual and the broader academic community of which we are all a part. After all, many of the great works that have touched both me and my students are products of the research university. And despite the obvious fondness that I feel for UW–Superior, it is not exempt from the pettiness, backbiting, and territoriality that are endemic throughout higher education. There are also challenges that are particular to public liberal arts colleges, most especially the stress that comes from juggling multiple competing faculty roles. And yet here, on the periphery of the academic world, there is an intellectual freedom that can be difficult to find in the centers of disciplinary life. Here, freed from constant publication pressures and from the intellectual jockeying through which scholarly status is established, we can engage in ways of thinking and ways of learning that defy the conventional standards of disciplinary life. And that, in the end, was what I had been searching for. Here, at this little school on the western tip of Lake Superior, I found a place where ideas truly do matter.

Works Cited

Astin, Alexander W. *What Matters in College: Four Critical Years Revisited*. San Francisco: Jossey-Bass, 1993.

Nelson, Craig E. "On the Persistence of Unicorns: The Trade-Off between Content and Critical Thinking Revisited." In *The Social Worlds of Higher Education: Handbook for Teaching in a New Century*, edited by Bernice A. Pescosolido and Ronald Amizade, 168–84. Boston: Pine Forge Press, 1999.

Pascarella, Ernest T., and Patrick T. Terenzini. *How College Affects Students: Findings and Insights from Twenty Years of Research*. San Francisco: Jossey-Bass, 1991.

Perry, William G., Jr. *Forms of Intellectual and Ethical Development in the College Years: A Scheme*. New York: Holt, Rinehart, and Winston, 1970.

Roche, William. *Why Choose the Liberal Arts?* Notre Dame, IN: University of Notre Dame Press, 2010.

Schneps, Matthew H. *A Private Universe: Misconceptions That Block Learning*. South

Burlington, VT: Annenberg/CPB, 1989.

Schuman, Samuel. *Old Main: Small Colleges in Twenty-First Century America*. Baltimore: Johns Hopkins University Press, 2005.

Sipress, Joel M. "Why Students Don't Get Evidence and What We Can Do About It." *The History Teacher* 37 (May 2004): 351–63.

Sipress, Joel M., and David J. Voelker. "From Learning History to Doing History: Beyond the Coverage Model." In *Exploring Signature Pedagogies: Approaches to Teaching Disciplinary Habits of Mind*, edited by Nancy L. Chick, Aeron Haynie, and Regan A. R. Gurung, 19–35. Sterling, VA: Stylus Publishing, 2009.

Sipress, Joel M., and David J. Voelker. "The End of the History Survey: The Rise and Fall of the Coverage Model." *Journal of American History* 97 (March 2011): 1050–66.

Tinto, Vincent. "Reconstructing the First Year of College." *Planning for Higher Education* 25 (Fall 1996): 1–6.

Notes

1. The notion that small colleges are fundamentally different from large universities is the central theme of Samuel Schuman's *Old Main*.

2. Schneps, *A Private Universe: Misconceptions That Block Learning*.

3. Perry, *Forms of Intellectual and Ethical Development in the College Years*. It was a workshop presented by biologist Craig E. Nelson that first exposed me to Perry's work. Nelson provides a summary of Perry's model that discusses its practical application in the classroom in "On the Persistence of Unicorns: The Trade-Off between Content and Critical Thinking Revisited."

4. Sipress, "Why Students Don't Get Evidence and What We Can Do About It." Nelson's application of Perry's model to the science classroom had a profound influence on my course redesign; "On the Persistence of Unicorns."

5. Sipress and Voelker, "From Learning History to Doing History"; Sipress and Voelker, "The End of the History Survey."

6. For a discussion of the ways in which overspecialization can distract from engaging great questions, see Roche, *Why Choose the Liberal Arts?*, 15–50.

7. We were particularly influenced by the work of Vincent Tinto. See, for instance, Tinto's "Reconstructing the First Year of College." See also Astin, *What Matters in College*; and Pascarella and Terenzini, *How College Affects Students*.

2

Detours, Intersections, and a Few Bumps in the Road

M. *Therese Seibert*
Sociology, Keene State College

As a young pre-teen in Louisiana, I had already mapped my life out as a good Catholic wife, mother, and social worker. Academia was nowhere in the horizon. But a college education has a way of derailing the best-laid plans; it opens up pathways to the mind and detours to the most unforeseen places. Reflecting on my twenty-five years in academia, I initially viewed my professional life as one of serendipitous twists and turns. But with additional introspection, I realize it is not by happenstance that for the past fifteen years I have been working at Keene State College, where personal choices and long-standing values intersected with new experiences, professional opportunities, mentoring, and, most of all, student interaction. I have ended up where I want to be and where I am most comfortable, but my path to Keene State has been nothing short of circuitous.

As a child active in community service, encouraged by my Catholic school, I was excited to discover that I could continue this kind of work as a social worker. The sisters, however, informed me that I would have to obtain a college degree. Two obstacles lay in my path: no one in my family had ever graduated from college, and my grades were generally below average. Undaunted, I buckled down, studied hard, and improved my grades significantly, because now grades mattered. This childhood expe-

Acknowledgments: I want to thank Dr. Jay Kahn, who encouraged me to participate in this project while he served as interim president of Keene State College, and for his helpful feedback on an early draft.

rience anecdotally reinforces what educational research reveals: that students perform better when coursework is personally relevant.[1] I went on to attend the University of Southwestern Louisiana (now called University of Louisiana) where I obtained scholarships and campus work that were much needed since I was putting myself through college. While pursuing a major in sociology, I participated in the department's internship program and worked as an undergraduate research assistant. Little did I know that in years to come those two things would intersect into what we now call community-based research, a form of engaged scholarship that has defined much of my academic life.

After college graduation, I secured what I thought was the job of my dreams with the Comprehensive Employment and Training Act (CETA), a federal program designed to help recipients of Aid to Families with Dependent Children develop skills and training they needed to exit welfare. Unfortunately I got this job in 1980, the year Ronald Reagan was elected president. True to his campaign speeches, he moved swiftly to terminate CETA's Public Service Employment Program, the program that I managed. With piles of federal legislation and streams of paperwork undermining my ability to assist clients effectively, the political attacks on CETA added to my disillusionment with social work. I left this profession to pursue a doctorate in sociology.

To say that I was clueless about all aspects of obtaining a doctorate is an understatement. I chose to pursue this degree at Louisiana State University because I could commute there from my home in Lafayette. Quite naively, I envisioned my future work as a professor to entail teaching a few hours a week and conducting some research at home, a perfect fit for raising a family. Enter my mentor, a hardworking, ambitious assistant professor and a specialist in quantitative methods. During my first year of graduate school, he hired me as a research assistant for his grant-funded research on race inequality. Working with my mentor introduced me to the realities of academic life at a Research I university (to use the category name of that time). That same year, my research methods instructor invited me to co-author an instructor's manual for a methodology textbook. I was now on the road to becoming a quantitative researcher. By the time I obtained my master's degree in 1986, I had presented three conference papers, received a student award for my research from the Southern Sociological Society, published a book review, and produced a master's thesis on occupational gender inequality. With a research agenda like this, who had time for community service?

At that point, my mentor and his wife moved back to their native state of Texas, so that he could work at the Population Research Center (PRC), housed at the University of Texas at Austin. My first husband and I followed suit so that I could pursue a doctorate in sociology and work on population-related research as a PRC research trainee. I worked the hardest in my life at University of Texas. Plagued by self-doubt, I was determined to transform myself into a worthy academic and demographer. Fortunately, theory always came easy to me; mastering statistics did not. I therefore took every advanced statistics course I could, became a teaching assistant with a seasoned statistics instructor, and worked on several demographically based grant projects, in addition to my work as a PRC trainee. Moreover, I presented papers at professional conferences, publishing one of them in conference proceedings, and I published my master's thesis in an academic journal. After obtaining grant funding, my mentor and I also started work on a research monograph. It was during this busy time that I gave birth to my daughter; she arrived two weeks after I completed my coursework and took my comprehensives, and one week after I defended my dissertation proposal. Female role models for managing the conflicting demands of my academic and personal life were few and far between. Fortunately, I was awarded two dissertation grants, one from the National Science Foundation (NSF) and the other from the American Association of University Women, to help me navigate the different directions my life was taking. Secure in my professional identity as a social demographer, I left Austin with my family intact and my doctorate in hand, to start my academic career at the University of Virginia.

My graduate school experience prepared me well for my six years at Virginia. My quantitative training and research on gender and women's issues provided a solid foundation for the related courses that I taught. I received another NSF grant soon after arriving at University of Virginia and published an article from my dissertation. My mentor and I finally published our research monograph titled *Long Time Coming: Racial Inequality in the Non-Metropolitan South, 1940–1990*. Using advanced statistical methods, we assessed a number of hypotheses derived from human ecological theory. We received favorable reviews for this mainstream sociological work. Yet despite their policy implications, the many statistical summaries and discussions of sociological theory were hard for civic leaders to grasp, much less draw from in formulating policy.

After becoming a single mother post-divorce, I decided to leave University of Virginia without going up for tenure. In 1997, I began work as a visiting professor at Colorado College. Teaching at a private liberal arts college differed greatly from my previous experiences at research institutions. While I occasionally attended campus functions with students at University of Virginia, Colorado College went so far as to provide take-home dinners for faculty members so they could host student gatherings in their homes. Suffice to say, much more was expected of me with respect to student support and interaction. Perhaps the biggest difference between the two institutions lay in the classroom. At University of Virginia I taught social statistics to about fifty students with two teaching assistants; at Colorado College I taught a similar course to about fifteen students, some of whom actually came to my house for tutoring. At Virginia, I primarily lectured, while Colorado College promoted engaged forms of learning.

It was at Colorado College that I discovered service-learning and received much support for infusing it in an ethnic relations course. This class produced a report for the local Urban League chapter that documented racial inequality in Colorado Springs. Interestingly, this report required my students to apply some of the same research skills and theoretical insight found in *Long Time Coming*. A remarkable difference, however, was that the Urban League used the report to effect changes in social policy, improve social programs, and increase support for its goal of racial justice. Even more impressive was the impact this project had on motivating students to develop research skills. Students requested that I teach them qualitative research methods to complement their quantitative work. Indeed, they were willing to meet on Saturday mornings to receive this out-of-class instruction. Needless to say, I embraced this newfound pedagogy that motivated students to learn, and that steered me back to community service.

My work with students on this report inspired my transformation from a *pure* sociologist using quantitative research to advance theory to a *public* sociologist who uses sociological research and theory to advance the local community. Although Herbert Gans coined the term "public sociology,"[2] this approach did not receive widespread attention until Michael Burawoy's 2004 American Sociological Association presidential address.[3] Burawoy pointed out that theory development, sociological research, and community service are not mutually exclusive activities. I agree. In fact, American sociology was founded on this three-pronged approach at the University of Chicago by sociologists like Jane Addams, who established Hull House for the purpose of advancing society through sociological research. Working with residents of impoverished neighborhoods, she produced data that informed social policy and program development aimed at alleviating poverty and other social problems.[4] I left Colorado College with the dream of creating a research center based on the sociological tradition of Jane Addams.

This dream became a reality sooner than I expected after another academic detour emerged. As a social demographer, my sights were still set on a research institute that would support my quantitative research. To be honest, Keene State was my backup college, that is, until I interviewed there and was diverted from a job interview at Colorado State. Nestled in the bucolic foothills of the Monadnock region in southwestern New Hampshire, Keene State is surrounded by awe-inspiring natural beauty. Keene, a small city of about 23,000, and its hinterland mirror the scenic places I fantasized about as a child growing up in a concrete-ridden, working-class neighborhood outside New Orleans. Its cultural vibrancy captivated me. The fact that Monadnock residents come together annually at Keene's Pumpkin Festival to break the *Guinness Book of World Records* record for most jack-o-lanterns lit simultaneously provides insight into this city's local color. Its strong commitment to health and well-being are summed up in Keene's Vision 2020, a citywide project designed to make Keene the healthiest community in the entire United States in the next decade.

During my interview, Keene's reputation as a tight-knit community with significant social capital became evident. I was therefore surprised to see such a significant divide between the campus and the local community when I arrived in 1998. Only a few faculty members were incorporating community work into their courses. Indeed, only a few faculty members expressed any interest in community engagement. What makes this observation especially surprising is that Keene State College grew out of Keene Normal School, which was founded in 1909 for the purpose of preparing the best teachers in New Hampshire to serve their communities. Indeed, walking through Keene State's Appian Way is an archway that reads, "Enter to Learn: Go Forth to Serve."

What I soon learned, however, was that the seeds of engaged teaching, learning, and scholarship were being scattered across the campus. Though small in number, a vocal group of faculty was cultivating an engaged campus. Equally important, the college's administration provided strong and steady leadership for creating sustainable partnerships with the local community. As an outgrowth of the college's 1993 master plan, the college's president and vice president of finance worked with local leaders to develop community goals, remodel a historic theater, and engage in workforce development. As a first-generation college graduate himself, Keene State's president reached out to students who were the first in their family to attend college. Indeed, he founded the Early College Awareness Program for middle-school students living in an impoverished town close to Keene.

My dean, a longtime advocate of engaged learning, approached me and a colleague to submit a Campus Compact of New Hampshire grant proposal to institutionalize service-learning on campus. While the vice president of academic affairs supported this pedagogy, even creating a service-learning task force, Keene State was far from an engaged college. With Campus Compact funding, we expanded service-learning through faculty development activities and community events. Additional funding allowed us to hire a service-learning coordinator who brought the program to a whole new level. By the end of the grant, assessment data indicated that we had become an engaged campus, a conclusion validated first by Keene State's 2005–2009 strategic plan, which aligned service efforts with instruction, student success, and faculty evaluation; second in 2006 by the Carnegie Foundation's classification of Keene State as a community-engaged college; and third in 2007 by recognition on the President's Higher Education Community Service Honor Roll.

A new president joined the college in 2005 and a new provost arrived in 2006. Under their leadership, Keene State continued branching out into different directions of engaged teaching, learning, and scholarship, which is not surprising since their search committees screened for candidates who embraced the college's culture of academic excellence and community engagement. In 2006, Keene State replaced its General Education Program with the Integrated Studies Program (ISP), which places greater emphasis on connecting knowledge and skills from different experiences and applying them to a variety of settings. That same year, the college transitioned to a four-credit model, thus expanding class time for skill development, community and global connections, undergraduate research, and creative projects. By 2010, Keene State housed a well-staffed Center for Engagement, Learning, and Teaching (CELT) with three divisions: Instructional Design, Experiential Learning, and Academic Technology.

My own growth as an engaged teacher and scholar parallels or, more accurately, intersects with Keene State College's development into an engaged college, given my efforts to foster this structural and cultural change. Because of my work with the Campus Compact grant, I participated in many institutes, workshops, and conferences, and eventually became a consultant. All of these experiences were professionally helpful, but in my own community service initiatives students have been the primary impetus. Annually, Keene

State students contribute about 400,000 hours in credit-based service and another 17,000 in volunteer community service.[5]

Soon after arriving at Keene State College, I wanted to model focus group interviewing during a research methods class. I therefore conducted one during class, which centered on how the research methods course could be improved. The students were vocal and united in their response: they wanted to be out in the community conducting real research that counted. A departmental survey of students confirmed interest in community research. A survey of area agencies also revealed a need for research assistance with surveys, program evaluation, and needs assessments. I thus began building the Community Research Center (CRC) by interviewing directors of similar centers and by securing funding from Monadnock Community Foundation to hire an office assistant.

The CRC was based on a community-based research (CBR) model. As Strand et al. discuss in their book *Community-Based Research and Higher Learning*, CBR occurs when students, faculty, and community partners work cooperatively on research that will advance and empower community agencies, while providing students with a meaningful and challenging research experience.[6] Sociology students participated primarily by taking my third-year sociology course, Community Research, though they could also work for the CRC through independent studies or college work-study. Working with city officials, community professionals and leaders, board members, consumers, and active citizens provided students with a model of community engagement that I could never replicate in the classroom. Agencies used most of the CRC research for program development, strategic planning, and to secure funding.

One criticism I often hear about service-learning, including community-based research, is that it lacks academic rigor. My first response is to invite critics to look over CRC student reports. All of these projects required students to collect, analyze, and summarize data following scientific guidelines and ethical principles. Students also revised their papers numerous times based on feedback from me, fellow students, and community partners. My second response is that community-based research is like any other teaching method; it can be rigorous or it can be easy. In his book *The Courage to Teach*, Parker J. Palmer cites education research showing that a passion for the subject matter, commitment to academic excellence, and love of teaching are more important than a specific method.[7] Ultimately, we need to use methods that work best for us and our students.

Over time the Community Research Center became a victim of its success. In 2001, nineteen students produced reports for ten different agencies.[8] With advice from Keene State administrators, I began charging agencies a nominal fee after the Community Foundation Grant ended. Charging partners, even just a small fee, changed the nature of the center. To keep up with demand, I started completing a number of projects myself and started demanding more from my students. I soon realized that the CRC had become a kind of a research factory with students working furiously to meet deadlines for paying customers. I started scaling back on the number of projects, but the scope of reports seemed to grow. For example, in 2005, the center conducted a large-scale program assessment for a local mental health agency that involved surveying consumers, interviewing professional counselors, and conducting focus group interviews of consumers' family members. We repeated projects of this caliber many times. I eventually stopped charging clients, which painfully meant terminating my office assistant. A sociology adjunct professor began working on CRC projects with me and became its director in 2004 when I stepped down to become departmental chair. The silver lining is that as the number of the Community Research Center's projects declined, there were more and more professors using service-learning across the campus who could alternatively address the needs of community partners.

My work with the CRC resulted in a scholarship of engagement I never anticipated when I entered academia. To be honest, I did not see my CRC research as worthy of promotion to full professor. When I went up for my first promotion, my vita displayed articles published in academic journals and a research monograph; now it listed CRC reports. I only assembled my promotion file after the urging of a colleague. In preparing the file, however, I realized that my community-based research had resulted in scholarly growth unmatched by many years of "pure" research. Virtually all of my early research involved statistical analyses of secondary data. In contrast, my community research called for analyzing primary data either by mail, phone, or e-mail surveys or by conducting personal or focus group interviews. Indeed, every new project challenged me to expand and refine my research skills. My work on the report "City of Keene Community Goals 2002 Telephone Survey" provides one example. Before this project, I had never conducted computer-assisted telephone interviewing (CATI). Nevertheless, CATI clearly was the best research method for this project. I therefore obtained an Alumni Grant to set up a CATI lab in the Advancement Office, worked with students and community leaders to design a telephone questionnaire, contracted with a marketing group to generate usable numbers for random-digit dialing, trained and supervised student interviewers, and analyzed CATI data. The students and I produced a report summarizing the direction in which Keene residents wanted to see the community advance. Community administrators and leaders used the report for strategic planning. Each CRC project presented research exigencies as challenging as the ones in this project, and I had worked on no fewer than twenty-five projects over a five-year span. Maybe I was worthy of going up for full professor after all. I was promoted in 2007, the same year that I was named Keene State's Teacher of the Year. I am truly fortunate to be at a public liberal arts college that values and rewards engaged scholarship and teaching.

When I returned after a sabbatical, the CRC's director had secured a tenure-track position in another department on campus. I took this opportunity to limit class projects to two or three in order to build a better sense of community and to give students more time to study relevant theory. For example, in the spring of 2009, CRC students crafted grant proposals for AIM High, an agency offering support for at-risk youth; administered a mail survey to sociology alumni; and interviewed residents of local homeless shelters as part of the state's Bureau of Homeless and Housing Services' needs assessment. The students were most excited about the homeless project. Our class had taken on this project because the bureau had lost its funding to conduct the assessment and thus relied on college students to collect data. In preparation for this project, the students and I visited three local shelters. By the third and last shelter, the class was moved to tears realizing how blind we had been to the extent of this problem. In response, we searched the literature on homelessness, read articles on theories and research in this area, and shared what insights each of us had gained.

A community of scholarship and service emerged among students during this class. The following year, three students in this class and two others they had recruited indicated that they wanted to work on the homeless project as independent studies. They knew that I was not teaching the Community Research course, and they wanted to be sure the bureau's surveys were conducted. One of the students who had already worked on this project agreed to lead the students in studying homelessness, conducting surveys, and presenting their semester's work at Keene State College's 2010 Academic Excellence Conference. The students did a wonderful job at the conference. Right before graduation, they encouraged me to create a service-learning course specifically on homelessness to replace the skills-based Community

Research course. The course was introduced the following year. It challenges students to review scholarship on homelessness; converse with professionals, advocates, and residents; volunteer at the local emergency shelter; conduct the surveys; craft grant proposals for an emergency shelter; make a public presentation to educate the community on homelessness; and pull all of these projects together in a reflective portfolio. This rigorous course, the brainchild of sociology students, keeps me on the path of community service.

My post-Katrina course provides another example of how students steered me toward community service. While teaching a statistics course in 2006, not long after the devastation of Hurricane Katrina, I mentioned to my students that I grew up in New Orleans and often worried about my family and friends there. A couple of students who had assisted in post-Katrina recovery through Keene State's Alternative Spring Break program approached me after class about creating a sociology course on the aftermath of the hurricane. They requested that the course include service on-site. At that point, I had not been to New Orleans since Katrina, but these students brought me home. I created the summer school course titled Race, Class, and Katrina, designing it to be a sociology capstone with community service and community-based research that included participant observation and informal interviewing. My best friend from childhood provided a home base for seven students, my husband, and me for one week in May 2007. Unfortunately, the non-profit organization we worked with turned out to be a disaster, with the exception of one day working at an animal shelter. The community-based research component, however, was a success; we listened intently to many Katrina stories from people of all walks of life, who urged us to tell their stories up north. The students and I organized a fund-raising event where they presented their research and Katrina stories and sent the donations to the animal shelter. Despite positive feedback from the students, I promised myself never to teach this course again, given the exasperating service experience. Keene State College students, however, are a force to be reckoned with.

The next year, two students who had worked in New Orleans as part of the Alternative Spring Break approached me after a statistics class about resurrecting the capstone course. I declined, noting that I was taking students to Rwanda that same summer. They suggested that I teach the course in the spring and take students to New Orleans during the following winter break. I then recounted my frustration with the service component of the previous course, on top of simply not having time to recruit students and organize the course. Undaunted, they told me that they would take care of recruitment and the service project. I challenged them to recruit twelve students and create a service plan before the semester ended. I assumed they would be too busy with end-of-semester coursework to meet this challenge. In two days, they had recruited twelve students, taken steps to organize the community work, and even thrown in some ideas for fund-raising. I still had an out: surely my colleagues would vote against adding this course to the spring 2009 schedule on such short notice. Impressed with these students, however, they supported the course. I am grateful to these students for their tenacity. The course, in particular the service component, was a success. This story exemplifies what is good about teaching at a public liberal arts college where engaged learning and research often emerge from students who take ownership of their educational experience.

While working with students on research continues to be my greatest professional joy, my academic journey also reflects a long detour that needs explanation. I was hired to replace the newly retired sociologist best known as the founding director of Keene State College's Cohen Center for Holocaust and Genocide Studies. With support from the administration, the center's next director assembled a committee to create our nation's first undergraduate minor in Holocaust studies. He invited me to join the committee even though I knew very little about the Holocaust. I was not alone. In preparation for teaching courses in the minor, committee members participated in a Holocaust reading group and a myriad of professional development activities and events. Our hard work led to an active minor and major in Holocaust and genocide studies.

While teaching a course on genocide, I became acquainted with a survivor of the Rwandan genocide who spoke publicly about her harrowing experience. We eventually developed a friendship, and my interest in this genocide grew. I started teaching courses on Rwanda in the summer of 2006. One year later, I traveled to Rwanda for the first time on a grant from the Marion and Jasper Whiting Foundation to develop a Rwanda-based course and to explore the feasibility of launching a research project on rescuers during the genocide. While there, I forged a fruitful and sustainable partnership with the organization Never Again Rwanda. In 2008, six students traveled with me to Rwanda as part of my summer school course, Rwanda: Then and Now. We explored Rwanda, absorbing this country's beautiful ecology and rich culture. We also participated in a weeklong human rights workshop sponsored by Never Again Rwanda. I repeated this trip in 2011, but this time Never Again Rwanda organized a two-week International Peace Building Institute for ten American participants and ten Rwandan participants. The Institute connected us with government and NGO leaders and took us to places like parliament, the Ministry of Justice, and Mpangao Prison. Virtually all aspects of the course were successful, and I plan to repeat it.

One of the students on this trip was a first-year student who had taken my Introduction to Sociology course. Even though she had not yet declared sociology as her major, she completed this fourth-year sociology capstone course that required her to produce a research paper grounded in sociological theory. I was so impressed with this student's paper on post-genocide reconciliation in Rwanda that I encouraged her to present it at the Academic Excellence Conference. After additional work on the project, she presented her research at the Northeast Regional Undergraduate Research Conference sponsored by the Council for Public Liberal Arts Colleges (COPLAC). The following spring, her research article titled "Reconciliation in Rwanda: Is It Really Working?" was published in COPLAC's undergraduate journal *Metamorphosis*. As a recipient of the Class of 1969 Bruce LeVine Mellion Grant, this student will embark on a new research project: a comparative analysis of rape during the Rwandan genocide and during war, ethnic cleansing, and genocide in Bosnia-Herzegovina.

Working with this student has rejuvenated my own research on rescue during the Rwandan genocide. After the NSF and the Harry Frank Guggenheim Foundation rejected my grant proposals for this research, I started losing motivation to move the project forward. Interestingly, one of the NSF reviewers voiced a concern that I could not carry out the proposed research at a college like mine and with undergraduates as research assistants. My student's own research on Rwanda defies the reviewer's misconception of liberal arts colleges and a lack of understanding about how high we can set standards for undergraduate research. But more than anything, it has been this student's wide-eyed enthusiasm that has jump-started my own research. It also reminds me how much I feel at home working closely with undergraduates on research at Keene State College. Perhaps the fact that I once worked on a grant-funded project as an undergraduate makes me more open to working with undergraduates, who can benefit from an absence of graduate research assistants.

It is not surprising why I generally feel at home at Keene State College. According to our Graduating Student Survey, 37 percent of our students are first-generation students, just as I was.[9] While this fact may present some challenges with respect to college preparedness, it has also allowed me to be a part of tremendous intellectual growth among our students.

For example, when I first started teaching at Keene State, I confronted a student whose remarks in my ethnic relations class made some students feel uncomfortable. This student told me that he had been raised by a single mother on welfare and grew up in public housing, and he could not stand to hear some of the remarks made in class. After coming up with a class participation model mutually acceptable to all, the class got back on track. More significantly, this student not only completed the ethnic relations course, the following year he raised $10,000 to bring Cornel West to speak to a packed auditorium because he was so inspired by West's book *Race Matters*. This student went on to study and work in Ecuador for several years. It was even more rewarding to have this student come back to Keene State College years later to speak to one of my sociology classes about ethnic relations in Ecuador.

When I lament my lack of peer-reviewed publications in academic journals or prestigious grant awards, as I often do, I need to remind myself of the possibilities Keene State has given me and the profound joy I have experienced in working closely with undergraduates on projects that have taken my students and me across the country, indeed across the world. No, my professional life did not pan out as I envisioned it years ago. I neither became a social worker nor stayed at a Research I university to conduct quantitative research, but these experiences have intersected and informed my community-based research. Moreover, these detours have led me to a place where I am at my best, a place where my teaching, research, and community service intersect synergistically. And while I may have encountered some bumps over the years, the institutional structure at Keene State is such that I have been able to transform problems into creative opportunities, together with students, to conduct research, address community problems, and intellectually engage a world beyond the campus. Yes, a college education has a way of derailing the best-laid plans. Thank goodness.

Works Cited

Burawoy, Michael. "For Public Sociology." *American Sociological Review* 70 (2005): 4–28.

Caine, Renate, and Geoffrey Caine. *Education on the Edge of Possibility.* Alexandria, VA: Association for Supervision and Curriculum Development, 1997.

Gans, Herbert J. "Sociology in America: The Discipline and the Public American Sociological Association." *American Sociological Review* 54 (1989): 1–16.

O'Connell, Thomas. "Jane Addams and the Vocation of Sociology." *Sociological Imagination* 36 (1999): 18–34.

Palmer, Parker J. *The Courage to Teach: Exploring the Inner Landscape of a Teacher's Life.* San Francisco: John Wiley & Sons, 1998.

Strand, Kerry J., Nicholas Cutforth, Randy Stoeker, Sam Marullo, and Patrick Donohue. *Community-Based Research and Higher Education.* San Francisco: Jossey-Bass, 2003.

Notes

1. Caine and Caine, *Education on the Edge of Possibility.*

2. Gans, "Sociology in America."

3. Burawoy, "For Public Sociology."

4. O'Connell, "Jane Addams and the Vocation of Sociology."

5. Keene State College's Admissions Web page, accessed May 14, 2013, http://admissions.keene.edu/student-involvement.

6. Strand et al., *Community-Based Research and Higher Education.*

7. Palmer, *Courage to Teach.*

8. The list of agencies includes AIDS Services of the Monadnock Region, Cheshire County House of Corrections, Housing Focus Group of the Monadnock Region, Keene Housing Authority, Keene Middle School's Together Against Violence, Mentally Ill in Need of Diversion, Monadnock Collaborative Service-Link, Rachel Marshall Outdoor Learning Lab, Swamp Bats, and Town of Hinsdale.

9. See Table 1 on page 2 of Keene State College, "Graduating Student Survey 2012," accessed May 14, 2013, http://www.keene.edu/ir/gss/GSSReport2012.pdf.

3

The Outsiders
Undergraduate Research in a Liberal Arts Institution

Dylan Fischer
Forest Ecology, The Evergreen State College

I remember the exact moment I first thought about teaching at The Evergreen State College. I was twenty years old, a sophomore at a community college in Eugene, Oregon. I had gone back to school after a brief dropout period at the end of high school. I was financially strapped, having grown up in a low-income single-parent household. That also made me a candidate for federal student aid, and I took full advantage of it. My friends from my childhood were nearly all struggling with choices they made, or the choices being made for them, in the non-college life. Early pregnancy, addiction, suicide, dead-end jobs—I had examples of all of these among my peers. I also had examples of friends who entered a permanent party phase that oscillated from endless streams of summer festivals to snow-crusted winters as ski bums in the Cascade Mountains. Eugene was a town whose recent history was built on a foundation of 1960s radicalism, which also formed the foundation of my childhood and that of my peers. "Anything goes" was the social framework we inherited, and had to make sense of, in the post-hippie 1980s and early 1990s.

In that lens, The Evergreen State College was known as a special enclave where making sense of this new era seemed to be taken seriously, and people really were trying to do things differently. It seemed to us (my

Acknowledgments: I would like to give a special thank you to the other authors of this volume for constructive feedback during the writing of this essay.

friends and me) as if Evergreen had reinvented higher education based on a new ethos of no hierarchy, equality, and experimentation. In fact, to some of the early architects of the college, that was exactly the goal. This institution was trying to be the change that we wanted to see in the world. Among institutions, Evergreen was not just an alternative college, it was THE alternative college, the Harvard of its kind, a leader in the movement to find meaning in the complexity of the alternative universe we all found ourselves in, in the late twentieth century. Global warming was happening, there was a hole in the ozone layer, nuclear war was a possibility, struggles for social equality and justice faced new hurdles as it became clear that the 1960s did not erase racism or sexism from our experiences in everyday life. And at the same time the American dream was "biggering and biggering" in suburbia everywhere as if none of the environmental and social justice hurdles we faced were real. It was strangely like a page of *The Lorax* was being acted out by Americans everywhere in sport utility vehicles driving between the mall and newly constructed homes. Against all that mess, Evergreen stood out as THE place where many of these struggles were at least being talked about in a serious way. It had abandoned grades and the curriculum bent to address the big issues of the day.

So why would a twenty-year-old community college student be audacious enough to imagine teaching at this college more than a decade in the future? Why not? At the time I was hopelessly idealistic. I had gone back to school with a clear sense of mission. As a result of either a misplaced sense of environmental guilt or a genuine desire to make a better mark in the world, I believed that it was my responsibility to excel in college and work toward making a better world through my own education. And for some reason, in between a calculus exam and a ten-minute plant taxonomy dichotomous key quiz, I stood on the sunlit lawn near the forest edge of my community college campus and I thought about the future. I got a clear image of what I wanted to do with my life. Then I quietly put the vision away and dedicated myself to my studies for more than a decade until I found myself in a faculty position here at The Evergreen State College— destined to face the realities that were hidden in my rose-tinted view of the institution. I'd say be careful what you wish for, but the world is never really that black and white. As it turns out, the audacious belief that an outsider can make significant contributions to academic work was a theme that I would carry with me. The belief is integral to my work with undergraduate research at a college that seems hell-bent on helping the outsider succeed. Evergreen's official mascot is the geoduck (pronounced "gooey duck"), a large, slow, phallic-looking bivalve native to the south Puget Sound, but our real mascots are the outsiders. Any underdog, zero, rebel, or refugee can call us home, and the institution celebrates these outsiders with glee. After all, outsiders have a special power—a power to see beyond the mundane realities to which the rest of us get accustomed. Indicatively, renowned Native American novelist Sherman Alexie gave our commencement speech in the spring of 2013. His speech was based entirely on the premise of being an outsider to education, the United States government, pop culture, and life itself, since he barely escaped death as an infant. The audience ate it up! It turns out that being an outsider is also a very helpful pattern in research, where, as I learned in my graduate training in ecological science, the best questions often come from people with fresh eyes.

I began teaching at Evergreen in fall of 2005. It was my dream job in my early career as an undergraduate student and it was still my dream job when I finished my PhD, but for different reasons. I am a forest and ecosystem ecologist. I had spent my graduate education days studying carbon and water cycles in forested environments. I became especially excited about conducting research because you could see changes happening before your eyes. In forest ecology research, you could also see things that were non-intuitive, like the dynamics associated with carbon, water, and nutrient cycles. We can't see carbon water and nutrient flux in real time, but you can see these cycles in the data. My research gave me tremendous appreciation for the complexity in these cycles. It also helped me appreciate how important it was to have hands-on experiences in order to understand these cycles that are fundamental to the climate changes our planet is currently undergoing. I wanted to share that experience with students. Suddenly there was a job opening at Evergreen, this medium-sized college nestled in one thousand acres of forest in western Washington. I could take students right out the door and measure carbon, water, and nutrient cycling in intact forests! I applied to the college and got the job offer. I knew the college was different, and I still thought that in that difference was the possibility of better answers about how to engage with science education in the twenty-first century. As I've matured into a faculty member, I face the realities that many college professors face where our hopes for our students don't always materialize, our bureaucracy can be both frustrating and cumbersome, we are often stretched too thin, students are not always happy, and we are at once in a profession where we are destined to be wrong and at the same time be responsible for providing answers. But what I've learned is that it's much more valuable to ask questions than memorize answers.

"Evergreen is a little different." I start out nearly every introduction to the college I work at with that phrase. We have a constantly evolving curriculum (set by the faculty) that adjusts to the current needs of our students and both local and global issues. We also have our students full-time; the students take one class at a time (sixteen credits), and we teach one class (twenty-five students). Faculties have no departments, and our office locations are assigned irrespective of discipline. We have to teach together, and almost all classes are interdisciplinary. Okay, now if you heard this for the first time, some inevitable questions start bubbling up to the surface about how this works, but for now, suffice to say that it does work. It works wonderfully for student-centered liberal arts education. Students are free to ask the questions they care about, and because they care so deeply, they have an unparalleled engagement with their work. When first teaching on this campus, almost every new faculty immediately notices that these students really care! Students talk about having been transformed into lifelong learners—and lifelong question-askers. If they don't come in intellectually curious, they inevitably leave that way. They get to explore the world in all its complexity and interdisciplinarity as if they are at the center of the academic stage, not just passive observers. They are outsiders to academia when they enter the college, but they leave as active participants.

From the start, my approach and my thinking went like this: If undergraduate research can work at all, it should work at our Evergreen. We have no institutional structures to blame if it doesn't! As a faculty member, I can devote quarter after quarter to classes in undergraduate research if I choose. I can design classes around research topics. I can have all my students learn hands-on research skills as their full-time academic work and teach courses that focus on getting students doing research. I can really focus on research methods and critical analysis of data in each course. In essence, our institution can be a laboratory for figuring out what works. Note that this may seem like a small departure from the rose-tinted, world-changing role I imagined I would be playing when I first dreamed of teaching here in my sophomore year! But when dreams meet reality, we have to choose graspable goals. The process of undergraduate research is important because it mirrors the transition from outsider to educated participant—and if the world needs anything from us, it needs us to be those active and educated participants. I saw breaking down the barriers between introductory college education and research as a civic contribution. What if students were introduced to research opportunities from day one of their education? What if they were invited to come up with their own research questions and follow their own ideas from the beginning? What if they were empowered to answer questions in a research framework—not just the upper-crust students, but ALL of them? They could get excited about the scientific process first, and then they would be motivated to do the grunt work required to learn the basics of mathematics, statistics, biology, and chemistry. My first classes were a testament to these ideas.

In my first ecology classes, I encouraged students to pursue their own research questions in rapid cross-country field trips in wild, off-the-beaten-track places. I have fond memories of waking up in our frost-tinged sleeping bags, under the fading stars, in remote deserts. We spent all day in the sun and wind coming up with questions and taking measurements for projects that had been thought up the night before around a campfire. We paraded through slot canyons measuring piles of debris trapped in trees (technically referred to as "hovels"). We enthusiastically measured plants along elevation gradients in the Olympic Mountains that make my legs hurt just thinking about them. These were large classes for the field—between twenty and fifty students—and we were likely somewhat of a circus to behold! Imagine being a hiker exploring the serenity of nature when suddenly a swarm of college students with sampling frames, sampling gear, binoculars, and other scientific paraphernalia suddenly descend and begin doing instant field science! Needless to say, some of those early classes were a little over the top.

I encouraged the students to pursue questions far from my own specialty area—shining examples of what is called "mission creep" in the business world. The ideas were far-out, the preparation for research was minimal, and the results were predictably mixed. I found great support for what my PhD advisor, Thomas Whitham, had said about letting students come up with their own research projects: "They will always come up with ideas you would have never thought of, sometimes for a good reason." Nevertheless, many of those projects bore fruit. Students continued to work on some threads of these projects for years, presenting them at national meetings and working on papers. Students from those first classes became foundational members of our research lab, and after five years we began publishing undergraduate research papers in high-profile scientific journals at a rate of about one per year. Many of the first papers from our lab came from those first classes and the freedom students had to ask their own questions. Many of our lab's current projects also stem from what students found in those first classes. I have added Linus Pauling's adage to my collection about research: "The best way to have a good idea is to have a lot of ideas." And I have come to realize that a great way to have a lot of ideas at an undergraduate institution is to unlock creative potential by opening up the doors of possibility. In our lab, the cornerstones of effectiveness are based on having a large community, inviting creativity, and building on the good ideas with everybody involved. We then encourage the hard work and attention to detail necessary for success by encouraging the students to see the possibility in their research and to do the work needed to realize it. The important lesson from that early work was not that it was too open or that mission creep was too easy, but rather that it was community and question-asking that were the most essential pieces of a good research program. I realized how important it was to teach your students to build bridges and recognize opportunity. I learned it was important to let them come up with unworkable ideas, and encourage the ones that seem more workable. This kind of approach builds excitement and it helps the students stay critically engaged in their work—because they care. But of course, even if it works in the long run, research at a public liberal arts institution is also not easy. I still constantly struggle through the minefield of potential problems. The problems with developing an undergraduate research program can be bureaucratic, financial, or institutional. They can also arise from simply making bad, or unlucky, decisions and not having enough time to follow up.

Even among the more successful outcomes of a decade running a research program, my first years as a beginning faculty member were strewn with missteps. In one of the lab projects, a group of five undergraduates and I spent three summers working on the best ways to analyze plant communities that were being exposed to prescribed fire. Each summer we were convinced we had the right approach. After three summers we had learned enough about measuring plant communities and what it takes to train outsiders that we could feel confident with our data. Our early errors came from multiple sources. I was not fully committed to a new study system. I was a forest ecologist and I had been pulled into some research in local prairies. As somebody new to the system, I didn't always make the right connections. I might have had great conversations with management technicians at my field site, but there were higher-ups with whom I needed to network to be an effective researcher. My students were excited but unsure. Sometimes they were haughty and overly proud about their work, and they were unwilling to share it with other students. Our process did not always foster open questioning and idea generation. It took time to help cultivate an atmosphere in the lab where sharing resources and data was better than an approach that favored fear, privacy, and competition. Our lab's forest carbon cycling research was similarly plagued, and we had a large learning curve to come to terms with the best ways to measure forest carbon flux in western Washington forests—even though I thought that was my specialty area! Luckily, I had a group of students who were willing to work through the kinks and contribute to a research program that has produced several nice papers[1] and an active blog-site (blogs.evergreen.edu/ecology). These students have gone on to work as fishing observers on ocean vessels, land managers in remote wilderness areas, remote-sensing specialists, urban ecologists, arborists, medical students, and successful graduate students in ecology. I'm proud of their work, but I'm more proud that they found out how to work together through the challenges the work presented. Our technical methods have evolved and our lab has grown more sophisticated in many ways, but we have kept alive the idea that our current approaches might be wrong, that every student can make a contribution.

At a public liberal arts school like Evergreen, though, we experience a double-edged sword in that we have freedom to pursue ideas wherever we choose, but we also struggle against both a national stereotype for liberal arts colleges versus Research I institutions and a local stereotype of our institution. At the national level, people I meet at conferences always know about Evergreen, but they don't recognize it as a place where we do research. Inevitably I end up discussing our unique pedagogy instead of research ideas. This is a problem common to almost all liberal arts colleges and so we are not alone here. The local stereotype is that we are a hippy-dippy school with low standards. Ironically, because of the freedoms we have and my pursuit of research for my students, I know I actually hold my students to an incredibly high standard. I want them to act like grad students at a research institution, something that would never be asked of undergrads elsewhere. At a recent national meeting, my former advisor summed it up in the midst of a student talk when he leaned over and said, "You really throw them into the fire, don't you?" But the amazing thing is that the high standard works. Even for those who don't end up pursuing research after college, their experience means they have a better understanding of how to interpret research in the real world. If they thought science was absolute, a process of finding the correct answers to things, they instead find the uncertainty that makes up the actual intellectual territory with which scientists deal every day. If they thought they would like to do ecology research because they like being outside, they learn that being outside is not always a walk in the park, and that logistic constraints and time management are key to successful outcomes. On a recent trip to a remote research site, we spent four days getting eaten alive by mosquitoes in 95-degree heat, but we got our data! Students learn that science is not really about memorizing arcane facts; it's about having creative ideas and thinking about worlds that are different from your own. That's the fun part and that's the part that really takes some students by surprise. It CHANGES their lives. We ask them to determine answers to questions about why questions are important. We ask them to place their academic work in the context of a bigger picture. Doing that work makes them better candidates for going into graduate programs at research institutions, if they choose that path. It also makes them better citizens because they start putting everything they encounter into a bigger picture and they never stop asking questions.

At a small school, the other faculty also makes up a lot of the community that makes or breaks an undergraduate research program. At our institution, we are mandated to teach cross-disciplinarily with partners nearly every quarter. Teaching partners always have a different background. Their reasons for ending up at our public liberal arts college are various. Some are here because they went to a small liberal arts college themselves and wanted to teach at a similar institution. Some are here because they wanted to get away from other liberal arts colleges. Some are here because they wanted to do something different—and this was the place to do it. And some are here because this was the job they were offered and it looked pretty good at the time. Almost nobody comes to a small liberal arts institution in order to do research. Many, though, hope to maintain some connection to their graduate research lives. Especially in the sciences, association with active research is held in highest esteem, and when faculty come to smaller institutions they often bring that hierarchy with them, whether they know it or not. They may think subconsciously that to be doing research is to be doing "real work," and to be "just teaching" is valuable, but not respected in quite the same way. Others come fleeing that dichotomy! Whether they excelled as graduate students or not, they come to a small college precisely to not be involved in research—an uncertain, highly stressful, and often frustrating world. They also bring with them the value system from another place, only they reflexively employ it in reverse: that is, to be doing research is the opposite of what they came here for. The faculty may have come from that world recently or they may have memories of that research-teaching divide from thirty years ago.

At my college, though, I have to teach with all of them. I am mandated to keep switching those with whom I co-teach. If I want my undergraduate research work to flourish, I need my teaching partners to either share my enthusiasm for undergraduate research or at least be sympathetic with my attempts. I need to understand their approaches and have them understand mine. They haven't always understood—and maybe I haven't either. In one meeting early on I was told by a fellow faculty member that I was in the wrong place: "You don't want to be here." (Indeed, I suddenly did want to be someplace else after I heard that!) In another case, a dean reviewing my work for the year told me to slow down and not work so hard or I might burn out. But in other cases, I've found faculty who not only commiserate, but have been great allies in doing research work that goes beyond the classroom. Sometimes these have been colleagues from completely different disciplines. I once taught with a poet and fiction writer, for example, who intuitively understood the importance of engaging students in research work, and together we challenged our students to write great poetry on the backs of some great scientific research experiences. We compiled the research papers and the poetry from the class into a single book and the students learned about typesetting and publishing to boot. Other faculty from other disciplines have become tremendous friends as together we grapple with the logistical constraints of trying to merge teaching with research in new and innovative ways. Geologists, ornithologists, virologists, biologists, historians, and anthropologists—we all deal with the same issues trying to help students at once escape the confines of individual disciplines and do meaningful work that lives professionally beyond the classroom. We are all trying to bridge the gap from outsider to full participant.

When I first arrived at the college, I thought the desire to emphasize research might be a struggle associated with my generation of relatively young faculty. Maybe we were raised academically in an environment (in the late 1990s and 2000s) that favored research over teaching and we were just trying to hold onto that? After almost a decade, though, I know that this is a longer-term issue. I learned recently of a class early in the history of The Evergreen State College that ran for three years straight, taught by two faculty members (Steve Herman and Michael Beug) and involving a rotating body of students. They published twelve papers in the course of those three years and did foundational research on marine animals in the Puget Sound. This was an undergraduate class in the 1970s! One woman at our college (Elizabeth Kutter) has stubbornly held up a world-class research lab through cutting-edge undergraduate research on phage since the 1970s. I met another alumnus recently who conducted forest ecology research as an undergraduate at the college in the 1990s and then went on to independently publish the paper in a well-respected journal without most of the faculty even knowing it happened! For faculty, past, present, and future, the struggle to work with the tensions between teaching and professional work in our disciplines, between the realm of the classroom and the realm beyond the classroom, between relevancy in our disciplines and teaching about what has come before, between content and process, is present in some form. Regardless, I now know that faculty at our institution have worked to merge research and teaching at the undergraduate level since its inception. We have several amazing long-term faculty whose professional work and students demonstrate that. My guess is that it's about the same everywhere, despite our distinctiveness.

So if Evergreen is a little different, but also a laboratory for work at other institutions, what do these experiences tell us in the larger scheme? What do they tell the new faculty member who has just arrived at their dream job at a liberal arts college? I suggest a few things. First, it is important for professors to remain open to new ideas. Enjoy being at an institution where exploring new ideas can be prized more highly than obtaining large grant dollars—and if your institution is not already that way then fight to get it there! Focusing on ideas makes us valuable outsiders in a world structured by funding given to insiders. Have fun and remain enthusiastic about engaging your students in the real world even if it drags you into broader territory than you expected. The benefit of that enthusiasm will outweigh the costs associated with unfamiliarity. Second, grow a large and supportive community on campus. If you can't get it at your institution as is, grow your own! Encourage a community of students and journal clubs and invite visitors from other institutions to make guest appearances. Third, don't fear the inevitable missteps. We all make mistakes. Modeling dedication to an idea and learning from those mistakes is much more important to our students than showing them we know "everything" (especially because we don't). Fourth, embrace a diverse community of colleagues. Pursuing undergraduate research works for me, but it may not be for everybody. Others have really good reasons to teach and be scholars with different approaches. Good for them! We can learn from each other without needing to adopt one another's approaches. At a small college, it's also important to remember that you may have others who share your approach in completely different disciplines. I'm a scientist, but my closest colleagues in terms of a pedagogical approach may be in the humanities. Modeling those connections is important for our students. Fifth, know your history. In nearly everything we do, we stand on the shoulders of giants. Many came before you who struggled with the same issues. Knowing who they are and what their struggles were can help you at a small college when you worry, "Am I alone?" and "Am I the first to face this challenge?" The answer is probably not. We are not alone through history, even if we are alone in our locality and time. And finally, don't fear either being or welcoming the outsiders. If you're not careful, you might just learn something. There are student outsiders on our campuses right now, staring at the horizon, imagining impossible futures. It's our job to help them try to get there.

Note

1. These papers were E. J. Rook, D. G. Fischer, R. D. Seyferth, J. L. Kirsch, C. J. LeRoy, and S. Hamman, "Responses of Prairie Vegetation to Fire, Herbicide, and Invasive Species Legacy," *Northwest Science* 85 (2011): 288–302; C. W. Elliott, D. G. Fischer, and C. J. LeRoy, "Germination of Three Native Lupinus Species in Response to Temperature," *Northwest Science* 85 (2011): 403–40; J. L. Kirsch, D. G. Fischer, A. N. Kazakova, A. Biswas, R. E. Kelm, D. W. Carlson, and C. J. LeRoy, "Diversity-Carbon Flux Relationships in a Northwest Forest," *Diversity* 4 (2012): 33–58; and W. D. Bretherton, J. S. Kominoski, C. J. LeRoy, and D. G. Fischer, "Salmon Carcasses Alter Leaf Litter Species Diversity Effects on In-Stream Decomposition," *Canadian Journal of Fisheries and Aquatic Sciences* 68 (2011): 1495–1506.

How Everything Influences Everything Else
The Strange and Wonderful Journey to an Integrated Academic Life

Jeffrey Trawick-Smith
Education, Eastern Connecticut State University

> We pass through the present with our eyes blindfolded. We are permitted merely to sense and guess at what we are actually experiencing. Only later when the cloth is untied can we glance at the past and find out what we have experienced and what meaning it has.
>
> —Milan Kundera, *Laughable Loves*

I am often invited to speak to new faculty members at my university about how to juggle the demands of teaching, research, and service. I am a senior faculty member and hold an endowed chair in early childhood education. These things apparently qualify me to share my insights on traversing the complex world of our small public liberal arts university. Usually the faculty I address are bleary-eyed young newcomers, struggling with the transition to a new life. They may have just defended their dissertations, uprooted their families and moved across the country, rented apartments or homes that their entry-level salaries will allow, and settled their children into school. Their minds are drifting to the syllabi they need to prepare for classes that start in a week. My talk also competes with the minutiae of campus life they are trying to absorb: where to get a parking sticker, how to log into Blackboard, or which retirement plan to choose. They are polite but distracted, and it is clear that my words won't completely connect. The experience always reminds me of trying to share life's lessons with my grown children so that I might help them avoid the challenges I have faced. Like my children, the new faculty nod, smile, and then do whatever they will do. They will make their own way, as it should be.

Over the years, I have reframed this presentation to become a profile in human development—my own—rather than a "how to" on survival at our unique university. It has become a study of the various ecological niches in which we find ourselves—the diverse contexts of a university like ours that shape our development as professors. There are fewer practical tips in my most recent version of this speech to new faculty. It has become simply a preview of the wondrous journey on which they are embarking. And I become not just a little wistful that I am not traveling along with them on this road, all over again. My approach is to tell my own story, to describe the stages that I have passed through on my way to a fully integrated and satisfying academic life. I present that story here.

The Splintered Identity of an Emerging Scholar

Like so many of my peers with whom I was an undergraduate in the 1960s, I became downwardly mobile, much to the chagrin of my middle-class family who had worked so hard to get me to college. I had become radicalized in the Vietnam War era and highly sensitized to the disparities between the haves and the have-nots in our world. During a community service requirement for my African-American studies minor, I began tutoring children living in low-income neighborhoods and witnessed firsthand the devastating effects of poverty. So, after graduation from a prestigious university, I sought employment that ensured I would live below the poverty level and as one of "the people." My life goal was to help those in need and to avoid joining the ranks of the bourgeoisie. I considered a job with the United Farm Workers Union for fifty dollars a week and a place to sleep and as a Head Start bus driver in an inner-city school. What I finally settled on was joining the Teacher Corps as an intern, working with five-year-olds living in one of the most deprived neighborhoods in Louisville, Kentucky.

But in this early stage of young adult development, my identity was hardly clear or complete. Lurking within me as I taught kindergarten was a very different self—an active scholar who wanted to study more and grow intellectually. Inspired by the lives of the families and children with whom I worked, I simply could not read enough about children's development and its cultural influences. I gobbled up scholarly books and research articles. I read *Death at an Early Age, Teaching as a Subversive Activity*, and even Urie Bronfenbrenner's seminal article, "Toward an Experimental Ecology of Human Development."[1] My colleagues would shake their heads on Monday mornings when I arrived at my school with another wild educational idea that I would share after a weekend of reading.

Graduate school was inevitable. I chose to leave teaching and enter a full-time doctoral program in child development and early childhood education. I believed that I was leaving behind one identity in pursuit of another. Entering an advanced degree program and becoming a scholar was, in my mind, a distinctly separate pursuit from my work with children in schools. I had made a choice: an academic life over work with real children and families.

Just prior to settling into the role of graduate student, a new identity emerged in my life, suddenly and wonderfully. I met and married my wife and became a husband and eventually a father. This new identity would clash in minor ways with my scholarly work. As my wife sought work in a university town saturated with smart, overqualified professionals, we struggled to live for a time on a tiny stipend I received as a graduate assistant. We shared a car—a rusted, rumbling Chevy—and discovered hundreds of new ways to prepare soybeans for dinner. My wife would sit for hours, smiling sweetly, as I explained to her the cognitive benefits of young children's symbolic play—the focus on my dissertation research. Likely, my mini-lectures at the dinner table only added to the tastiness of a soybean casserole! It was a happy time, but challenging.

A New Faculty Member Attempts to Piece the Puzzle Together

During and after graduate school I was faced with a minor crisis of identity. Which of these many roles—community activist, scholar, father—that seemed to pull me in various directions, would eventually define me? What kind of faculty position would I seek? On the one hand, my role as a scholar had come into clearer focus. My dissertation had received much attention in my field and I now viewed myself as a researcher. My mentors in my graduate program encouraged—no, *expected*—that I would join the faculty of a Research I university. On the other hand, my first son was born and my wife had narrowed her career interest to providing services to the elderly. What kind of position could I take that would be the very best for my family? Where would there be good schools and opportunities for my wife to pursue her career? I am proud to say that I accepted an assistant professorship at a small, public liberal arts university, bypassing positions at research institutions. I had made my choice, I thought. My role of father and husband held primacy; goals of academic greatness or lasting contributions to society would take a backseat.

However, these other identities still bubbled below the surface as I began my new university career. I worked hard to maintain a research agenda, conducting small studies and presenting papers at important conferences. This was difficult. I had to find time to record and code the behaviors of children attending a small child-care center on campus and write up my findings while planning and teaching four different courses each semester. I would squeeze in an hour of writing time in the morning before a class or just before bed. Over time, I learned to coordinate the activities of my complex life. I would modify an article I had written so that it would become a session in a class I taught. I would use video from my studies to illustrate key concepts in my child development courses. I even used a set of lecture notes as the beginnings of an article for publication and for a paper to present at a conference. All of these efforts helped me cope with time constraints. However, I was still viewing my work as comprised of distinct and sometimes incompatible pieces that needed to be somehow fit together into the puzzle that was my academic life.

I made room for my other roles in this same puzzle-piece way. Still eager to contribute directly to the community, I joined a number of groups and sat on boards. I tried to work directly with teachers or families in workshops or presentations at least once a semester. I would write small articles in non-refereed publications for teachers or parents. Some of these activities took me away from home in the evening—a time when I wanted to be with my family. When our second child was born, it was a critical time to be attentive to my home life. My solution was to become involved in community activities that related most directly to my scholarship and teaching and in which my family and my students could all become involved. For example, I chaired a committee to plan a community event for children in which all of these important people could participate.

To torture the puzzle metaphor just a bit longer, my various roles fit together in a messy way. My life resembled a five-year-old's best efforts to complete a puzzle that was too difficult, so that she needed to force the pieces together in places they didn't belong. I was able to turn, move about, and squeeze together the disparate parts of my life—my responsibilities as a father, scholar, teacher, and community member—but it was a tight fit. Here is what I had not yet discovered: placing together splinters of my work into a picture that made some sense was one thing; integrating them into a coherent whole was quite another.

A Tenured Professor Begins to Integrate His Academic World

After five years at my university and a positive tenure decision, I was catapulted into my next stage of development as a scholar when I finally got around to reading a book that had been recommended to me long ago in graduate school. I can remember the moment when I first picked up Yvonna Lincoln and Egon Guba's *Naturalistic Inquiry* on a summer day at a coffee shop where I was plotting out my next study on young children's symbolic play. It is not the kind of book one would immediately think of as life changing. Remarkably scholarly, dense, and drawing from such fields as history, philosophy, physics, mathematics, and education, the book was the furthest thing from a light summer read at Starbucks! Yet I was enthralled. It took me the full summer to get through it.

To explain my response to this work, I need to describe my worldview at the time. I was a card-carrying positivist, believing that simple, causal, unidirectional relationships always exist between one thing and another. As a researcher, my goal was to identify the variable or variables—teacher behaviors, classroom materials, or peer interactions—that produced complex symbolic play in young children. I sought to discover these causal relationships in other aspects of my life as well. Earlier in life, as a kindergarten teacher, I would ask, What things can I do in my classroom that will lead directly to positive outcomes for my five-year-old students? Which classroom practices *cause* them to learn to read, do math, or interact in more positive ways with their peers? In my family life, I believed that if I engaged in "good parenting," my children would turn out well. (Only later was I to discover that my children would turn out in the ways they would turn out, regardless of anything I might say or do!) As a university professor, I believed that if I prepared engaging class activities or presented material in a very organized way, my students would learn. Simple as that. A causes B.

I saw each linear relationship in my life as distinct and parallel, with little connection to any other such relationship. When I planned and taught classes, I was exclusively promoting student learning. When I conducted research projects and wrote about my findings, I was contributing insights to my field. When I played ball with my children in the yard, I was enhancing their development (and, sure, also preparing them for lucrative careers with the Red Sox). Each activity was important; but each produced a narrow, distinct outcome. Then I read Lincoln and Guba.

The premise of these authors is that causality is simply not viable. They argue persuasively that, in any field, as soon as one determines that one thing causes another, an exception will be discovered. This is as true in history or physics as it is in human development. Eventually, too many "causality violations" are found for us to trust that a simple causal relationship truly exists. In my own research, for example, the relationships I have reported between teacher behaviors and child outcomes have been contradicted by too many outliers—individual children for whom my causal conclusions don't apply.

One thing that contributes to this problem, according to Lincoln and Guba, is that there are multiple and often bidirectional influences at work in the world. When I discover that a particular interaction by a teacher promotes early math learning, can I be certain that there are not many other unknown effects that are also at work that explain this? Do gender, cultural background, socioeconomic status, temperament, IQ, social competence, emotional health, physical health, dispositions toward mathematics, or even a bad head cold at the time of the study affect a teacher's impact on learning? More important, do children's behaviors and learning affect what teachers do? To what degree do children elicit specific teaching strategies from teachers, rather than the other way around?

Lincoln and Guba conclude that the world should be viewed as a system, rather than a collection of simple relationships between one thing and another. In their words, "everything influences everything else in the here and now."[2] The role of researchers is to provide an elaborate description of all they experience as they study a phenomenon, rather than try to isolate linear causal relationships.

What does any of this have to do with my development as a scholar, the reader is surely asking? Once I carefully considered Lincoln and Guba's thesis (and, based on this, conducted an ethnographic study of children that focused on rich descriptions rather than linear relationships), I began to view my life and work differently. I came to recognize that my teaching and research were endeavors that were too complex and interrelated to be neatly teased apart. My research—not only the discoveries I made, but my methods of inquiry—affected my teaching. For example, when I conducted an ethnographic study in which I wrote a "thick description"[3] of children's interactions—rather than conducting the spare regression analyses as I usually would—I also became more descriptive and less linear in the college classroom. I was now more inclined to move beyond questions of *what* influences children's development (to be covered on the next quiz) to grapple with the far more interesting questions of *why* and in *what alternative ways* children turn out as they do. I began to guide students in forming their own working hypotheses about the multitude of ecological factors that might explain the development of a single child, just as I was doing in my research. I was careful to point out that children have as much effect on adults—parents and teachers—as the other way around. My teaching, it was clear to me now, influenced the research questions I asked. One startling revelation I experienced during this time was that student questions in class were a rich source of ideas for forming my own research questions. When a student asked a challenging question about child development, I would, without full awareness, be inspired to investigate it. Sometimes the investigation turned into a full research project.

My work in the community or with parents and children shaped the content of my teaching and my research methods. For example, I noticed that I more often taught or studied the impact of families' culture or socioeconomic status on children's development when I served on a Head Start advisory board with parents who lived in poverty. I could even see the ways my family life intertwined with my work. Because of my unique area of teaching, I would regularly share stories, recorded language samples, and video of my own children with my university students. I would offer examples of the challenges of parenting that my wife or I had experienced firsthand. My students' opinions, questions, and positions on parenting and family life—unique to their own backgrounds and cultures—caused me, at times, to reassess my own parenting beliefs and child-rearing practices.

I now recognized that, in my life as a whole, everything was influencing everything else, as Lincoln and Guba propose. Many of these multidirectional interrelationships among my work and family experiences already existed in my life, but my discovery of them transformed how I approached my work. I began to see that I could make each hour of work contribute at once to many, or even all, spheres of my world. When I spent an hour planning a class, I was in some way influencing my research; an hour of research, conversely, was shaping my course planning and teaching. My experiences in the community and with my family were affecting and being affected by these areas of my professional work. Lincoln and Guba call this "mutual simultaneous shaping."[4]

No longer was I trying to fit disparate puzzle pieces together to accomplish distinct and competing goals. I was striving to fully integrate life's activities into a network, a coherent whole. When approaching the world in this way, not only was my life easier and my work more productive—I had never published more and was recognized by my university for excellence in both teaching and research—but my day in, day out life was so much more meaningful.

An Endowed Chair Is Inspired by Undergraduate Student Insights

Another twenty years passed and I had become a senior faculty member and a teacher-scholar-parent-community advocate with no clear boundaries between these different roles. I had published my most successful book, on child development and culture, which was a model of my integrated life. The book was conceived when I taught an introductory course on child development. I came to realize that available textbooks for this course focused too exclusively on the behavior and learning of white, middle-class children. After some extensive reading of research on children of color—some of it hard to find and sometimes unpublished—I presented a paper at a conference and later published an article on the gaps in our knowledge of developmental diversity. I integrated this paper into several class sessions for my course and then developed a new course on families, culture, and community. At the same time, I planned a study on the play of children at home and school in Puerto Rico, which I carried out during a sabbatical leave. This study too was woven into courses, conference presentations, and several publications. My book was the culmination of all this research, writing, and teaching. Even my family life contributed to this new network of scholarship I was engaged in around children and culture. I had been collecting drawings and early writings of my own children and eventually included these in a new edition of my book, alongside similar work done by children in other societies. (I argue that my children were among the best-published preschoolers in the world!) So every part of my work in this area influenced every other part in the here and now.

Having settled into a very satisfying academic life, I could not imagine any other event further transforming me. Yet several interrelated developments sent me in a new direction. A dynamic, forward-thinking new president was hired at our university. In one of my earliest interactions with her, she invited me to apply for a new endowed chair in my field; after a search, I was offered this position. There was a nice budget attached to this chair for my research; I began considering the ways it could be used. At this same time, our new president was inspiring us to transform our campus into "an elite, but not an elitist" public liberal arts university. She engaged our faculty in discussions about how to achieve this. Our work culminated in a new strategic plan, an element of which was a goal to increase opportunities for undergraduate student research—an important benchmark for liberal arts universities, but one I had rarely even considered.

So I was at once inspired by a charismatic president who proclaimed the benefits of undergraduate research and needed to find an important use for funds attached to my endowed chair. I decided to implement a plan to engage my students in my own studies of young children's play. I would use my available resources to bring students who worked with me to national conferences and, in some cases, to employ them as research assistants. These initial attempts were interesting, but not always successful. I came to learn that some students were more eager to conduct research than others. Some were better able to handle quantitative methods; others could contribute most to qualitative or descriptive studies. It was a trial-and-error process over a number of years before I learned how to individualize students' involvement in my research based on their strengths and interests. During this process, however, I slipped into a simpler mode of thinking, believing that the professor-student researcher relationship was linear and unidirectional. I imparted research knowledge (and assigned tasks) to students, but I was not fully aware that my students were having as great an impact on me.

One year I received a research grant from a prestigious foundation to conduct a very complex study on preschool play and mathematical thinking. Did I dare include my undergraduates in such an important grant-funded study? I assembled a team of six capable students and we conducted the investigation together; our findings were important and students accompanied me to two national conferences to present them. But here was the most important part of the experience for me: I came to understand how fresh and unique the insights of undergraduate students could be. These students challenged and inspired me and set my thinking in new directions. They raised questions I would not have asked and shared perspectives that someone overly immersed in the field would never have thought to consider. Not only did their ideas guide the conduct of the study itself, but their perspectives influenced our interpretation of findings and found their way into publications and presentations. So students were influencing me as much as I was guiding them.

I have not conducted a research project since that time that did not include undergraduate students in vital roles. In fact, over the last few years, I have given over complete responsibility to students for a series of studies on children's toys and have assisted them only when they have needed help. They are now taking the lead on some of my studies and enlightening me with their findings and conclusions. They present their work in my classes and in workshops for parents and teachers. Through all of this, my research has had as much impact in my field as it ever has, as evidenced by the many conference presentations and published articles that I have co-authored with my students. But my scholarship is now comprised of a complex network of learning, teaching, and research, in which everything influences everything else.

Work with student researchers has now become one of the most satisfying aspects of my academic life. I wonder how well the integrated and meaningful life that I now live could have been achieved working at a large research institution, as I had once hoped to do. Would I have come to know my undergraduate students well enough to have heard and learned from their fresh perspectives? Would doctoral candidates, who are so intensely focused on their own research and who already hold strong preconceptions in their fields, have provided such unique viewpoints on my academic work as my undergraduates do? Would I have had a chance to work with and touch the lives of undergraduate students at all at a research university, given their emphasis on guiding doctoral students? Would work with more advanced graduate students have been as satisfying? Could I have played as powerful a role in helping undergraduates consider—often for the first time—that they have the abilities to pursue careers as researchers and scholars? Finally and perhaps most important: Would doctoral students have been nearly as much fun as my undergraduate students can be?

My Speech to New Faculty

In my most recent speech to new faculty, I shared much of what I have written here. I presented clever graphics of the interrelationships among areas of my work, described the stages of my professional development, gave many helpful tips, and told terrifically funny jokes (at least I found them to be so). But the expressions on the faces of my audience showed they were distracted, anxious, excited, and bewildered. And I thought, maybe the journey to an integrated life at a liberal arts university is something one must simply experience, not something that can be conveyed in a one-hour presentation (or a chapter in a book). It may be that liberal arts scholars must fit the pieces together on their own and actively construct their own lives in ways that hold meaning for them. I might lend some emotional support to these newcomers along the way, as can other faculty mentors. But the road to a satisfying academic career may be an act of self-discovery that can only be achieved by living one's life. Indeed, this integration of all that is important in the world may only be fully understood in hindsight. The sole message I should try to convey to new faculty is that work at a small, public liberal arts university will be filled with wonderful surprises. It will take you in unanticipated new directions, allow you to learn things you would never have learned in another setting, and provide opportunities for you to contribute to your field in novel ways. Most important, the liberal arts university is a place to truly touch the lives of others.

Works Cited

Bronfenbrenner, Urie. "Toward an Experimental Ecology of Human Development." *American Psychologist* 32 (1977): 513–31.

Kozol, Jonathan. *Death at an Early Age.* Boston: Houghton Mifflin, 1967.

Kundera, Milan. *Laughable Loves.* New York: Harper Perennial, 1999.

Lincoln, Yvonna S., and Egon G. Guba. *Naturalistic Inquiry.* Newbury Park, CA: Sage, 1985.

Postman, Neil, and Charles Weingartner. *Teaching as a Subversive Activity.* New York: Dell, 1969.

Notes

1. Kozol, *Death at an Early Age*; Postman and Weingartner, *Teaching as a Subversive Activity*; Bronfenbrenner, "Toward an Experimental Ecology of Human Development."

2. Lincoln and Guba, *Naturalistic Inquiry*, 151.

3. Ibid., 125.

4. Ibid., 151.

5

Notes from an
Academic Odd Couple

Lee Rozelle and Jill A. Wicknick
English and Biology, University of Montevallo

Two professors with wildly different personalities shed preconceptions and abandon sacred cows to put together an original environmental program for the University of Montevallo community.[1]

Lee

When I arrived at the University of Montevallo in 2003, I had just finished my dissertation in environmental literary criticism while working as an instructor at Louisiana State University. Having felt myself swallowed up by the LSU mega-campus, I was quietly relieved to land a job at a small college in my home state. When my graduate school major professor visited Montevallo shortly thereafter, he cocked his head and whispered into my ear what major professors whisper when their acolytes wind up with big teaching loads: "publish your way out of there." But I found myself quite at home at a COPLAC university. I was taken in by the University of Montevallo's historic campus and its unique role in Alabama higher education. In 1896, the Alabama Girls' Industrial School opened in Montevallo with the goal of training self-supporting women. In 1923 it became Alabama College, opened its doors to males in 1956, and in 1969 became the University of Montevallo. Ten years later the Alabama legislature affirmed

Acknowledgments: Special thanks to the following persons for comments that improved the manuscript: reviewers Brian Becker, Alesha Dawson, Stefan Forrester, Adele Leon, and Kelly Wacker; and our fellow *Roads Taken* chapter authors.

Montevallo's mission statement "to provide students from throughout the state an affordable, geographically accessible, 'small-college' public higher educational experience of high quality, with a strong emphasis on undergraduate liberal studies and with professional programs supported by a broad base of arts and sciences."[2] I knew none of this during my campus visit, but I noticed that the place had a different feel than the research universities I had attended. Somehow the students seemed more at home. Students and faculty alike were definitely more "artsy" and also seemed more engaged with local issues.

As an undergraduate, I was involved with the University of South Alabama's Environmental Club, but in graduate school my environmental efforts became increasingly theoretical. There was a growing disconnect between my sense of environmental responsibility and my evolving career. Writing about environmental issues in order to help the humanities consider issues of place is a worthy pursuit, but while writing my dissertation I felt myself growing pale in the library's fluorescent lights. As I focused my energies on *The Ecocriticism Reader*,[3] I was reminded everywhere I turned of such urgent issues as ozone depletion, global warming, deforestation, droughts, and food insecurity. I wrote frantically as a means to fill the void of a more tangible and concrete social activism, and reminded myself that my writing scholarship was indeed "doing something" to help.

Jill

It has been easy for me to figure out where I fit: biologist, environmental advocate, professor at a liberal arts university. They feel so natural that they don't seem like decisions, although they were.

I have been an animal lover since I was young. In elementary school, I was an active member of the Ecology Club, which recycled newspaper—even then I knew that saving trees meant saving habitat. I joined the Girl Scouts solely for the year-end camping trip on which I was lucky enough to touch a bullfrog.[4] From a young age, I was on the path to biology and environmental activism. In graduate school, I focused my research on ecology and conservation biology, which are the foundations for understanding the environment and human interactions with nature. My undergraduate time was spent at a small liberal arts college; I knew I wanted to be at a similar place. Although I had grown up in the north—Philadelphia, Cleveland, Chicago—I completed my graduate degrees in Texas and Louisiana and liked the warmth of the southern latitudes. Coming to the University of Montevallo was the perfect combination of biology, liberal arts, and sunshine. And, as it turned out, environmentalism.

I moved to Montevallo in 2003 eager to begin my first tenure-track position. Newly divorced, three-year-old son and two elderly dogs in tow, I was ready to start the next phase of my life.

Lee

Ecocriticism is by definition an interdisciplinary approach with a social mission, but as an environmental literary critic I had little sense of how far I would have to get out of the classroom to make sense of my new career. Though I published articles about the importance of environmental stewardship and lectured on how place informed poetry, no evident structure existed for me at that time to apply these concepts on the (college) ground. What I did find as a new professor at University of Montevallo was a nascent environmental community involved in numerous undertakings: a university legal battle with a limestone company over a wetland, a biology course that singlehandedly developed an effective campus recycling program, a mad philosophy professor who taught a Sustainability Banquet course, a new campus-community organic garden, and plans for an elaborate walking trail that would connect town, campus, and local parks. I noticed that most of these projects were faculty/student collaborations but that professors had no release time and very little financial support for these ventures. Although our student Environmental Club was quite fervent—huge for a campus our size—there were almost no academic courses that dealt with either environmental studies or environmental science.

Jill

The University of Montevallo campus is charming: bumpy red-brick streets, towering pecan trees lining the walk to the president's house, and purple wisteria that drapes in bloom over the entrance to Main Hall. A healthy population of redheaded woodpeckers appears in spring, along with flocks of eastern bluebirds. Our peaceful campus lake is home to softshell turtles and territorial dragonflies. The university has distinctive elements too. We have the oldest homecoming tradition in the United States, in which students compete to create the better theatrical production of their own plays, and an architectural history that includes a small family cemetery from the 1800s, buildings used during the Civil War, and landscaping designed by the Olmsted Brothers.

As I was unpacking my books and biological specimens in an office painted the color of the sky, a student, Sally, introduced herself and said,

"I want to start an environmental club and a campus recycling program. Will you be the faculty advisor?" I was shocked that there was no recycling program on campus or in town (I had to teach my son to throw his recyclables in the garbage), that we had students who had never recycled, and, of greatest concern, that we had students who didn't care about their impact on the planet. With Sally's question, I became immersed in local environmental activism. We started the club and I found a county recycling dumpster that everyone on campus and in town could use. Over time, we created a campus organic community garden, volunteered for our city's Arbor Day celebration, held cleanups in our town park, and raised $2,000 to purchase a composting toilet for UM's Shepherd Observatory. By design our foci were education and activism; in practice our activities centered on making positive changes both on campus and in the local community.

This was an exciting and rewarding start to the service component of my career. But my work with the club was surprisingly time consuming and exhausting. We had passionate students who wanted to be active but they needed a lot of support and guidance, which required that I be fully involved in almost every club activity. Weekly club meetings and almost daily conversations with club presidents were the norm.

A few years later, my Conservation Biology class worked with campus housekeeping to organize a recycling pickup service for all offices and classrooms. Recycling was so popular on campus and in the local community that we could not handle the demand, so we eventually built a city-university cooperative recycling center. In the meantime, fellow biology professor Mike Hardig and I gathered information and testified in court to help the university protect our Ebenezer Swamp from eventual destruction by a potentially multimillion-dollar limestone operation. Remarkably, we won; the quarry was not built. Surprise was the reaction all around, specifically *because* we are in Alabama where the prevailing attitude was that little wetlands do not beat big business. It turned out that Alabamians do care about recycling, about a sixty-acre swamp, and about the environment.

The undercurrent of student excitement about environmentalism was becoming stronger and more noticeable around campus. We were in need of formal education to complement this enthusiasm, but there were few campus-wide courses with environmental content at the time. My Conservation Biology class was designed for majors and has two prerequisites, which prevents general reach into the wider student body. Art historian Kelly Wacker's Landscape to Land Art course addresses environmental issues but is similarly discipline-focused and was not widely known. A newly developed class, Sustainability Banquet, taught by philosophy professor Michael Patton, was attracting attention and held promise: this unique course addresses ethical issues about food sources while challenging the students to serve a multicourse dinner to one hundred people using ingredients found within one hundred miles of campus. In addition, the university had no sustainability committee and no organized way to think about its environmental impact. But an energy was building. We had a growing group of faculty who were expressing their interest in environmental issues. The emerging environmental community on campus gave us a starting point.

Lee

Little did I know how many other faculty members there were out there ready to get involved—not only biologists but also art professors, writing teachers, historians, business professors, philosophers, and social workers. I was really surprised how many people on campus and in the surrounding region were working on environmental projects. Jill and I knew the students were hyped—the Environmental Club was pushing hard on a range of issues—but I had no clue how much support we were going to ultimately receive. I did notice, though, that the faculty members who seemed to have made the greatest impact on campus—faculty who deserved the most credit in terms of service and academic achievement—also seemed to be the most exhausted and dispirited. This showed me that successful projects were often done in isolation and their creators perhaps did not receive proper recognition.

I rarely make great first impressions and often come across as somewhat of a kook. Sputtering, stuttering, trailing off in midsentence . . . I do that. Also, I have this habit of tossing off really bad one-liners when I'm nervous. So trying to wedge my way into various university subgroups and offering elaborate speculations about yoking their projects all together in some utopian campus vision would have failed miserably, I think, if Jill hadn't been there to add credibility and levelheadedness. When I first met her, Jill seemed quite cordial but distant, and with a healthy degree of skepticism. She was—and indeed still is—a no-nonsense type of person, and that gave her the gravitas that I very much lacked as an academic lackey. So I came to realize that if I could convince her that my proposals were sound,

I would have a better chance of persuading the others. Moreover, as a biologist she had practical expertise in environmental scholarship that I did not have. And, perhaps most importantly for environmental studies, she was the faculty advisor for the hardest working and most capable student organization I've ever seen.

Jill

Lee and I are so different! In personality, in approach, in background, in point of view. He is, indeed, exactly as he describes—a kook who is all over the place with his ideas—but he thinks big. He's really good at seeing the whole picture, sometimes carrying it quite far into the future. At times I have to bring him back into the present to get things done, but his vision is admirable and has value. Big-picture vision is something that I am good at contributing to but not so good at initiating. Together, Lee and I have come much further than either of us could have come alone.

I can be a difficult committee member. I pick apart every idea to find the problems. This is a vital role that has at its core the goal of strengthening a project, but it can be discouraging to others. To compound this, when I am busy, I am so focused on my tasks that I skip over pleasantries; for instance, I often forget to place the greeting on an e-mail message when I'm asking for assistance or information (though I have learned to check this before I send). As a result I can come across, quite unintentionally, as personally distant. Lee stuck with me, however, perhaps at first because he had to do so. We butt heads, but our dissimilarities have helped us and we've learned a lot from working together. One bonus is that we each enjoy doing specific tasks the other one dislikes—guess which one of us writes the unit plan describing our direction for the following year and which one does the budget? Neither of us is fond of administrative work, but our strengths balance nicely.

We were behind the other COPLAC schools in developing an academic environmental program and a defined sustainability agenda, but we were ahead of the other universities in Alabama. This combination, being behind our peer institutions nationwide but poised to be a leader in our state, provided a compelling argument in favor of our proposal to start both an environmental studies minor and a campus Sustainability Committee. In other arenas, our vice president for academic affairs was supportive of the newly developing service-learning initiative on campus, and the university's recent strategic plan included developing interdisciplinary studies (IDS) courses that would be made available to all students.

We saw that we could incorporate both of these new initiatives by merging elements of service-learning and IDS into the minor, and in the process we would further strengthen our case. There were discipline-specific service-based courses being offered around campus, but the environmental studies minor would allow more students to be involved, since the work of environmentalism happens, in part, through service. Faculty were already discussing innovative interdisciplinary courses that they'd soon be ready to teach. Since environmental studies is an interdisciplinary field, it was a natural fit for IDS courses; we presented environmental studies as an obvious home for them.

Lee wanted to include an independent study experience in the minor, with both academic and hands-on components. Though we don't have senior projects for other minors, the students interested in the developing environmental studies minor wanted to get their hands dirty so they could be truly involved. Volunteer faculty mentors were happy to embrace endeavors in the local community via an academic avenue. Since faculty were mentoring projects in their own fields, they were combining their own interests with both teaching and service to the community.

Lee

As I began to negotiate the faculty terrain in my third year at the University of Montevallo—serving on university committees, getting to know various segments of the Montevallo community, and finding my place in the English department—I wanted to get to a place where my career made sense. I was teaching a plethora of classes, serving on the General Education Committee, writing grants and ordering kebabs for the Montevallo Literary Festival, and working on the departmental Web page. It was all pretty scattered, and I realized that I needed to figure out how to make my efforts work somehow as a piece so that I could control where my job was headed.

There are a number of pitfalls for new hires at small colleges as they near their tenure year and begin to grow out of their roles as service minions. You can get tenure and then simply fade out—avoid meetings, volunteer little, teach your classes and go home. You can keep working incessantly for everybody else's endeavors and then burn out in a blaze of exhaustion and disappointment. Some professors become martyrs as they cling to their underappreciated pet projects like Ahab flailing in a torrential sea. Others turn into paranoiacs and live only for the bedevilment of campus politics. Some see scholarship as the sole yardstick for their accomplishments as human beings . . . oh what grievous lives they lead. And then there are those who go to the dark side and become administrators. I wasn't content with any of those options. My desire at that time was to make all the parts of my career—scholarship, committee work, community service, teaching, writing—all part of a unified structure that used the energies from one segment to fuel the others. My plan would involve students, the physical plant, faculty members across the disciplines, administrators (and their resources), and the wider community, with Jill Wicknick beside me at the helm. We would all work hand in hand as an organic whole to spread the environmental values that are a true expression of the University of Montevallo community! I was filled with zeal! It all came together! It made perfect sense!

Jill

Lee was pissing me off. He wanted to hold a meeting to gather information about environmental interests on campus, which was great, and he asked me to help. But in the process of creating his event and heading toward his personal grand plan, he was exploiting *my* efforts. I had spent several years developing a campus environmental community and he was merging our successes with his ideas as if it had been part of his design all along. I was working on a variety of projects around campus, mostly focused on environmental issues, but I was overworked in service and not in the mood to have my students' and my work claimed by a Johnny-come-lately who wanted to say, "Look what *we're* doing!" I'd been going it alone with my students for a while and things were great; we didn't need a white knight to show us what to do.

What Lee really wanted was to develop something that was big and all-inclusive, a grand plan for an environmental focus on campus that included academics. I needed to see his commitment and I needed time to integrate it all within my own mind. When I think back, I recall that in his vision-telling, Lee alternated between enthusiasm and almost shyness—tempering himself so as not to overwhelm me. In the meantime, what I was already doing was distinct from our new work on the environmental studies minor and it continued to function well separately. I worked to keep it that way; I was not yet willing to be assimilated. It took me about a year to agree that the right way to go was to combine all of our environmental efforts.

But back to gathering interests. Lee wanted to hold an open meeting to find out what students, faculty, staff—everyone in the campus community—wanted to do about everything and anything environmentally related. He put up flyers inviting people to attend. I had to teach a lab during the meeting and couldn't be there, but the meeting was held in the large classroom next to my lab and I could hear the voices. Much to our surprise and delight, the large room was completely packed! He gathered a ton of feedback. I and a handful of others at UM had already added recycling, an organic community garden, and a few specialty courses. The campus wanted more: sustainability efforts, fair trade, and local foods. And what the students wanted was an academic understanding of environmental issues—an environmental studies program.

Lee

Luckily, about 80 percent of COPLAC universities offered formal environmental education programs that we could emulate. Many of these schools now offer environmental studies majors, and The Evergreen State College even awards a master's in environmental studies. Because a time-honored role for environmental studies in public liberal arts existed, we could easily make the case that University of Montevallo needed to teach "green" courses at long last. Montevallo biology professor Mike Hardig had just taught a successful one-hour honors class that had different weekly lecturers discuss environmental issues from the vantage point of their own disciplines as a means of synthesizing their approaches and bolstering the students' understanding of concepts ranging from pollination to post-apocalyptic film.[5] Mike was convinced that any successful environmental studies program would need to shed disciplinary thinking altogether if students would have a chance to comprehend ecological issues in unconventional and proactive ways. Using Mike's honors course and interdisciplinary ethos, a small group of faculty members began to hammer out a proposal to submit to the vice president for academic affairs and the Undergraduate Curriculum and Standards Committee.

An eclectic bunch of faculty members came to the first ad hoc meeting to design the minor: a botanist, a business professor, an eighteenth-century literary scholar, an art historian, and a professor of management. I was nonplussed. What were they doing here? I had serious reservations about letting *my* program get bushwhacked by a bunch of Milton Friedman types, business professors who would probably infect our idealistic arts and sciences students with their corporate propaganda. And what was that wonky art historian trying to prove? I clutched elaborate diagrams scribbled on multiple pages of a legal pad, and as I stood in front of them red-faced and sputtering, I realized that I had no choice but to just sling my ideas out into the crowd—expecting a thud, expecting hostile wheezes, expecting the sound of ravenous beasts ripping my proposal to ribbons. Instead I found that this group was the faculty committee equivalent of the Flying Wallendas. They maneuvered, spun, tossed, and caught one another's ideas with grace and ease. They rushed to the chalkboard and etched out elaborate curricula. They encouraged. They gracefully erased. They bolstered the plan by incorporating dimensions that I hadn't considered. And, perhaps most importantly, they gave me a firsthand understanding of why an interdisciplinary approach was essential to making our program work.

Jill

It was one of the business professors who insisted that ecology be a required course, which shows that we were all focusing on the nature of environmental studies and developing a good minor, not on ensuring that our own specialty courses be included. Developing the minor was in some ways very standard: determine which foundational courses should come from the general education curriculum and select a number of course hours required. On the other hand, we wanted both an overall interdisciplinary approach to the minor itself, and we wanted specific environmental studies interdisciplinary courses. Keeping the number of required hours reasonable, a mix that would include foundational science courses, courses from arts and humanities, social sciences, and business, plus environmental studies–specific interdisciplinary courses, was quite a challenge. In a bit of a Lee-Jill role reversal, I was the one who kept adding requirements while Lee kept the number of credit hours manageable. On the positive side, we found that there were a lot of courses already being taught around campus that fit environmental studies and our goals. We retained the one-credit Introduction to Environmental Studies course that Mike Hardig developed, added an environmental studies interdisciplinary course (different each semester), and the environmental studies independent project, along with options for environmentally related coursework from all over campus.

At present, about 25 percent of our faculty from all four colleges are involved in the minor. We continue to find additional faculty who want to be involved, along with bringing in guest speakers. We've even had two guest faculty teach entire courses. Over three hundred seats have been filled in our environmental studies–specific courses in just three years. It's been a great success and has brought the campus together in a new way, while extending our arms to the local community more than ever.

Lee

Part of the environmental movement's lure is its grassroots style. Green-leaning activists like to work together as autonomous parties who share common motives, not function as employees. We like to feel that corporate-style hierarchy is less effective for our aims than decentralized self-regulating coalitions, and that meetings have less value than actions. Sacrosanct is the basic premise that everything remain interdependent, and it is also felt that since many small, individual missteps caused our current environmental problems, many small, individual steps might prove redemptive in the future. Therefore, even the most modest effort can be seen as an important contribution, especially when it is performed within the context of a loose organizational style that promotes internal motivation and creative problem solving. So when I was approached by the Faculty Senate to chair a new university-level Sustainability Committee, I was hesitant. My own experiences with university committees and boards led me to believe that they were useful for things like salary issues, grade complaints, and accreditation, but might suck the life out of our burgeoning campus movement. A directorship, regularized meetings, and long, useless bloviations from faculty cranks . . . I feared it might backfire and we would lose our momentum.

On the other hand, I craved—for myself and for our efforts—both credibility with the Faculty Senate and a line of communication with University of Montevallo's president. I had to decide whether we were going to remain an oppositional movement on the margins, which is certainly more romantic, or become a recognized facet of the university community with larger responsibilities. After seeking advice from the Environmental Studies Council—the faculty group that designed the minor—we decided that Jill and I would co-chair the new Sustainability Committee. After some trial and error, we also decided that a majority of the members would be students, and interested faculty could join on a voluntary basis.

The new committee kicked off, fizzled, reinvented itself, and after a year really began to integrate itself into the life of the university. Environmental studies students would work with Environmental Club members to highlight campus issues—the need for a bigger organic garden, a desire for a bike-share program,[6] more local food on campus—and the Sustainability Committee would take up these issues with faculty and the administration. Environmental studies professors would teach classes that offered an intellectual and ethical backdrop for community issues, with support from the committee. Students from the Environmental Club would get the word out for generating surveys and petitions regarding campus issues, and the Sustainability Committee would lobby faculty and staff for solutions. It was working. Jill and I labored like fiends, organizing guest speakers, generating unit plans, making posters, promoting the minor, finding new places to put recycling bins, and cajoling dining services to give up Styrofoam. We were working out of my office suite, so the university offered us a circular office at the bottom of the iconic tower at the center of campus. We dug old couches and moldy tables out of a campus shed to use as furniture for our new office, and we claimed two computers that had been circulated out of a writing lab. We desperately needed resources.

Jill

Since the environmental studies minor is interdisciplinary, it has no place to call home—it, at once, belongs to everyone and no one. Within the environmental studies minor, we were doing a lot with no money, scrounging castoffs and begging supplies from the biology and English departments, which were kind in their support. But we had to have funds because we had needs: faculty to teach environmental studies specialty courses, office support staff, a garden manager, guest speaker honoraria, advertising supplies, and our own course releases so we could do the necessary work to run and grow the minor. We didn't need a lot of money, but we couldn't do it without any. Over time, the administration awarded us funds for our most essential needs. This support covered the operation of the minor pretty well, but it did not cover green campus improvements.

In stepped the University of Montevallo Environmental Club at just the right moment. The club's president, Cameron, attended a student conference and returned with an ambitious idea—she wanted to start a Green Fund. This is a small fee paid by all students into a single university account that is used for sustainability improvements on campus. Most green improvements require an initial cash input with savings returned later, thus it can be difficult to find funds for green ventures. The Green Fund would help to solve that problem and, although similar funds were starting around the country, there were none in Alabama. We would be first! The benefits were obvious, but would the student body want it? And would the administration and the Board of Trustees approve it? Cameron and club members Annie and Aaron worked diligently to write a well-argued proposal for the president and to gather petition signatures in favor of the fund. During the process, we found out that UM students were willing to increase their own fees for this cause. After a full academic year of hard work, the Green Fund was approved all the way up the ladder.

The university created a new account into which five dollars per student per semester is deposited, along with five dollars in total for the three summer sessions, generating about thirty thousand dollars per year. By year two we had funded a sculpture and plant garden for the Recycling Center, shades to keep the hot Southern sun from heating the library, a solar generator for the Shepherd Observatory, rainwater collection for the community garden, sculptural bike racks, recycling containers, the refurbishing of musical instruments, and guest speakers who have discussed eating local foods and reusing materials in clothing production. Best of all, anyone on campus with an idea and a plan can apply to have a project funded. The student-majority Sustainability Committee selects the grant awardees who then do the work to make their own project happen. The Green Fund was the icing on the Montevallo sustainability cake.

Lee

Having an advocate in administration, we found, is essential to launching any new campus project that requires annual funding. Dean of Arts and Sciences Mary Beth Armstrong supported our program at every stage of the process, and she was even there for the very first brainstorming session in 2007. She funded us when she could, slashed our budgets when she had to, yet always encouraged us. But in 2011 she and the vice president for academic affairs (VPAA) tossed us a challenge that almost drove me nuts. Dean Armstrong had been talking to the VPAA about new courses, and the suggestion was made that Jill and I cobble together a new summer class—I think we had about three days to get a course on the books—that would somehow incorporate environmental studies, a service project, and the honors program. *Oh, is that all?* I thought to myself as I grinned in mock appreciation. *Why not add ballroom dancing?* Of course we wanted environmental studies to be taught in the summer, but why this? At that point in the hectic semester we just didn't have the extra time to concoct brand new multifaceted courses for our fledgling program. It's as if we were tasked to do something that would be so sketchy and ill conceived that it was bound for failure. The e-mails began to fly back and forth, with Jill and me having multiple conversations going on at the same time as we took turns constructing bad proposals and conspiracy theories. At night I tossed and turned in bed, my addled brain spinning as I tried in vain to triangulate seemingly arbitrary components for a class made of hot air.

As I tried to think up something useful, I came to understand that the balance between liberal arts education and pressures for applied training must be met at the University of Montevallo by the capable problem solvers and creative artisans who graduate each year. In this tradition, any new environmental studies class must engage students in collaborative projects that tackle local problems with solution-oriented approaches. But how? I was complaining to my wife during a walk when in my head the class just materialized. Environmental studies would host a class in the new Organic Community Garden that would give the food to the needy and also cross list with the honors program! Students would work the garden, learn how to preserve fresh foods, make strawberry jam, produce a Google food map, and learn about growing organic veggies. Jill and I would collaborate to teach the class and garden lab in the summer. Jill liked the idea, and in a matter of minutes she had fleshed out a proposal. She gave it some substance, produced an itinerary, and named the class Summer Harvest. We forwarded it to our dean, and to our great relief she loved it.

Suddenly and without warning I was operating a tiller.

Jill

Noon. July. Alabama. Me, Lee, garden manager Holly, and twelve students. We worked together to till the soil, plant seeds, pump water, build trellises, and harvest vegetables. We learned about food insecurity, human nutrition and disease, and soil nutrients. In the first three years, the Summer Harvest classes, along with Holly and a variety of volunteers working year-round, donated more than two thousand pounds of fresh, organic vegetables to our local food pantry. And we all learned about more than gardening; we have learned about the role and value of community. When Lee stepped out of Summer Harvest instruction after the first summer, members of the social work faculty stepped in to join me, and the class continues on as one of a growing number of interdisciplinary environmental studies specialty courses.

The environmental studies minor culminates in a student-designed independent study that combines academics with a hands-on experience. These projects are required to be interdisciplinary, thus they require two faculty mentors. The effect has been students' involving faculty mentors with each other and in projects that improved the city's Recycling Center, educated local people about sustainability initiatives, mapped city and campus walking trails, raised public awareness of the importance of a watershed, and created a garden labyrinth. Overall, the environmental studies program has intertwined members of the campus with the local community in a rewarding way for everyone and has fostered common goals among previous strangers.

Lee

In three short years, the University of Montevallo community overcame a number of challenges to create a promising new interdisciplinary program. Jill and I had to get out of our respective disciplinary shells, trust each other, work incessantly, guide and recruit students, plan and create a curriculum, and then deal with the consequences of our shared success. In the process, I had to integrate my own self-image as a college English professor in the ivory tower with practical environmental concerns such as aluminum recycling bins, cafeteria meals for vegans, and composting. The result has been more fulfilling than I expected. In fact, one result of witnessing the campus in this transformative phase has been a scholarly reconsideration of my entire approach to physical landscape. It has been curative in this age of environmental despair to see the campus and other places perhaps considered ecological dead zones understood instead as liminal spaces. Anthropologist Victor Turner describes initiates in rites of passage as going through liminality, which is "an interval, however brief . . . when the past is momentarily negated, suspended or abrogated, and the future has not yet begun, an instant of pure potentiality when everything, as it were, trembles in the balance."[7] And I think that it was seeing the abandoned campus archery range transformed into the Montevallo Organic Community Garden, and watching free local food go to members of the Montevallo community in the Summer Harvest class, that made me understand the pure potentiality of this unique institution. As a result of my evolution as environmental studies co-chair, I have published two articles on the topic of liminality and a third essay is forthcoming. Frankly, I do not think that I would have been able to produce these articles if Jill hadn't helped me conflate my abstract theorizing with my own life practice at the University of Montevallo.

Jill

I have been immersed in environmental activities on campus since I arrived ten years ago. I have been personally acquainted with the recycling bins and the mechanics of the solar water pump at the garden since their acquisition. I can help students organize a weeklong Earth Day event and volunteers for a cleanup in town. I know how to start a student club, create a one-acre garden, and design and administer a grant fund. A few years ago, my nine-year-old son asked me, with a kind of amazement, "How did you know how to start a recycling program?" I told him that I didn't know how to do it when I began. "You just start doing it and you figure it out along the way."

Immersion in service was not my plan when I arrived at the University of Montevallo. Although I have loved working with the Environmental Club students and I'm proud of all that we've accomplished, I came to realize that service was taking more of my time than I cared for and that I was increasingly pushing aside my research (one clue that your professional equilibrium is off balance is the honor of receiving the annual Faculty Service Award). It's not unusual for a faculty member at a liberal arts school to get overly involved in service, as good projects that create numerous volunteer opportunities abound. It is, however, essential to find a healthy blend in order to be both professionally successful and personally content.

I want concern for the environment to spread; in an ideal world everyone would care and everyone would act. For UM, combining the new environmental studies minor with our ongoing campus and local environmental work was the way to create a vibrant activist community. For me, working with Lee and many others at Montevallo released me from some of my service and allowed the local movement to spread. The momentum is building and our city is now becoming more involved in making Montevallo into an eco-friendly place. Environmentalism at UM and in Montevallo now has a life of its own.

The University of Montevallo has been a wonderful place to create, direct, and develop an academic program for many reasons, but especially because we were able to experience firsthand the impact of our efforts. While Lee and I are now ready to step back into our own disciplines and pass the leadership reins to someone with new ideas who will take us in new directions, we will continue to participate enthusiastically. As the Montevallo environmental movement grows, it will impact more students, more faculty, and more members of the local community in a positive way. We couldn't ask for more.

Coda

Environmental Studies at the University of Montevallo is an interdisciplinary minor grounded in the natural sciences that incorporates perspectives from the social sciences, the arts and humanities, and business. The purpose of the program is to provide students with the skills, knowledge, and attitudes they will need as citizens and as members of the workforce to make informed decisions with respect to ecological issues and to foster leadership skills for building a sustainable society. The overarching objective is to help students learn to balance present needs with those of future generations while promoting environmental justice and biological sustainability. Recent class offerings include Environmental Aesthetics and Ethics; Lore of Appalachian Eco-Resistance; Environmental Law and Policy; National Parks, Landscape Art, and the American Imagination; History of Global Capitalism and the Environment; and Summer Harvest, which includes time in the Montevallo Organic Community Garden growing food for donation to a local food bank while learning about social and environmental justice issues. The minor is an innovative option for UM students looking for an interdisciplinary honors college experience in step with COPLAC environmental programs. Environmental studies prides itself on bringing faculty, students, staff, administrators, and the community together to solve environmental problems and make the UM campus a veritable sustainability lab.

Works Cited

Glotfelty, Cheryll, and Harold Fromm, eds. *The Ecocriticism Reader: Landmarks in Literary Ecology*. Athens: University of Georgia Press, 1996.

Turner, Victor W. *From Ritual to Theatre: The Human Seriousness of Play*. New York: Performing Arts Journal Publications, 1982.

University of Montevallo. "Mission & Vision," accessed June 20, 2013, http://www.montevallo.edu/about-um/um-at-a-glance/mission-vision/.

Wicknick, Jill A. "Becoming." In *Courting the Wild: Love Affairs with Reptiles and Amphibians*, edited by Jamie K. Reaser, 197–203. San Francisco: Hiraeth Press, 2009.

Notes

1. A great number of people have worked on the development and success of the University of Montevallo's environmental studies program and on sustainability projects at Montevallo. Thank you to all UM Environmental Club members and environmental studies students, past and present. Thanks to the Environmental Studies Council and Sustainability Committee members, the UM Physical Plant, our burgeoning environmental studies faculty, and the staff and administrators who supported, and continue to support, environmental studies. We appreciate those persons in the local community who contribute to the greening of UM and the City of Montevallo.

2. University of Montevallo, "Mission & Vision."

3. Glotfelty and Fromm, *Ecocriticism Reader*.

4. Wicknick, "Becoming," 197.

5. Professors Mike Hardig and Kathy King were the first faculty members to conceptualize and lobby for an environmental studies program at the University of Montevallo.

6. With the help of the University of Montevallo undergraduates, the Montevallo Service Learning Office and the City of Montevallo have created ValloCycle, the first city-university cooperative bike-share program to be implemented in Alabama.

7. Turner, *Ritual to Theatre*, 44.

6

" 'Tis the gift to come down where we ought to be"

Gary Towsley
Mathematics, State University of New York at Geneseo

Firenze

We were on our way to Italy, a two-week tour. My wife and I had been married for seven months and I had just completed my first year of teaching at the State University of New York (SUNY) at Geneseo. The tour was a gift from my mother-in-law. We arrived at Ciampino, Rome's charter airport, and boarded a bus for Florence. The air conditioning didn't work and the traffic was awful, but the countryside was completely new to me.

Early the next morning we were led by our guide for the day, Giovanna, to the center of Florence, to a point equidistant from the Baptistery, the Duomo, and Giotto's Campanile. Giovanna's first words to us, pointing to the Campanile, were, "Giotto. Imagine it." She told us about Dante's love for the Baptistery and for the city of his birth. Her words sparked a love for Italy and Dante that endures after almost forty years and fourteen trips.

One effect on my career has been to lead me into team-teaching courses that are not usual for a mathematician. One in particular stands out. Every other year or so, Ron Herzman of Geneseo's English department and I have taught a course called Poetry and Cosmology in the Middle Ages. We read Plato's *Timaeus*, Boethius's *Consolation*, and several other works that heavily influenced the medieval European view of the universe. Then with that background we "read" the cathedral of Notre Dame de Chartres and *Il Paradiso*, the third canticle of Dante's *Commedia*.

Rochester

I really enjoyed graduate school. It wasn't my first choice. While at Case Institute of Technology, which became part of Case-Western Reserve University during my senior year, I had applied to and been accepted into the Peace Corps. My job was to build a school in Ethiopia (I had had some construction experience) and then teach in it. My local draft board intervened to tell me that there was no deferment for the Peace Corps. I then chose to attend the University of Rochester in the fall of 1968.

The graduate department at Rochester was a good fit for me. Its moderate size (an entering graduate class of twelve), high-quality graduate faculty, and selective undergraduate admission allowed me to advance as both a mathematician and a teacher. I had the opportunity to meet and speak extensively with many of the top mathematicians in the world. Several Rochester faculty had solid international contacts and we enjoyed a steady flow of talks by noted scholars from Europe and Latin America. I met my future wife in the math department. She would eventually become my colleague—more on that later. As a graduate student I did, however, nearly cause an international incident. I spent a couple of months writing a translation of a book on Kähler manifolds from the original French. I had to understand both the French and the mathematics. One day, a very highly regarded French mathematician who was spending the semester with us sat down next to me in the little library space I was using. He kept glancing over at what I was doing and appeared to be getting more and more incensed. Finally, when his outrage at the brutality of my work with his native language became too much, he stormed out. Luckily there were no repercussions.

It was clear in graduate school that learning, doing, and creating mathematics were the priority. Teaching was secondary. I enjoyed the courses the faculty offered us but in those days we were expected to be self-motivated and the quality of teaching was very rarely a topic of conversation. However, graduate students came very quickly to appreciate the opportunity to teach recitation sections under a professor or to teach a full course. When your primary task was to prove a completely new theorem or solve a heretofore-unsolved problem, each day provided a bountiful harvest of frustration and solid evidence of one's intellectual shortcomings. Walking into a calculus recitation became a source of joy: "I know something and I can speak about it intelligently." Perhaps I spent more time preparing my teaching efforts than was necessary but it felt good. The focus of everything was mathematics and there was no real consideration of why we were teaching what we were teaching or discussion of any kind of best practice.

Finally I had a research result. I showed that the standard results on the homotopy classes of continuous maps from compact Riemann surfaces to the Riemann sphere did not carry over to classes of meromorphic functions. Then on March 31, the day before I would register my dissertation, a fellow graduate student discovered an error in my proof. Luckily I was able to correct everything within about two weeks but the delay meant that graduation and an earned PhD would be held up a whole year. The good news was that all the work was done and I could go forth and seek employment as a professor. But it was 1974, an awful year for job seekers in mathematics. Vietnam and avoidance of the war had produced a glut of PhDs in the scientific fields (where deferments were much easier to get) and the effects were fully felt in that year. I applied to about 150 colleges and universities and had exactly one mild nibble. Only one of my classmates, a very applied probabilist, was set with a position for the next year. The faculty at Rochester seemed genuinely surprised that I had no offers by July. I talked to the chair at a nearby community college. He said he would love to hire me but that the other faculty in his department would object since earning a doctorate meant I clearly couldn't and didn't want to teach.

Then it happened. SUNY restored funding to several of its four-year colleges and allowed them to restart searches that had been cancelled in the late spring due to fiscal problems. But it was now August. The chair at Geneseo, about twenty-five miles south of Rochester, called and asked if I was still interested in their position. I successfully contained my joy and excitement. I drove down the next day and was verbally offered a job that afternoon. Little did I suspect the import of what had just happened. Little did I suspect that thirty-nine years later I would be at SUNY Geneseo writing this piece.

Geneseo

SUNY Geneseo is a mainly undergraduate college (we offer a few master's degrees in education for teachers) of about five thousand students. It is a very selective public college with a strong tradition in the liberal arts. Founded in 1871 as a normal school (my grandmother was to attend there in the early 1900s but illness prevented her from enrolling), it became part of the SUNY system in 1948. The college is in the county seat of Livingston County in the village of Geneseo, also with a population of about five thousand. Located thirty miles south of Rochester, Geneseo is on the northern edge of rural western New York, an area from which we draw many students.

Once my contract came in the mail, I met with the assistant vice president for academic affairs, from whom I learned about the bureaucratic side of being a professor, and then with members of the math department, from whom I received my teaching schedule. Little did I know of the strained relations between the chair and the committee that did the scheduling.

My teaching assignment for the first semester was not a very interesting one: two sections of MATH 100 (Mathematics for Elementary Teachers) and one section of Calculus II. Indeed, no new faculty member since then has started with a schedule like that one. I didn't care. I didn't know anything about MATH 100, its clientele, or its purpose. I did know that a fall semester Calculus II was out of synch, a class to be made up of those who had failed either Calculus I or II and were off a semester from the standard flow through the curriculum. It didn't matter. I enjoyed that first semester even if I was teaching in the do-what-comes-next mode. It would take a few more rounds with MATH 100 before I could figure out how to make this course useful to the large number of elementary education majors who were required to take it. It took that long before I knew that that was an important consideration. None of my colleagues talked about the course at all. But I wasn't giving all As and the students weren't complaining about me to the chair, so I must be all right.

It was this course, MATH 100, that began my own questioning of my role as a professor. Calculus and the upper-level math courses didn't raise any immediate questions. I thought I knew what I was doing. MATH 100 was a carryover from the New Math, adapted for elementary education majors. Its curriculum was both dry and abstract. In theory the students would absorb set theory, logic, an axiomatic presentation of algebra, and numeration at a certain cognitive level, and then use what they had learned in later pedagogy courses. There were many problems with this assumption. First, most of the professors in the education department didn't know the material of MATH 100 (and why should they?). Second, the students didn't really absorb the mathematics at a level that would be useful to them in later education courses. Slowly I looked at ways to make this course useful to the students in front of me. They would be required to teach mathematics at some level as part of all their other duties. To some of my colleagues it was sufficient that the students could execute the basic arithmetic algorithms and use Venn diagrams as a shortcut to logic.

Talking to students during the course, I realized that for a large number of them math was simply magic. It happened correctly if the incantations were correct. It could not actually be understood. Certainly many of my teachers in elementary school believed that. They also thought that the algorithms (addition, long division, etc.) were simply a matter of memorizing procedures and that students who failed to learn them were either lazy or deficient in some other way. For many, the fact that math could not be understood but only accomplished led to a real aversion to it. (My fourth grade teacher had a very personal take on this aversion. When the class got noisy she would yell, "Be quiet or we will do math.") Finally, I began to see my way into the course. The students didn't appreciate that the algorithms actually could be understood and that the procedures were difficult; I began to give them concrete ways to think about a topic like the division of fractions. They could reduce it to "invert and multiply," which was simply a magical procedure. But behind it there was justification and intuition. I'm sure my students tired of hearing that this stuff was not magic.

One of the topics in MATH 100 that was a clear holdover from the New Math was number bases. Using a base like seven and the symbols zero to six, one could do all of arithmetic. But to what end? I discovered a reason. By having my students, who by and large had no real difficulty doing addition or long division, execute their procedures in some other base, they were forced to relive their original learning experiences. This resulted in some new empathy for their future students and it also brought the reasons for the steps in the algorithms to the fore. At this time students did not have four-function calculators. Everything was done by hand. As calculators became more readily available, the nature of the course began to change. By the time I felt I could actually teach MATH 100 in a useful fashion, it had become a series of one-credit modules. But I was well on the way to a fundamental intuition about teaching—that it's really about learning and not about teaching at all.

The rest of my teaching flowed very smoothly during the pre-tenure stretch. I taught lots of calculus and several different upper-level math courses. None of it challenged my conceptions about teaching. I did run an experimental course called Mathematical Models in Ecology, a foray into mathematical biology. I was warned against such efforts by a senior member of the department, who told me that nothing I did was as valuable as another paper in print. My first five years, however, did involve another influence that would eventually end up changing my teaching. My office-mate was Rudy Rucker, formally a logician and a budding science fiction novelist. He shamelessly ignored syllabi and course descriptions and taught what he and his students were interested in. He transformed the Foundations of Geometry course from an axiomatic presentation designed to prepare high school teachers to teach to the Regents Exam into a course in relativity and the fourth dimension. This change didn't sit well with many in the department and would be one of the many straws that led him to leave the college. Rudy showed me the possibilities in the driest of our courses and the importance of a narrative to flesh out the run of definitions, theorems, and proofs. Rudy was also responsible for my talking to Kurt Gödel, one of the most important and influential mathematicians of the twentieth century. Gödel had read a paper of Rudy's and called our office to speak to him. I answered the phone. The great man asked, "Is Rucker there?" I answered, "No." He hung up after saying thank you. But I did talk to him.

In the run-up to my tenure year, the college was reforming its general education program. The program had been a very loose set of distribution requirements with the student choosing two courses each from four sets of departmental prefixes (any two courses from philosophy, history, or English fulfilled the humanities part of the core, for example). Mathematics was not included in the possibilities. I became involved in the reform effort partly to help mathematics become part of general education. The outcome was a general education program that was much more tightly focused and rigorous. It contained a new area—critical reasoning—that included courses from any department that satisfied certain criteria. The criteria were stringent and there were not many courses that met them. Calculus I was one of them. Since I was the one who wrote the proposal to bring calculus into the core area, I had to take a serious look at the course. It became clear that somewhere between all the mechanical procedures with which calculus is filled and the proofs for all the important theorems, there had to be a middle ground that was critical reasoning. I had to take a serious look at the course content for the first time. I identified several parts of the course that fit the criteria, wrote the proposal, presented it to the faculty in the math department, and finally adjusted my own teaching of the course to the new schema. I was slowly moving away from the content of the course toward the purpose of the course. The department accepted the proposal and so did the core committee. I am not sure it changed the way many of my colleagues taught the course, but it certainly affected my teaching.

The quest for tenure can be nerve-racking. I was lucky to have received a SUNY award, the Chancellor's Award for Excellence in Teaching, the semester prior to the decision. Since the vice president for academic affairs had very publicly begun the year with a call for improvement in teaching on the part of the faculty, I felt confident enough to put in an offer on a house in town. My wife was pregnant and we needed a bigger place. We went to a realtor and looked at many houses. Finally we chose one and submitted a purchase offer. The offer contained a rider to the effect that in order to close the purchase I needed to receive tenure. The seller accepted the rider, knowing that the decision would be made within two months at most. As it turns out the seller was the sister-in-law of a very good friend of the VPAA. Thus on a day early in June of 1980, I received word from my realtor that I had been granted tenure. A few days later the official news came from the college. Geneseo is a small town.

At the point of tenure I had become proficient in teaching most of the courses the math department offered in a way that students seemed to appreciate. I taught in a very standard way—mostly lecture—to large but not huge classes. We never went the route of large lecture calculus, but kept to single-instructor sections of thirty to thirty-five students. As a softie, I usually allowed overloads so my sections were closer to forty. One frustration was that I had not been able to bring my own mathematical specialty, compact Riemann surfaces, to my undergraduate students. The area required a large knowledge base encompassing several different parts of higher mathematics: complex analysis, algebraic geometry, and algebraic topology. Instead I had tried to develop mathematical ecology as a tie between research and teaching. Unfortunately my colleague from biology took a new job in the Midwest and it became hard to sustain work in that area. Fortunately my chair offered me a new opportunity. A well-known historian of mathematics was coming to give a colloquium on the history of calculus and asked the chair if there was someone in the department who could give a talk on Descartes and the importance of the development of coordinate geometry prior to his colloquium. The chair asked me. I had always been interested in history generally and in the history of mathematics in particular. Now I had an excuse to spend some time reading. From a professional historian's viewpoint, my initial effort was at best very naïve and at worst a textbook example of Whig history, but I hadn't heard that term in 1982. In retrospect, this initial effort has borne fruit.

A part of the new general education program was the requirement of two specific interdisciplinary courses—Humanities I and II—with a common reading list that all students would take. Teaching these courses was open to all faculty at Geneseo, but one first had to team-teach with a faculty member who had already taught the course. One of the faculty who had developed these courses, Bill Edgar, a philosopher, had originally wanted the history of science to be a strand within both courses, but that was too much in 1980. But a few years later, Bill and I offered one-credit courses in the History of Science I and II to parallel the humanities courses. My growing interest in the history of mathematics was coming into use. I learned how to teach with someone else in a single class where we both attended and often both spoke on the same day.

Another pleasant aspect of being a faculty member was the ability to sit in on colleagues' courses. I used the opportunity extensively—various philosophy courses, quantum mechanics, medieval history, and of course Dante. The interdepartmental course, The Age of Dante, taught by Bill Cook and Ron Herzman from history and English, respectively, was legendary on campus. It would eventually become a best seller for The Teaching Company. Bill was on leave so Ron was teaching the course solo when I sat in the first time. I made a few comments about Dante's use of mathematics (perfect numbers) and cosmology (the Aristotelian cosmos). Ron found them interesting and asked if I could speak to the class when the *Paradiso* came around. Afterwards we talked about team-teaching a course that would concentrate on the last canticle (the *Paradiso*) of the *Commedia*. Out of those discussions came Medieval Studies: Poetry and Cosmology in the Middle Ages. It is this course that really crystallized my view of my role at Geneseo.

Our two children were born in 1980 and 1983 and my wife joined the math department in 1982. Since I was doing most of the course scheduling for the department, I could produce non-conflicting schedules for Olympia and me; as a result, child care became much easier. The period from 1980 to 1989 was heavily devoted to raising the children and less devoted to building a career. During this period, though, I chaired the Academic Standards Committee, which heard appeals from students in academic difficulty. Geneseo was in the process of becoming a very selective college, but in the period roughly from 1977 to 1983 there was a dip in the high school population and there were students enrolling who had great difficulty with the curriculum. What I saw as chair of the committee was first, the effect that faculty had on students, both good and bad, and second, the wide variety of reasons for which students actually attended college. All this too would slowly alter the way I saw myself at the college.

In 1989 I was asked to co-chair the Middle States reaccreditation effort with the associate vice president for academic affairs. Suddenly, I learned almost too much about the non-academic side of the college. I formed committees of faculty, staff, and students to study the aspects of Geneseo that Middle States wanted to know about. From their reports I helped write a self-study for the accreditation team's visit. Then our president took another job. We hired Carol Harter as president and she immediately put a halt to the reaccreditation process, receiving permission to delay the visit by a year. This of course involved rewriting the self-study, but with a new emphasis: planning. The process went smoothly and we received a painless reaccreditation. The planning emphasis led to the creation of the College Planning Council with the president and me serving as co-chairs. For the next six years, the council met about once a week to craft a new mission statement, develop strategic goals for the college, and run a small grants program on campus designed to move the college toward meeting the goals. The mission statement was five paragraphs long (much too long) and the set of goals covered about sixty items. It was unwieldy but effective in getting the campus community moving in new directions. The very first goal was to "encourage students to become active rather than passive learners." At the time I didn't realize just how loaded that phrase was. But from that goal and the actions of the Planning Council came Geneseo's emphasis on student research and faculty-student collaboration. It is stunning to see the difference in the campus from 1989 to 2013 regarding the ways in which students now have opportunities to direct their own education.

For the entire period of Carol Harter's presidency, I was heavily involved in various aspects of the governance of the college. I worked on the new Honors Program and created a Freshman Seminar Program. But then Carol Harter was hired away from us and our new provost, Chris Dahl, became interim president and then after a year president, a position he would hold for seventeen years. This change in leadership allowed me to step away from the heavy involvement with governance and concentrate again on teaching, on mathematics, on the history of mathematics, and on Dante.

The course I was co-teaching with Ron Herzman on Poetry and Cosmology in the Middle Ages led to a wonderful joint paper called "Squaring the Circle: *Paradiso* 33 and the Poetics of Geometry," published in 1994. We looked at the last thirteen lines of the *Commedia* and took Dante very seriously when he spoke of "squaring the circle." Most commentators had simply seen that phrase as a metaphor for a very difficult problem, an image that could have used any difficult problem in math equally well. We showed that it was the actual problem that was important. This joint work and other work have contributed to the richness our course has developed.

In the past decade, two of our students have won the Student Paper Prize from the Dante Society of America for their final papers in the course. All in all, the course is a wonderful example of collaboration in teaching and research, across two disciplines that are not often linked. (I also just had to go to Italy several times to give a lecture on Dante and cosmology to the National Endowment for the Humanities seminar on Dante that Ron and a colleague from the University of Vermont run almost every other year.)

In 1994 I was named Lockhart Professor. This was a supported three-year professorship that included the opportunity to create and teach a new course on anything at all each of the three years of its term. I decided to aim the three courses at different levels. The first one was an introductory-level course with few prerequisites called The History of Mathematics Outside the Western Tradition. The second was for science and history students called Galileo and His Medieval Predecessors. Finally I taught an advanced course for math majors called simply Elliptic Curves. That was a hot topic at the time since elliptic curves were a principle tool in the proof of Fermat's Last Theorem in 1995 by Andrew Wiles of Princeton University. After my stint as Lockhart Professor I taught History of Mathematics on a regular basis and folded in what I had developed for the Lockhart courses.

In 1999 my career took two new turns. I received the Deborah and Franklin Tepper Haimo Award for Distinguished College and University Teaching of Mathematics from the Mathematical Association of America (MAA). This is the national teaching award for undergraduate mathematics. The only real duty attached to this award is to give a talk at the Joint Mathematical Meetings. So in January 2000 in Washington, D.C., I spoke on the subject, "What does Dante have to do with mathematics?" As a side effect, I became heavily involved in the MAA, and in particular in the Seaway Section of this national organization. For the last fourteen years, I have served the section in a variety of capacities. I am presently governor of the section (and a member of the MAA Board). The section consists geographically of New York State outside of New York City and Long Island, and the provinces of Ontario and Quebec. This work has introduced me to a large number of mathematicians concerned with teaching undergraduates. We discuss problems, best practices, reforms, and teaching styles, both formally and informally. One example came early on in my involvement with the section. A set of faculty from a private college spoke on their efforts in what was called Project Calculus. This was a calculus sequence partly based on student research projects. It was quite inspiring as presented. It was a good way to turn calculus students into active learners. At the end of the presentation a faculty member from one of our sister SUNY colleges asked the embarrassing question, "How many students do you have in the calculus classes?" The answer was, "While we are under the NSF grant the enrollment is held to eight. When the grant ends we will extend the effort to our usual class size of twelve to fifteen." The questioner was considering the feasibility of Project Calculus in a class of thirty-five.

A new wrinkle in my career at Geneseo came with my election to the Faculty Personnel Committee. This is a collegewide committee of professors and associate professors that makes recommendations to the provost and president on all continuing appointment and promotion requests. I was elected chair of the committee and served in that capacity for ten years. During that period, I read dossiers for about 120 continuing appointments and two hundred promotion requests. It was a new lens through which to look at undergraduate education. I read all the student evaluation forms that came to the committee. I learned to appreciate the comments students made and fold them into my own decisions. The variation in expectations about teaching and research across the departments was far greater than I had imagined it would be. It became clear that one could not judge these matters with one set of rules for all faculty. Some departments paid little heed to any publications short of books or major articles, while others saw the value of textbook writing. Some departments valued collaborative work with students highly, whether it led to a publication or conference presentation or not. In others there were strict rules about what counted. I slowly developed my own baseline for each of the decisions—tenure, promotion to associate (these are not linked at Geneseo), promotion to full. All my past experience told me that some of the people before me made real contributions to the learning of their students, whatever their publication record, while others would always simply float on the top of teaching without ever really engaging their classes. I found the committee to be the most serious and thoughtful of any on which I had ever worked. As chair I was responsible for bringing each case to a vote and then reporting the vote, the reasons behind the vote, and a fair representation of any disagreement to both the provost and the president. After a decade chairing the committee, enduring two lawsuits over our decisions, and writing letters of recommendation and non-recommendation to almost all of my colleagues, I decided to not stand for reelection, but I took away a deep feeling for what professors do and what they believe in all their variety.

As I entered my thirty-eighth year at Geneseo in fall 2011, the provost asked if I would chair the General Education Committee. The general education model that had been developed in the late seventies and early eighties had served the college well. Programs up and down the line had become more focused and more rigorous. Students could not avoid courses in which they confronted views with which they were uncomfortable. They had to do something serious in both the arts and the sciences. But after thirty years, it was evident that our students had grown beyond the old structure. Student research involves about 25 percent of our students at any given time. Over 30 percent study abroad for a summer or a semester. Our students had been calling for more languages, more global content in the curriculum, and more interdisciplinary work. Reforming the program was the task given to me for the committee. It has been exhilarating simply to consider this challenge after thirty-eight years of teaching at Geneseo. My vision for general education is so completely different from what it had been. The committee has decided on a program structured by four baccalaureate learning outcomes: first, specialized knowledge (a major); second, broad/integrative knowledge (a combination of introductory and intermediate-level courses with an interdisciplinary flavor); third, intellectual and practical skills (a long list); and fourth, a high-impact experience (such as student research or study abroad, with a reflective component). I have learned, however, not to presume how the college senate will respond to such a recommendation.

The request by the provost that I chair the General Education Committee led me to go back through my career at Geneseo and recall the changes I have seen in the whole academic endeavor. Starting as a recent graduate student, I viewed teaching as a careful presentation of a set body of material. This material could be best offered to the students through lectures. Today "lecture" is a relatively bad word. But I defend lectures. A lecture can be a dialogue if there are as many questions as there are assertions. A lecture can be a dialogue if the students sense uncertainty and ambiguity in what is presented. What a lecture should not be is an excuse to allow a note-taking pen to run on autopilot. Over the years I have certainly changed my lecturing style and have introduced many other forms of teaching-learning interaction. The big change has been simply the focus on student learning rather than teacher presentation. It took me a while to figure out how my lectures could make me more than just an audible textbook, more valuable than a good set of notes (or an online course). This change in me has followed what is happening generally in higher education.

Actually my whole career, in all its aspects, has mirrored what is happening in higher education. I have seen a breaking down of the separation of research, teaching, and service. I have seen some tearing away at the disciplinary walls separating divisions, departments, and subdepartments. I have seen the shift from teacher-and-course-centered education to student-learning education. I have participated in these changes on my own campus in a variety of ways through a variety of roles. One of the major bits of enlightenment came in a college retreat in 1993. President Carol Harter brought together key administration, faculty, and staff to discuss our mission and strategic goals. The keynote speaker for the retreat was Robert Zemsky, who has been talking and writing about reforming higher education for decades now. I took to heart one rather pithy comment he made: "The faculty have to get beyond the idea of the university as a jobs program for people with PhDs." In a stark way he made me change my whole focus to the students. Rather than live up to the inherited role of a faculty member, I had to help my students accomplish what they want to accomplish. That one statement changed forever the way I viewed my role. I had been on the road to that realization from my first classes at Geneseo, but Zemsky made it unavoidably obvious.

I will close with one small story. On a Tuesday in April each year the college has held GREAT Day. Classes are cancelled and the day is devoted to student posters, presentations, and performances. This year over 950 students participated directly and twice as many of their colleagues attended. The quality of the presentations is always very high. In 2013 the keynote address for GREAT Day was given by Dava Sobel, author of *Galileo's Daughter* and *Longitude*, among many other works. She had recently published a book on Copernicus, *A More Perfect Heaven*. At the center of the book is a play she had written about Copernicus and his reluctance to release his revolutionary work. She asked me if I would assist her in the talk by reading two passages from the play. I would play Copernicus to her Rheticus, a young mathematician. The play itself is very easy to read in that fashion and with very little preparation I pulled off my acting debut (not quite—I had been a carrot on stage in first grade). It was well received. Several friends spoke about how I had been hiding my acting talent all these years. My wife, as usual, was able to ground me instantly. She said that in the reading I was an elderly mathematician patiently dealing with a young scholar who just didn't quite get the issue at hand: "You weren't acting. That's you."

7

A Kid for Life

Quan Tran
Mathematics, University of Science and Arts of Oklahoma

As far back as I can remember, I always *knew* I was going to be an astronaut, an astronomer, a geologist, biologist, botanist, zoologist, an artist, photographer, architect, carpenter, inventor, engineer, a cook, and a writer when I grew up.[1] When I was five years old, I remember looking up at the night sky with my father and being completely mystified by the stars.

"*Bo*, what are people who go to the stars called?"

"Astronauts," was his short reply.

"I want to be an astronaut when I grow up."

When the weather was warm enough, my parents sometimes took me to the zoo. I remember marveling at all the different kinds of animals. My favorite was the monkey because it swung around in the trees all day and reminded me of myself.

I asked my mom, "*Me*, what are people who work and play with animals called?"

"They're called biologists, darling. Is that what you want to be when you grow up?"

"Yes," I affirmed, "I am going to be a biologist when I grow up."

On one occasion, during a family trip to the beach, I built an elaborate sand castle that came up to my chest. As I stood proudly next to my masterpiece, I asked my parents, "What are people who build sand castles all day called?"

They both broke out laughing and my dad wittingly replied, "Children."

Acknowledgment: I would like to thank my parents for satisfying all my curiosities growing up and my daughter for being a model for me to emulate as I grow older.

My mom added, "No one is going to pay you to build sand castles, honey. The closest you can get to that is to be an artist. But you have to be good at drawing and painting to be an artist."

I do not recall if I was any good at drawing or painting as a child. But growing up, because my parents could not afford to buy me very many toys, I found a great deal of amusement in drawing, painting, folding paper, and building neat things out of sticks and scraps, and so I agreed, "Okay, I will be an artist when I grow up."

My father often went to thrift stores and would bring home broken electronic devices and appliances. I used to sit by my father as he took them apart and delighted in watching him fix them. I was seduced by all the electronic complexity and array of buttons.

"*Bo*, what are people who make up these things called?"

"Inventors."

"I am going to be one of those when I grow up."

I think I had as ordinary a childhood as any healthy kid did growing up. I had all the same curiosities and aspirations of any wide-eyed child I knew. Every time I see my two-year-old daughter tilt her head to the side and watch with alertness and curiosity at every strange sight and sound she comes across and make intelligent comments on what she has just experienced and learned in a language I cannot understand, I am convinced of the ordinariness of my own childhood. But somewhere along the line, I think most people grow up and find one or two things they really love to do, and they work hard and focus their energy to develop these interests and talents while leaving behind many of their previous recreations and not really exploring any new diversions. In this sense, I do not think I ever grew up. Much like a kid, I still like to poke and piddle around in all sorts of different things. I get excited about new things and get absorbed in them until I bump into something new or want to revisit something old. I feel as if I love just about as many things today as I did growing up. I still want to learn and know about everything that I come across, and remain as curious, confident, and impressionable as I was in adolescence.

College Years

In college, I enrolled close to home at the University of Oklahoma and decided to major in computer science. Because computers are used to solve problems in nearly every professional field I could imagine, I thought choosing it as my major was a smart way for me to continue to dabble in various academic and professional areas. My parents, knowing my penchant for distraction, pushed for me to focus singularly on my degree and finish early. "Don't waste your time taking extra classes," they advised, "you can always come back and take them later." But I knew I would never come back to take any courses once I graduated. I decided that this was my chance to explore as many of my interests as possible. So instead of buckling down, I enrolled in several extra courses that did not count toward my major.[2] Little did I know at the time that my decision to take these extra courses would end up making me a prime candidate for my current position as an assistant professor at a public liberal arts university.

After graduating from college with a bachelor's degree in computer science, I changed course and went on to graduate school at Oklahoma in mathematics, an area I became enamored with during my study of computer science. The first few years of graduate school were exhilarating. I was introduced to pure mathematics for the first time in my life. New concepts, new terminologies, new approaches—my mind felt as if it was working on a Lego farm. I was building proofs and tearing them down, modifying and rebuilding them from scratch. I started to make connections between rules and laws in mathematics and filling in holes I had ignored when I was younger. Study was fun and challenging, but still allowed me to explore and audit courses outside of mathematics.[3] Most significantly, I was given the opportunity to teach lower-level mathematics courses. That did it for me. I was hooked. I knew teaching was what I wanted to do for the rest of my life.

Teaching was so much fun. It provided a venue for me to share with others the fields of academia I had unearthed and found fascinating. Even though I was assigned to teach mathematics, I often gave my students riddles, brainteasers, short stories, and creative writing assignments as extra credit. One writing assignment I continue to use is from a list of exercises found in John Gardner's book *The Art of Fiction*:

> Describe a building as seen by a man whose son has just been killed in a war. Do not mention the son, war, death, or the old man doing the seeing; then describe the same building, in the same weather and at the same time of day, as seen by a happy lover. Do not mention love or the loved one.[4]

When I discovered Gardner's list of exercises, I felt compelled to share it. Had my English teachers when I was growing up given assignments like this that teach about tone and diction in a fun and creative way, perhaps fewer of my classmates and friends would have spurned reading and writing, and more would have learned to appreciate what goes into good writing. Challenging students with trinkets of mind puzzles and pushing their creativity were a few ideas I had adopted to reach, engage, and turn students on to learning. I had other ideas on how to teach differently and how to teach better. Some were original ideas and some were ineffective or bad ideas. But that is a bit beside the point. The point is that I was having fun, my mind felt alive and was constantly racing with new and different things to try, and I had finally found something I could settle on doing for a long time.

An Interview

Toward the end of my last year of graduate school, I drove to Chickasha, forty-five miles outside of where I was living in Oklahoma City, to buy a used car. Chickasha is a small, rural town known throughout the state for its massive plates of barbecue, onion burgers, and its annual Festival of Light, a holiday celebration at a local park. At the time, I remembered a small university in town called the University of Science and Arts of Oklahoma (USAO) from when I was scouting regional towns two years before to possibly open a local music store with a friend of mine. Since I was in the midst of applying for teaching positions, I stopped by to see if there were any math positions available. There was one. And after applying, I earned myself an interview.

At that time I had been married for over a year, and after my wife had given birth to our daughter we made the decision that we wanted to be near family. I had applied to three other regional universities in the area, all considerably larger than USAO and closer to our home in Oklahoma City. They were my first, second, and third choices for teaching. I did not know much about USAO. It was a small school in a small town forty-five miles from home. To be honest, I did not seriously envision myself teaching there. But USAO offered me my first interview, and so I took it with the idea that it would be good practice for when I interviewed at my top three choices.

On the day of my interview, I arrived early to tour the school's campus. USAO is a small, quiet, and quaint undergraduate college whose entire campus is recognized as a National Historic District. It is Oklahoma's only public liberal arts college. That is, it is affordable[5] and its educational model puts an equally strong emphasis on the general core courses of arts, sciences, and humanities as it does on a student's major. This is in opposition to the view that these general courses are peripheral to a student's major that I had become familiar with at the University of Oklahoma.

At my interview with the USAO search committee, I was surprised by the line of questions I received. The committee seemed more interested in the courses I took in college that were outside of my discipline than they were with my dissertation and the math courses I completed in graduate school. They were tickled and impressed that I offered writing assignments in the math courses I taught. Imagine going to an interview in which your interviewers asked only questions about your pastimes and nothing about the topics essential to the position you were interviewing for and you will understand the bizarre scene I found myself in. I am exaggerating of course. The committee did ask a number of questions about my approach to teaching mathematics, and I did perform a teaching demonstration, but the committee continued with questions like "What can you teach other than mathematics?" "What connections with other disciplines such as art and politics does math have?" "Can you explain and teach how mathematics has reshaped the world throughout history?" "What was the last book you read that was not a math book?"

So heavy was the committee's interest in my hobbies and knowledge outside of mathematics that at times I was confused about the type of position for which I was applying. I did not come prepared to answer such questions, but I found that my answers came quite naturally and effortlessly. That USAO put a great deal of value in what I had formerly deemed as academic diversions rejuvenated me and made me feel that all my natural curiosities and wide range of interests when growing up suddenly had a purpose.

I came to the interview at USAO thinking of it as a mere exercise, but I left with a transforming impression of how a professorial life could be. I was made for this job. The university's interdisciplinary curriculum particularly appealed to me. Through its interdisciplinary studies program, I would be encouraged to teach courses outside of mathematics, such as origami and World Thought and Culture—courses I surely would not have the opportunity to teach to a broad audience at many other places. When I received the offer for a tenure-track assistant professorship position from USAO, I accepted it ecstatically and withdrew my name immediately from consideration at the other three schools.

Culture

For some students, a public liberal arts school like USAO is the sensible next step in their academic careers. This is because USAO shares certain characteristics students valued in their high school that were conducive to

learning: small class sizes, student-centered pedagogy, and an earnest relationship with their teachers, professors, or mentors. It is because of these
similarities that, for faculty who arrived at this profession for teaching and
making a significant impact on their students' academic growth, a small
liberal arts college can provide an ideal environment to do so.

The size of a university can have tremendous influence on the culture of the institution. In many ways, it dictates how professorial life at
the university functions. For instance, because USAO is small, its student
body is small, which means the school can only afford a correspondingly
small faculty. This in turn means that each professor generally is required
to teach four or more courses each trimester so that students can finish
their undergraduate requirements in three to four years. This translates
to less time for research; however, what it results in is significantly more
exposure with students. Not only does every professor at USAO meet and
teach a higher percentage of our student body than we would at a large
university, we also have smaller class sizes and more face time with each
student in our respective programs. This extra time together forges a deep
and growing rapport and professional familiarity that is characteristic of a
healthy and vibrant classroom community.[6]

Though liberal arts colleges and high schools both center their work
and priorities around students, there are philosophical differences. One
important difference is that the role of the professor of a liberal arts college is thought of as a mentor, instructor, lecturer, or discussion leader,
whereas teachers at high schools generally have more of an authoritarian
role. This difference can greatly affect the academic atmosphere of each
institution. College students are taught to research, contemplate, question,
and to generate knowledge. This approach to teaching—where the gap
between teacher and student is narrowed—is not common in high school.
Students there are treated as academically less mature and are generally
given knowledge to regurgitate, formulas to plug and chug, and guidelines to follow. At USAO and other liberal arts colleges, students are taught
about the connections and interplay between different disciplines. This is
a distinct feature of liberal arts colleges that is lacking at other colleges and
research institutions. The hope is that interdisciplinary teaching builds a
solid foundation for creativity and innovation that is valuable for graduate
school, the job market, and each student's future goals.

Interdisciplinarity is one of the hallmark objectives at USAO and
other liberal arts colleges. By working with colleagues from other disciplines, we teach lessons and carry out investigations from different points

of view, needs, and expertise. For instance, like many public liberal arts colleges, USAO features team-teaching, where members from generally distinct disciplines join together to teach a course in a cohesive manner. By lecturing together, a team of professors can expose, through cordial dialogue and debate, the breadth and complexity of the human world in a way that individual teaching cannot achieve. Other interdisciplinary interactions among faculty come in the form of committees, meetings, outreach projects, gatherings, and recreation. One committee on which I serve at USAO, the Festival of Arts and Ideas Committee, includes faculty from each division so that the annual festival gets broad participation from all corners of the university to celebrate a chosen theme viewed from different disciplinary spectacles. One key difference I have found between the culture at a liberal arts college like USAO and the research institution from which I graduated is that it is common to see colleagues from across campus teaching together, working together, researching together, and socializing together as if they were part of a homogeneous intellectual community.

Challenges

As with any change of scenery, I had to meet many challenges and make several adjustments to adapt to my new professional surroundings. These ranged from teaching the courses I wanted to teach, to the type of research I could contribute to, to the kind of service I wanted to engage in. One of the first obstacles I ran into relates to the size of the institution. At USAO, the mathematics department has three faculty members and two adjunct instructors. This means we can only offer around twenty math courses per trimester, with a large portion of those courses devoted to servicing other majors, such as Elementary Statistics, College Algebra, Trigonometry, and Math in the Modern World.[7] This translates to only a handful of advanced courses USAO can offer a student majoring in mathematics. Advanced staple and special topics courses like Advanced Calculus I, Advanced Calculus II, Modern Algebra II, Graph Theory, Complex Variables, and Introduction to Topology are rarely offered. This stark contrast to the amount and variety of upper-level math courses available at larger universities troubled me. Why would a student wanting to major in mathematics come to USAO? And how could I feel confident about sending my students to a graduate program in mathematics if I know they have not taken certain fundamental advanced courses? But the reality is, even if USAO hires more math professors to offer more advanced courses, where will the school find the students to take them? Due to the small number of math majors at USAO, the class size of advanced math courses tends to be on the dangerously low end of the spectrum. Adding more advanced courses raises the possibility of courses competing for students and risks cutting class sizes even further.

Realizing that class size was the root of the problem, I knew that I could offer a new upper-level math course if I could get enough students to enroll in it without compromising enrollment in any existing advanced course. To do this, I needed to ask students to take extra math courses above the required number of elective courses. The only way I knew to do that was to generate excitement for mathematics.

I began by resurrecting the long-retired USAO Math Club. Because student interest in its rebirth came primarily from my calculus course, we ended up with math, physics, chemistry, and computer science majors in the club. So, in the spirit of interdisciplinarity, I asked our lone physics professor to cosponsor the club with me and renamed it the Mathematics Technology and Science Club (MTS). Among the goals of the club were to generate interest by establishing a venue to give math, technology, and science seminars, and to establish a forum in which students can lobby for additional courses they would like to see offered. The MTS Club was a huge success. It allowed us to interact with students on a more casual level and to introduce to them less rudimentary, more beautiful, exciting, and cutting-edge mathematics and science. Already we are seeing one of our primary goals met as Modern Algebra II was offered in the fall of 2013 as a course for the first time in school history.[8]

Along with additional advanced courses in mathematics, I also wanted to branch out and offer interdisciplinary courses. This was, after all, the primary reason I chose USAO over other institutions. In my first two and a half years, I developed and taught four interdisciplinary courses never before offered at USAO. Because interdisciplinary courses are open to all majors, the challenge here was not in trying to get the courses approved, but in promoting the courses to meet enrollment requirements and teaching each course in a format that is effective for the diverse audience.

One of the courses I developed is called Documentary Films. I came up with the idea for this course after years of watching documentary films with my roommate during graduate school and discussing them over beer and pizza. Documentary films have become increasingly well produced, engaging, and relevant to today's society. Most importantly, this bundle of knowledge is packaged and wrapped into a two-hour box that is perfect for a one-day-a-week, three-hour course. To promote the course, I e-mailed faculty, students, and various institutions in the community. I also had an article written about it in the student newspaper. The course explored a new twist on USAO's team-teaching model. This twist involved presentations by eleven different professors with all of the academic divisions represented by at least two professors. Each presenter was given an entire three-hour class period to show a documentary film of their choice and discuss issues raised in the film. The course was a huge success with students and audience members applauding the course, claiming that they found themselves "learning quite effortlessly."

Another course I developed and offered is in origami. The course was conceived one night about a month before my interview at USAO when I serendipitously came across a documentary film about the art of origami called *Between the Folds*.[9] Watching it rekindled a favorite pastime of mine from when I was younger. The timing could not have been any better because it turned out to be one of my key talking points at my interview. The search committee told me that USAO would welcome a new interdisciplinary course on origami. True to their word, two years later, Origami was offered for the first time. The goal of the course was to learn how mathematics can be used in the design of paper animals and other models.[10] The interdisciplinary art/math course consisted of a mixture of lecture days, lab/studio days, and a weekly show-and-tell day. The course turned out to be another success, with students clamoring for Origami II. It was a fun course in which everyone, including I, learned a great deal about the art of paper folding, play, and discovery.

Not all challenges fall under the category of teaching. One more obstacle I had to overcome involved adjusting my area of research. My dissertation in graduate school was on geometric group theory. GGT is a young, vibrant, and abstract field in mathematics and, as a result, it has a small, active, and narrow academic community. Unfortunately, this community has not yet reached the city of Chickasha.[11] In order to continue my mathematics research in this area, I would need to reconnect with the GGT community by way of collaboration and regular travel to attend and present at conferences. Because funding for research is limited at USAO, collaboration with my peers would be more feasible if done almost exclusively through e-mail, phone, and Web conferences; attending conferences would be more sporadic than ideal.

I think I could still be rather successful in GGT research if I truly wanted to be. Certainly a few of my former classmates who ended up at other small schools where undergraduate teaching is given priority over research continue to contribute to the field. But for me, GGT has lost its appeal. In the end, what made it most dear to me in graduate school was not the value of the research or even the beauty of the geometry (though this beauty is what drew me to GGT in the first place), but the ability and opportunity to share it with the on-campus GGT community of my professors, peers, and visitors. The absence of such fellowship at USAO to bounce ideas around with would be like playing four square by myself: it simply would not be any fun.

Consequently I have since turned my attention to research in mathematics education and recreation. A recently hired member of our mathematics department did his graduate research on guided reinvention, a movement in mathematics pedagogy that teaches mathematics through group work and carefully crafted problems that guide students toward creative and informal solutions that hold similarities to established mathematical theorems, laws, and processes. Intrigued and impressed with this new concept, I plan on collaborating with him on several future projects. Other scholarship possibilities I am interested in pursuing include where mathematics can be used in the fine arts (e.g., origami, perspectives, and symmetry), and in using mathematical ideas and logic in writing fiction and creative nonfiction.[12] These are areas of mathematics that students, colleagues, and friends of the university can all understand and appreciate, and are themes around which I can build a small academic community.

The final challenge of my work concerned making a contribution in the form of service. There was, of course, the usual committee work to maintain the functionality and governance of the university that is expected of all faculty members. Sponsoring clubs such as the MTS Club and Chess Club helped strengthen academic fellowship within the university, but I still felt I was doing minimal work in this area. A common theme at our division meetings is that service to the community is directly linked to service to the university. In the short time that I have been at USAO, my division has organized or been a part of several projects, events, and activities that serve our community.[13] I wanted to engage in some form of community outreach I could call my own.

In the fall of 2012, an opportunity revealed itself. I was given charge of managing the USAO Math and Science Tutor Lab (MaST). At the time, the lab served only USAO students. After I learned that our tutors had a lot of free time despite the amount of promotion we put out for MaST, I set out to extend its service to the local high school in Chickasha. The parents, teachers, and principal of Chickasha High School were thrilled. I have received several letters and phone calls expressing how much our MaST lab has improved their students' academic success and how valuable it has been for them to have a safe and academically conducive place to send their students and children to study. In addition to serving the community, opening our doors to them benefits USAO in several ways as well. Most directly, it solidifies the basic mathematical and scientific knowledge of our students who serve as tutors. It also increases the university's exposure to potential students and puts these students on the path to academic success. Less obvious is that it raises the university's standing with the community[14] by fostering healthy relations and communications with the high school. Leveraging these lines of communication the lab has opened, I am currently working to host the American Mathematics Competitions at USAO for local and regional high school students and to begin a series of workshops to prepare them for these exams.[15] My hope is to share with community students the joy I find in the mind games of mathematics and to show them that USAO can be a fun, challenging, and special place to learn. These forms of community outreach not only enhance USAO's image, but are also integral to the health of the math program.

If I were at a research university, I would not have had to work so hard to offer a particular math course, find a new research area or academic community, or concern myself with community outreach and service. The math department of which I would be a part would already be a well-established academic metropolis. But in meeting all these challenges, I have found it intensely fulfilling and rewarding, because here—at a small liberal arts college—I have a significant say in what is being done, I have a voice in its vision, and I have a hand in its success. The mathematics department at USAO may never be an empire for mathematics, but it is becoming a playground that sure is fun to run around and play in.

Reflection

I have now taught at USAO for a little more than two academic years. I have a cozy office on the second floor with a large window facing the sunrise that I can open and enjoy the fresh country air. I have three clocks so that depending on where I am sitting or which direction I am facing, I do not have to turn my head to know the time. I have a worn-in couch I bought from somebody's grandfather. I have the dartboard from my college days hung to regulation height on my west wall. I have colleagues with whom I enjoy having a beer or tossing around ideas. When people ask me about my job, I always smile and reply, "I have landed exactly where I was always meant to be."

I had a heavy reservation during my final year of graduate school about my ability to succeed at a research university. A lot of my classmates who made it to the end with me were excruciatingly dedicated to and brilliant at mathematics. They were the type of people I would have to be on par with to be successful at a research institution. My former office-mate lived for and breathed mathematics. That was all he ever wanted to talk about. At parties, at bars and restaurants, at football games, on the street, on the road, while flying in the air, while swimming—there was no place that was a bad place to discuss or work mathematics.[16] He had the kind of mind that would thrive at a research university.

It is not that I do not love and enjoy mathematics; it is that I do not love and enjoy *only* mathematics. I do not have peak ambitions for mathematical research. What I do have is a juvenile joy for playing along its foothills and learning and discovering new knowledge. That is why I feel so at home at a liberal arts college. USAO encourages me to do research and scholarship, but does not pressure me to publish on a regular basis. This ease from stress allows me the flexibility and luxury to wander outside of my mathematical base and comfort zone into other fields to see if new bridges can be built between those areas and mathematics. If I can build them, great! If not, that is okay too. My time spent on these endeavors is not viewed as a loss. In fact, USAO takes pride in the fact that their professors are well rounded and interdisciplinary. This flexibility to do any kind of research and the interdisciplinary culture at USAO are what make me look forward to going to work every morning.

So I may never be an astronaut or a biologist, but where I am now, I am having fun and I have the opportunity and freedom to jump around, to dibble and dabble, to poke and piddle, to learn and to explore whatever captures my fancy the way I used to when I was a kid. And who knows? I can still be an artist, and maybe someday I will invent something. But teaching at a liberal arts college has, in a way, allowed me to remain a kid—hopefully, for the rest of my life.

Works Cited

Gardner, John. *The Art of Fiction: Notes on Craft for Young Writers*. New York: Random House, Inc., 1983.

Gould, Vanessa, et al. *Between the Folds: A Film about Finding Inspiration in Unexpected Places*. [Brooklyn, NY]: Green Fuse Films, 2009.

Notes

1. Notice that neither mathematician nor teacher is on that list. Funny how things work out.

2. E.g., Photography, Ceramics, History of Judaism, Film and Video, Fiction, World Literature, and Creative Writing.

3. Even with class sizes of over three hundred seats, the two most popular courses at the University of Oklahoma, Freedom in Greece and Freedom in Rome, taught by classics professor J. Rufus Fears, regularly had the longest enrollment waiting lists at the university. I was able to circumvent these long lines to see what all the hubbub was about by unofficially auditing each course . . . twice.

4. Gardner, *Art of Fiction*, 203.

5. In 2010, on the "Great Schools, Great Prices" list of *U.S. News Best Colleges Guide,* USAO held on to its number-one spot among all baccalaureate colleges in the western United States (http://usao.edu/news/news/usao-ranked-no-1-best-buy-again).

6. This is in direct contrast to my experience as a student at the University of Oklahoma where I was one of nearly one hundred students in my Calculus II course, and my professor's only responsibility was to give lectures and to write exams. All interactions with him went through his graduate assistants since they were the ones responsible for grades and the discussion sessions.

7. This is USAO's version of liberal arts or general mathematics.

8. Though Modern Algebra II has been offered three times before as tutorials (which are like reading courses at other universities, where the faculty member's role is purely as a supervisor), this is the first time it will be offered as a lecture course.

9. *Between the Folds* aired on PBS stations as part of the Independent Lens series.

10. Robert Lang's TED talk was used as inspiration for this course. His fifteen-minute talk can be found at https://www.ted.com/talks/robert_lang_folds_way_new_origami.html.

11. Preparing students in this area would require more abstract courses (Introduction to Topology, in particular) to be taught, which as previously mentioned, we have not been able to offer yet.

12. Examples of mathematicians who have been successful in writing creatively include Charles Dodgson (a.k.a. Lewis Carroll), Raymond Smullyan, and Edwin Abbott Abbott.

13. E.g., Festival of Arts and Ideas, Mathcounts for middle school students, Oklahoma Junior Academy of Science meetings, high school scholastic meets, Earth Day 2013 for Girl Scouts, and a summer academy for junior high students titled "Where Does Our Food Come From and How Did It Get There?"

14. USAO, for several reasons, has had a strained relationship with its surrounding

community, particularly Chickasha High School. It has been suggested that one reason for this is that because USAO is so close to University of Oklahoma, many perceive sending their children and students to a local small-town college as a failure, that students go there because they either could not afford the big universities like University of Oklahoma or were not smart enough to get into them, even though USAO's admission standards are the highest in the state.

15. The American Mathematics Competitions are the first of a series of competitions for high school students that determine the United States team for the International Mathematics Olympiad.

16. My office-mate came from a part of India where recreational swimming was a luxury. Determined to learn to swim, he asked me to teach him one summer and I obliged. For several days in the summer, in his apartment swimming pool, I held him across my forearms like I would my own daughter while he flapped and flailed frantically for breath and progression. And when college girls came by to bathe in the sun and take a dip in the water, we played it cool on the edges of the pool and talked mathematics.

8

Dr. Monograph; or, How I Learned to Stop Worrying and Love the Liberal Arts

Janet Schrunk Ericksen
English, University of Minnesota, Morris

Driving to Morris, Minnesota, from Minneapolis–St. Paul can seem like driving off the map, out of civilization, into the wild. More than a hundred miles northwest of the Twin Cities comes a turn off the interstate to a two-lane road, with a subsequent hour spent moving through towns of decreasing size. When two wind turbines appear on the horizon, they signal arrival at a place that at least to some extent counters expectations set up by the journey. Morris has only about five thousand inhabitants—still far more than the last town on the route, which has fewer than three hundred—with two grain elevator operations along the main commercial street and three hardware stores, but it also has a food cooperative with local products, a cooperatively owned first-run movie theater, and two art galleries. And it has the University of Minnesota, Morris.

The wind turbines signify Morris in more ways than one. While I could make a long list of things that this small town on the northern prairie does not have, something we have in great abundance is wind. To students and university leaders, the perfect response to an abundance of wind is to build wind turbines, to take what is here and make something good from it. The campus has been particularly progressive in environmental initiatives. In addition to the wind turbines, which provide about 70 percent of the campus's electricity, we have a biomass plant that gasifies local crop debris, replacing most of the campus's natural gas consumption and reducing carbon dioxide emissions. We

117

have a solar-heated pool, a new dorm designed as an environmental living and learning center, and much more along these lines, but only because students and staff have had imagination and a willingness to consider ideas and actions other than the obvious or the familiar ones. Those who are happiest at this college, whether the four-year students or the longer-term faculty, seem to be those who have or develop broader comfort with things outside the familiar, whether that means adapting to the odd hours of the local coffee house—not a Starbucks but instead run by a consortium of local Lutheran churches—or learning to perceive successful academic research as having more forms and paces than it typically does at the kinds of institutions from which faculty earned their graduate degrees.

In significant ways, my research at the University of Minnesota, Morris has stayed in line with both my graduate school training and the expectations of my first academic position, which was at a Research I university. I work with books and so require no lab or special equipment. Expanding digital resources and interlibrary loans have meant equal or even improved access to library holdings regardless of location, and this in turn has allowed me to keep up with others' research in my field as well as to study texts in libraries around the world. When more direct access has been important, research grants have allowed me to work abroad—in two instances, for an entire semester—at the libraries that possess the primary materials I study. A network of colleagues in my field at other institutions, people to whom I send my work and whose work I have reviewed, has continued to develop and continues to support me, and throughout my career I have usually presented papers at one or two major conferences each year and published regularly, at least when I have been in a standard faculty appointment. I have, in addition, taught almost every other year at Morris and at my previous university the introductory course in my specialization (Old English literature and language), a course that is often for first-year graduate students but also widely available to upper-level undergraduates. Indeed where medieval studies graduate students are few, as they were at the research university where I worked, the majority or entirety of the class may be undergraduates, so the fact that I now exclusively teach the class to undergraduates is not remarkable. Even some of the most widely publicized contextual differences between a liberal arts college and a research university have not directly affected me: my field does not lend itself easily either to co-authored research or teaching assistants, whether undergraduate or graduate, or to community outreach—few communities have a clearly identified need for someone with expertise in early medieval literature.

My primary field is Anglo-Saxon literature, texts written before about 1100 in the now nearly foreign stage of English known as Old English. Like many of my peers, even those who (unlike me) had come from and hoped to work at liberal arts colleges, I chose my research focus primarily because of personal interest rather than because of career plans, and when I received an offer to work at a Research I university, it seemed the perfect next step. The graduate faculty in medieval studies had prepared me well; they were good teachers, kind people, and excellent guides to the field, and they nurtured their students exceptionally well both academically and professionally. My field seems strikingly remote to most people, more suited to research contexts than ones with greater emphasis on undergraduate teaching, and certainly much of what I work on seems to offer little to counter that perception, at least at first glance. I wrote my dissertation on a single Old English narrative poem, one composed sometime between about 800 and 1000 CE and preserved in just one manuscript, and my publications include articles that deal with not just Old English language and texts but also Old Norse, Old Irish, Latin, and the runic alphabet that predates English use of the Roman alphabet. What my publications do not yet include is a monograph, that standard marker of academic success in the humanities, the measure by which promotion is frequently determined and something I was well on my way to producing before I decided to move to a job at a liberal arts college. My place of employment has not put such an achievement out of reach—many of my colleagues have managed to publish monographs while working at a liberal arts college, and my own book, on which I have sporadically continued to work for years, is finally nearing completion. Indeed, had I given it highest priority, I am confident that I could have finished my book years ago. The choice not to do so reflects what I see as the largest distinction between research at a liberal arts college and at a more research-focused campus: research at a liberal arts college requires flexibility—sometimes by choice and sometimes imposed—of pace, of priority in workload, and of focus.

When I was visibly pregnant with my eldest child and in my first job, a senior faculty member in my department, rather in passing, commented to me, "I see you've made your decision"—or perhaps just "*a* decision." She said it with a smile. I do not recall quite how I responded, except to be fairly sure that my sense of position at the time yielded a bland reply. Yet the remark has remained with me, in part because I was never quite sure what it meant. It might have been a quite benign comment on the choice to have a child, but I assumed that the perceived choice was between aiming for high achievements in research and having a family, particularly since my department had apparently never had to deal with a pregnant faculty member before me. The comment played into other factors that seemed to be pushing me toward a different job, but my choice to leave was not an easy one.

Factors that played into that choice, just when I was finally beginning to feel somewhat comfortable in my position, included the nonexistent support offered by senior colleagues to junior faculty and the uncertainty of my chance at tenure. Two denials of tenure had just occurred in my department, and while the details remained unclear to me, I knew that both of these colleagues had published books with good presses and at least one was well known as an excellent teacher and was the recipient of an undergraduate advising award. The only obvious supporter I had among the senior faculty, before he retired in poor health, held a role among the other senior faculty that had become or maybe always was an antagonistic one, so that his support seemed more likely to work against me rather than for me. He still modeled, however, an intellectual life that extended to everything he did, such as spending much time with students and giving them energetic and demanding teaching, producing respected research in his field, and playing music in a band for fun. And he came from a liberal arts college, as did my husband. I found myself developing a sense of opposition between what I had and what a liberal arts college might offer. My department projected an atmosphere of self-importance and exclusivity, one in which attention-getting research and publication numbers seemed not just the primary but almost the exclusive goals, and I had a growing sense of wanting a broader view of intellectual life (a sense admittedly amplified by the fact that I gave birth to two children and had no tenure-clock extension or parental leave). Despite all this, I also had the nagging sense that leaving meant giving up what I had been trained for, what my advisors hoped for and fellow graduate students sought most, what the world esteemed most highly—and that my decision was a bad one.

I no longer wonder if the choice was a bad one, although adjusting to Morris took some time. Among other things, I had to adjust to no longer being at a university with a well-known name and research reputation. I have, however, definitely decided that a liberal arts college is a wonderful place to work, and I have also become a firm advocate of liberal arts college education. The public liberal arts college in particular appeals to me, with its egalitarian foundations; the University of Minnesota, Morris opened in 1960 as a result of citizen lobbying, of people's desire to make more widely available the kind of education provided at the more expensive private lib-eral arts colleges of Minnesota, and our students continue to reflect that goal. Roughly one-third of recent students at Morris are first-generation college attendees and another third come from low-income households. Approximately 20 percent are students of color, including more than 13 percent who are American Indian, a statistic that reflects both the egal-itarian impulse and an older, much less egalitarian history. The campus began as an American Indian boarding school in the nineteenth century, and when that closed in 1909—a few of those early buildings remain part of the campus—a residential agricultural high school opened on the site, succeeded by the university. With the transfer of the first boarding school property to the state came a requirement that any subsequent school on the site admit American Indian students without charging them tuition, which remains our policy. My advocacy of the Morris mission and cam-pus rests not just on my own experience but also on many discussions with faculty at other universities and colleges. Although I cannot say that I would promote living in rural Minnesota, I not only embrace the college's mission, but I also truly like my job, something I do not hear frequently from my peers at other institutions. My students are on the whole people I admire, and the campus is a genuine community of teachers and schol-ars who are interested in each other and each other's work. My research continues, and I still think of myself as an Anglo-Saxonist, whatever my teaching load might include—although somehow, despite the fact that my current department has fewer than a third of the faculty number that my previous department had, I am teaching very nearly what I taught at the research university, with what were once graduate seminars now replaced by advanced undergraduate courses. My teaching load increased by only one class per year with the move, and the internal research support did not dramatically diminish, which I recognize is relatively unusual among public liberal arts colleges. We have the advantage (sometimes also the challenge) of strong connections to the University of Minnesota system, through which we have access to competitive research support and where the vice president for research, for instance, acted upon the recognition that we wanted and benefited from research support as much as did our colleagues on the larger research campus.

The greatest quotidian change with my move to a liberal arts college was my degree of involvement in campus governance and with my stu-dents, and in turn my willingness and my freedom to move research to lower levels of priority. At my first job, junior faculty were largely to be seen and not heard; at the liberal arts college, every voice not only can be heard but is needed, right from the start. Even though I welcomed the chance to participate more in campus affairs and interact more with students, I knew that such commitments would reduce the time I put into research. In turn, I had to come to terms with the acceptability, to myself and to peers in my field, of a slower rate of scholarly work and of the value of sometimes putting other things first in my higher education career. Willingness not to focus on research as consistently the highest priority seems to me central to the success of the college, and faculty unwilling to adjust, in my experience, risk suffering from Research I envy and corresponding unhappiness with their liberal arts context. The research-is-not-always-first perspective runs counter to what most graduate students learn as they move toward completing the PhD, and, for me, it was further confirmed by my years working at a research-focused university. I would not, however, choose differently if I had the job choice to make again. Greater freedom to set my own priorities and directions came with the job change, and that flexibility suited my research and my career as a whole, as well as my desire for a life that was not consumed by the drive for publication. I certainly do not spend less time on my work now than I did at the Research I job, but it is more widely varied and in some ways more in my control, even if at times (and I think this is good) it focuses less on what I have to say and more on what I do for my students and colleagues.

The rearrangement of research priorities began as soon as I changed jobs. Given the short time I had until my tenure-decision year when I began at the liberal arts college, I decided to put aside the book temporarily. I was not yet happy with it, and I was worried about finding a publisher; books on Anglo-Saxon literature are not as highly sought after as books with potentially wider audiences or more obviously splashy potential. The humanities equation of tenure and book, or any single comparable achievement such as a solo exhibition at a major gallery, has always seemed to me narrow and mechanical. Such equations are standard at research universities and also at many more universities and colleges, despite their obvious limitations. If two assistant professors are both fine scholars and hard workers, and both produce books, their books are not the automatically comparable achievements that the single tenure bar proclaims them: one could produce a semi-autobiographical monograph that is among the first studies in a particular field, and the other might work in a long-established field that still has much to explore but requires research in multiple languages and subfields before any respectable study can emerge. I do not mean to diminish the value of any project or field, rather the contrary. Making the monograph the single measure of academic success inevitably distorts research by forcing it into one model and one timeline. The development of that perception may have been one of the first signs that I was suited to the greater flexibility of a liberal arts college. I decided to pursue, instead of the book, a series of shorter projects that I felt more capable of doing well at the time and that excited me more. Part of me does still sometimes think of this decision as a diminishing one, and indeed the dean told me during my exit interview that he doubted I would ever be able to finish the book if I went to the liberal arts college—the Research I mind-set is firmly entrenched.

Putting off the book project, however, allowed me not just to pursue what interested me most at the time but also to prepare some new courses. One of these was a study abroad short course on medieval literature that I have taught repeatedly and from which I have developed new research avenues, and another was an honors seminar co-taught with a chemist and a historian that has been one of the highlights of my teaching career (a student, now a successful lawyer, who took that class more than a decade ago was very recently singing its praises on Facebook, so the perception was not mine alone). Focusing on other projects also allowed me to return to the book when I was better able to consider its arguments and spend time framing them, which I have now done. My own delays as well as those by some of my peers have led me to wish I could find a way to convince more academics that not producing a book—on a one-size-fits-all timeline or indeed ever—does not mean not being a good scholar or a valuable member of a field. If we become scholars because we relish learning and arguing and writing, then perhaps we can find a variety of ways to measure the continuation of scholarly involvement and achievement. Indeed, the monograph measure is relatively new and primarily the product of increased competition for jobs rather than of more dedicated or better scholars. We do need ways to evaluate our work, but the book or indeed any single achievement need not be the automatically revered measure and universal standard, particularly at a liberal arts college with its varied demands and opportunities.

The chance to choose the order and pace of projects is a considerable freedom in any job, and one I think I value more for having felt my research shaped by a single standard in my first job. Delaying the book project allowed me to think a bit more broadly and to be pushed in directions I had not expected, even when doing so meant at times putting research into a position of lower priority and slower pace. Within my first five years at the liberal arts college, I began down a route familiar to many faculty at small colleges. I began to take on administrative responsibilities before I had achieved tenure. I had no intention of pursuing such roles and no desire to make them my goal, but in a small department with a combination of about-to-retire senior faculty and new hires fresh from graduate school, the candidates for leadership roles were few and I seemed a reasonable option. At first, I managed to add on the relatively small roles of search committee chair and then of discipline coordinator without much effect on my research. (Rather than actual departments, we have disciplines with collective administration, although with eleven faculty in English, we function much like a small department and many of us cannot quite get past using the term.) As I dealt with the form-processing and organizational work of such positions, I could still squeeze in research around the edges of teaching and in the summers. I gained tenure, took a sabbatical for which I managed to secure a fellowship at a British university, and was awarded a National Endowment of the Humanities grant to support a new research project. Despite my choices to take different directions in research and to play different roles on campus, my research progress seemed still to be largely consistent with my past experience. After the luxury of a sabbatical year in which research was the priority, however, other responsibilities crept, and then roared, into view.

Committees need participants, and most liberal arts campuses function with the same basic raft of committees as any campus: assessment, faculty reviews, awards and grants, searches, and more. Like most liberal arts college faculty, I have served on a wide array of committees; faculty cannot abstain from service and expect the campus to work well. Everyone truly is needed, even if not everyone participates as fully as they should. A similar understanding of the need for faculty involvement led me to another decision about my work priorities. When the possibility of serving in an administrative position, as chair of the Division of the Humanities, arose, I found myself considering applying. I was still only an associate professor, with two children under the age of ten, and with specific plans for research and teaching over the next several years. Only two of my senior colleagues, however, pursued the appointment, and neither seemed likely to shape the division in ways that would continue to make it a place at which I wanted to work. My husband and I talked about what the job would mean and what I might bring to it, and I had similar conversations with many other colleagues. When I decided to go forward with seeking the position, my primary motivation was the desire for continuation of the progress made under the last division chair, particularly the progress made in openness, clarity, and fairness. Besides, I told myself, the appointment would be only for five years.

Motivated by my experience at my first job in a department that had neither openness nor clarity—nor, in my experience, fairness—I gave the job of division chair precedence. The move meant that the five years during which I served as chair of the Division of the Humanities were not good ones for my research, but having found, more or less, a view of and place for research that made sense for me, I wanted to do what I could to ensure that others could do the same and in turn be evaluated on a range of paces and achievements, as individuals with varying professional circumstances, and that was something I could work for as chair. The chair of another division had served in the position for more than twenty years when I took the appointment, and he remains an associate professor, his research derailed by this other priority. His experience was my warning— although he had also been a highly effective leader—and I was determined to maintain some research progress. I managed to do so, but at a far slower pace and with little progress toward the kind of record I would need in order to be considered for promotion to full professor. At the same time, I learned an enormous amount, largely from evaluations of my colleagues about the variety of ways they have found to be active scholars as well as excellent teachers. Not everyone finds a way; I had the deeply unpleasant task of informing tenure-track colleagues that their contracts were being terminated, in no small part because of a lack of progress in research. Yet in every faculty review, we talked about our standards, our goals, and where research fits into our liberal arts college, and we gave a range of thoughtful, nuanced answers—not just one answer, but a range. Research at a liberal arts college is indeed different from what I experienced at a research-focused university.

The exposure to other fields and other standards that has come from serving as division chair and from serving on the humanities—not the English department—promotion and tenure committee has further shaped my desire to maintain a flexible understanding of scholarly accomplishment. Our division has ten disciplines as diverse as studio art, music, and philosophy, yet we all evaluate each other, and we all have to learn about the standards in each other's fields and interpret them within the framework of our campus and its faculty's responsibilities and possibilities. What I value perhaps most about such a process and such a place is the flexibility that this interpretative work includes. We have external as well as internal review for tenure and promotion, which means that faculty must produce work of which they can be proud and for which they can gain respect from peers in their field. Exactly how much must be produced or accomplished, however, remains unspecified. A few lengthy, very well-placed articles combined with excellence in teaching and service might, for instance, earn a person tenure, although a far more comfortable basis for that decision would come with a greater number of publications, and too-minimal accomplishments in research have led to denials of tenure or the chance to continue pursuing it. At the same time, I feel quite protective of allowing a range of achievements. As more of our faculty produce more research, reflecting changes in the market and in graduate school, I sense from some of my colleagues the desire to narrow the research requirements for advancement; as more tenured faculty in the humanities publish monographs, in other words, I watch warily for the desire to make the monograph the minimum standard. If our flexibility in evaluating research diminishes, then we correspondingly restrict our ability to reprioritize and to explore, and to be a scholar in more than simply one sense. In turn, the liberal arts college would become a far less appealing place for many of us to work—including those of us who value research.

While I know that many of my liberal arts colleagues are excellent and well-published scholars and I want to be able to continue my own research, at the same time I do not want the liberal arts college—the one at which I work or many others—to strive too much toward Research I values. The liberal arts college is different from the research-focused campus, with flexible possibilities for scholarship that can and often do work for both scholars and students, although we may have to fight to maintain that flexibility. In their recent review of David Breneman's 1990 study of liberal arts colleges, Vicki Baker, Roger Baldwin, and Sumedha Makker characterized the ways in which they found liberal arts colleges changing, and the changes appear to be ones that threaten the flexible spaces for scholarship. That nagging sense of diminishment that I felt on moving to a liberal arts college is widely shared and influential in at least one direction of change: "[s]ome liberal arts colleges have transformed themselves into 'research colleges' in order to attract students and faculty who value the mission of the research university." That move may in part result from a desire to keep a liberal arts college from moving toward being a "professional college," that is, "implementing more academic programs in professional fields in order to compete for students who see higher education primarily as a path to a career and financial success."[1] Primarily, however, I think a significant portion of the faculty at the liberal arts college where I work would welcome the designation of "research college" for the apparent distinction it conveys. We produce a remarkable amount of published research across all fields, and like many other liberal arts colleges, our campus has focused attention on providing plentiful opportunities for undergraduate research as well. The research college designation might help us clarify our distinctions from other higher education institutions in the state and beyond it, defining us more directly away from the equation of small and regional that people seem frequently to make and giving up on trying to explain to people what "liberal arts college" means. The designation seems, however, to reflect some insecurity about scholarly reputations and to focus attention on faculty more than on the bulk of what the campus provides to its students. Top-tier liberal arts colleges have long included excellent and well-known scholars (even if some of them end up with careers at Research I universities). The same institutions, however, have faculty who have been extraordinary scholars without publishing monographs or winning National Science Foundation grants. Instead, their attention has focused on continuing to explore ideas and passing on interest and exploration to their students. A colleague in chemistry embodies such achievement: he also studies Thomas Aquinas and Dante and writes sonnets and short stories. He is a beloved, challenging, and highly respected teacher and, although he is not a nationally known scholar, his intellectual engagement suggests strongly that he could have been had he made such accomplishments a top priority in his career. He has students who have gone on to achieve such status, and I have not seen the slightest evidence that he ever considered as a sacrifice his decision not to make research the career-long priority. Under the label of "research college," space for such scholars would seem at risk, prioritizing the narrow focus for everyone, all the time. Most liberal arts colleges have neither the funds nor the faculty numbers to support functioning as a research university in miniature, and if their mission lies in education across the liberal arts, then teaching and research have to work as variably coordinated priorities without giving research consistent precedence.

What liberal arts colleges do well, indeed do better than other institutions of higher education, cannot be achieved without willingness over the course of a career to be flexible in the amount of time in which research is given top priority. Pursuing the question, "Do Liberal Arts Colleges Really Foster Good Practices in Undergraduate Education?" Ernest T. Pascarella et alia found affirmative evidence, much of which reflects faculty time and effort:

> Students attending liberal arts colleges reported a significantly higher level on 12 of the 19 good practice dimensions than did similar students at either research universities or regional institutions. This included both first-year measures of student-faculty contact, level of cooperative learning, three out of five measures of active learning/ time on task, instructor feedback to students, three out of four indicators of high expectations, and both measures of effective teaching. Furthermore, liberal arts college students reported significantly more essay exams and computer use during their first year than did their counterparts at research universities, and a significantly higher scholarly/intellectual emphasis than similar students at regional institutions. All these significant effects persisted in the presence of controls for an extensive battery of student precollege characteristics and other influences.[2]

The study made no distinction between public and a private liberal arts colleges, something that might have modified their conclusion that liberal arts college students "have significantly higher levels of parental education and income" than students at regional or research universities.[3] What matters more is the distinction between liberal arts college teaching and research and regional university teaching; the former requires no small investment from faculty. To maintain these good practices, we have to be willing to be flexible for ourselves and our colleagues as we pursue goals in teaching and service as well as in research.

Yet if research cannot and should not be everyone's top priority all the time at a liberal arts college, it can still play a role when precedence is given to other kinds of academic achievement, particularly, of course, those directly related to our students. My research—even when it has been at low priority for some time—has influenced and been influenced by such things as the varying emphases of courses I teach, the interdisciplinary courses I have taught, and the advising I have provided to students. I have even found community interest in my field, or at least in one of my secondary fields: the swathes of Nordic immigrants to Minnesota yielded some of my students and members of the wider community, and they have a lively interest in medieval Norse sagas and culture. The same kinds of influences undoubtedly occur on campuses where research consistently ranks first among the faculty's responsibilities, but generally to a lesser extent. Because many of my classes are quite small and I often have students for more than one class, I find that my research helps me to piece together material and ideas in different ways, to provide a route for students to connect and develop across classes, and to make sure that I do not sink into rather automatic repetition from course to course or year to year. I find that trying to explain my research and literary interests to students who will not go on to graduate school in English, let alone in medieval studies, is often good for me, and I have, for instance, found interesting ways to connect early British literature and culture to American Indian cultures. I also find that my participation in my research field helps me prepare students to compete well with students from larger campuses for graduate school admission. Sometimes this has meant advising students to go abroad or take summer courses to fill in gaps that our limited offerings simply cannot provide; sometimes it has meant a directed study or two—one-on-one instruction in addition to my regular teaching load, which I am not always able or willing to do. More often, it has meant lots of talking to students inside and outside of classes and pushing them to think and reach, and to consider both tightly focused research and potentially broader connections. One of the best places for this to happen has been in co-taught courses, the most recent of which has been a course on environmental history in Iceland that I co-taught with a colleague in biology—he focused on the material record and I focused on the literary record—and that has yielded two conference papers and an article with which I am nearly finished. Not every such attempt to go a new direction has worked out as well, but a few failures do not mean career derailment. The relatively low-risk opportunities to try new directions in research or in teaching seem a precious benefit of and central to liberal arts college employment.

For reasons such as these, I am grateful too that I convinced a liberal arts college to hire me and hopeful that liberal arts colleges can continue to hire those who are genuinely interested in working at them even if little in their background ties them clearly to such an interest. My research field is not often represented among those of English faculty at liberal arts colleges, and increasingly is not one represented in larger English departments either. According to the admittedly incomplete listing in the University of Minnesota's database of less commonly taught languages, Truman State University is among the very few public liberal arts colleges where courses in Old English language and literature are offered with any regularity.[4] Larger or richer liberal arts colleges such as the College of Charleston, Vassar, and William and Mary—those more tightly bound to the traditional definition of a liberal arts college—have invested in an Anglo-Saxonist, but otherwise coverage of early medieval literature, where it happens at all, becomes part of the responsibilities of a scholar whose focus lies in Middle English or even Early Modern English literature. In small departments, faculty who can cover the widest range of material seem a particularly wise investment. Hiring faculty with highly specialized research interests may appear—and may at times turn out to be—dangerous, resulting in a faculty member who ineffectively navigates between research and teaching and who generally feels as if the liberal arts college is a temporary and insufficient location. Liberal arts colleges, particularly those that emphasize undergraduate research, want faculty to connect teaching and research, to be able to involve students where possible and to benefit from such interactions. Faculty with narrow, highly specialized research would seem, then, to be too limited and too limiting. Such faculty include those who sought and sometimes launched careers in a research-focused environment and who never found a way to embrace the liberal arts college in which they found themselves. But they also include people like me, who moved to a liberal arts college and found a place not only where a narrow field extended and diversified the department's offerings but also where research goals could be maintained and pursued with a greater sense of individual control and choice, so long as accompanied by the willingness to be flexible about the priority of research. Indeed, in my experience, my narrow research focus has largely been an asset at the liberal arts college, for my students as well as my colleagues, and rather than interfering with more generalist responsibilities, it has enhanced them.

With a mixture of relief and reluctance, I did not seek to renew my appointment as division chair when my five-year term ended. Instead, I took an overdue sabbatical and immersed myself in research, with the happy expectation of returning to full-time teaching after the sabbatical. The return to such a focus on research, after so long with my focus on administration, was not easy—I had much catching up to do in reading, in remembering old project arguments, and in mapping out new ones. Frustrating and difficult though I sometimes find it, I like the research I do. Of course at the same time I am motivated by external demands; the more I publish, the closer I am to promotion to full professor. Yet I am also happy that publishing alone or even primarily will not get me there, and I am very much looking forward to returning to closer work with students. I doubt that I will explain to any of them just what I have been working on (the audience for a study of how Latin texts were used in Anglo-Saxon schools is probably small, although I do think it useful in understanding how education changes as well as how the role of reading has changed and continues to change), but I will return to teaching with the feeling that I have a better sense of where my research fits into my field and my teaching. I cannot complain about the pace of my progress toward full professor because of course I chose to take on the administrative position. Instead, I try to see my path as just one option among many; other liberal arts faculty have chosen routes that have also diverted them, such as investing time and effort to guide huge student projects or to help a series of students gain national scholarships or to boost the enrollment in and success of a particular major. With too few non-teaching staff and a relatively small faculty, tasks such as these can take enormous amounts of time, but they also can have enormous value to all involved, both short- and long-term. Being able to give them at least temporary priority over research is one of the luxuries of a liberal arts campus, so long as administrators and other decision makers understand that such rearranged priorities inevitably affect other aspects of faculty life. To do research well in any environment requires dedicated time and access to materials, and most of us became professors because we wanted and expected to be able to continue doing research and to continue to be part of the larger community in our field. Even if we give research only an occasional position of precedence, we can stay connected to our fields and research projects while embracing, or at least accepting, other responsibilities, particularly those that put students first. At a liberal arts college, we can value and pursue research on our own terms to a greater extent than I have found elsewhere, and with wider benefit. I rather desperately hope that we can continue to do so, something that will depend in part upon liberal arts colleges' ability to explain and advocate better their distinctions from the generally lower costs of Research I institutions.

The challenge of broadening perspectives on research both within and outside Research I institutions is neatly evident in the responses from some of my Research I colleagues when I announced my decision to move to a liberal arts college. One senior colleague remarked, "I wouldn't touch that job with a ten-foot pole." The comment, though delivered with humor and focused in part on the small-town location of the job, reflects a widely held and firmly entrenched view of liberal arts colleges, and probably of anything other than a Research I institution. Liberal arts colleges, however, are only really understood from within and not even always there, something that adds to the risks that they and their important role face. Yet the comparison of my two experiences leads me not just to prefer the liberal arts college job, but genuinely to think it the better of the two. Liberal arts colleges do not suit every professor any more than they suit every student, but their balance of research and teaching, their often intensive and extensive interactions between faculty and students, and their collegiality and community allow me to pursue research influenced but not constrained by a standard defined at other places, in other contexts. At a liberal arts college out on the windy northern prairie, we can see farther than the research view with which we arrived.

Works Cited

Baker, Vicki L., Roger G. Baldwin, and Sumedha Makker. "Where Are They Now? Revisiting Breneman's Study of Liberal Arts Colleges?" *Liberal Education* 98, no. 3 (2012). http://www.aacu.org/liberaleducation/le-su12/baker_baldwin_makker.cfm.

Pascarella, Ernest T., Gregory C. Wolniak, Ty M. Cruce, and Charles F. Blaich. "Do Liberal Arts Colleges Really Foster Good Practices in Undergraduate Education?" *Journal of College Student Development* 45 (2004): 57–74.

Notes

1. Baker, Baldwin, and Makker, "Where Are They Now?"

2. Pascarella, Wolniak, Cruce, and Blaich, "Do Liberal Arts Colleges Really Foster Good Practices in Undergraduate Education?," 65.

3. Ibid., 64.

4. Less Commonly Taught Languages Database, Center for Advanced Research on Language Acquisition, University of Minnesota, http://www.carla.umn.edu/lctl/db/index.php.

9

Music, the Liberal Arts, and Rural Identity
The Not-So-Straight Road

Milton Schlosser
Music, University of Alberta, Augustana Campus

I. The Not-So-Straight Road

> It is a view that always creates a sense of wonder in me; I have seen it
> many times as a runner in the Alberta countryside. Before me stretch-
> es a straight gravel road that intersects along its way wild prairie grass,
> some stands of poplar trees, and dormant farmers' fields. It is late
> spring, with snow finally gone. Little green is in sight and the color of
> the gravel—greyish brown—pervades the land except for where the
> road in the far distance seemingly ends, making a final cut through a
> horizon of dark green spruce trees. These trees serve as a thin border
> between the barren landscape and what lies ahead: a sky so vast and
> so richly blue—there is not a single cloud in sight—that it overwhelms
> me, leaving me with a tender ache in my chest and surging pressure
> behind my eyes.

Much to the chagrin of my parents, I can never be accused of having taken
a particularly *straight* road in life. Despite having a love affair with straight
gravel roads as a runner, in my career and personal life I seem to gravitate
toward twists and turns. Apparently even when I try to be straight, it just
doesn't quite *work*. Take my handwriting, for instance. According to my
partner, Paul, I have a pathological aversion to straight lines. Keenly aware

133

that the French continue to use handwriting analysis to assess prospective employees, he conjectures that my writing between the lines—I never allow my handwriting to touch either line—might be construed as defiance against established conventions and codes. As he teasingly reminds me now and then, in tones of mock horror, "seemingly, Dr. Schlosser (that is, if you *really* are a doctor), rules are beneath you."

Looking back on my academic career at a liberal arts and sciences campus over the past twenty-eight years, I have delighted in stepping outside the bounds of disciplinary borders and expectations on more than one occasion. I suspect, for those outside my campus who have evaluated my C.V., that its content related to teaching, research, and service appears too broad, indicative of someone with lesser performing abilities who wisely chooses to be more academic in orientation. Ironically, for a concert pianist, I may look too scholarly to some. Those used to reading the careers of performers at so-called major research institutions would expect the dossier of someone like me to list lecture courses that are related to the piano in some respect (e.g., piano pedagogy, history of piano music). However, in addition to these courses, I have taught general music history, cultural criticism, feminism, music theory, and even music composition. In terms of research, classical pianists typically are expected to limit themselves to performing and recording and, when scholarly, to be involved in written projects rather conservative and sustaining of the extant musical canon. I, on the other hand, have maintained an active performing profile, including five CD releases, and have pursued written research projects that have extended all the way from queer theory to, most recently, intersections between neuroscience, contemplative studies, and sport psychology. In terms of service, I exhibit similar diversity, from being in key administrative positions as chair of the Department of Fine Arts and director of music, to starting early childhood music programming and designing a bachelor of music curriculum. Those expecting a stable, normative career outline might be perplexed at how I have allowed the boundaries of music and my institutional roles to be tested, expanded, and redefined—a disciplining or defining of music at the hands of the liberal arts that serves to undiscipline or redefine it.

Playfully, I would like to suggest that the disciplining/undisciplining of something as notoriously conservative and uptight as classical music is a good thing. University music studies need a good spanking, and who better to administer it than the liberal arts and sciences? I suspect that such an act would induce pleasure both in the one who administers and in the one who receives. Classical music needs to be freed from the constraints and dowdy appearance forced on it over the past century; it needs to reconnect with its unruly, haphazard history within the Western European tradition. As William Weber points out, the history of classical music has been for the majority of its existence one where only the music of living composers was highlighted; prior to the nineteenth century, there was no "canon" and it was expected that when a composer died, so did his or her music.[1] In essence, music was always cutting edge, and musical styles and tastes were always in contention with each other. Yet, in the 1950s in particular, music experienced a disciplining at the hands of the modern university that transformed its image. As a seeming response to centuries-old perceptions of music's beguiling qualities, music was made out to appear as mathematical, tamed, and scientific as possible.[2] Apparently the price of admission into the modern academy was music's freedom.

Sometimes I catch myself wondering what would happen to music if it was freed from the decidedly *unplayful* type of disciplining that it has received, only to realize that not only do I *know* what would happen, but also that I have already *lived* it. In this essay, I suggest that the freedom engendered to university music studies by liberal arts perspectives tends to become contagious in all areas of a person's life. Case in point: I take pride in telling my piano students that I have quit piano on at least four occasions in my life. This is something that most pianists would neither confess nor brag about. Furthermore, their institutions would probably see it as problematic given that faculty are usually hired according to discipline-specific specializations. However, something about the liberal arts frees me up to be—dare I say it—human.

Like musical taste within history, I have changed. Some of these changes have occurred because I was encouraged by my institution to be *interesting*. To see the process of learning as more important than course content, to dialogue with professors and students from other disciplines on important ideas and on contemporary issues, to reflect on the biases of my discipline and its subdisciplines, to learn how to become a better teacher at all stages of my career, to see students more as colleagues than apprentices—these are some of the ways I have been challenged to differentiate myself from others in the teaching profession. Because of my liberal arts context, I have been introduced to ways of thinking that have resulted in greater agency for me in my career. I tell students that I used to be as conservative, if not more, in my musical perspectives as they tend to be, and look at me now: a classically trained pianist inflected with queer, feminist, neuroscience, and sport psychology perspectives.

This broadening of my perspectives was uncharted for me in my initial training and it was not something I could have predicted or anticipated. Neither could I have known how such growth would affect both my performing of traditional classical repertoire and my exploration of contemporary art works. In writing this essay, my major intention is to highlight for others curious about or currently teaching at a liberal arts campus the ways that such employment can be uncommonly rewarding and meaningful. There are specific trajectories through which I will approach these aspects that serve to emphasize the nature of my journey. First of all, I delve more deeply into what it's like to be a music professor at a liberal arts campus. Secondly, I examine my experiences on a small-sized campus in a small town that serves a rural area within the Canadian context. Finally, I turn my gaze from behind me to the future. This might surprise some. While the look back at the road is important and will shape the bulk of this chapter, I maintain that reviewing the road I have taken seems incomplete without addressing what I see as the road ahead for music professors and students within the liberal arts. After all, beyond the horizon is a stunning blue sky that invites one to dream, if not proceed.

II. Going Wilde: Music and the Liberal Arts

> People point to Reading Gaol, and say "That is where the artistic life leads a man." Well, it might lead to worse places.[3]

Do people point to liberal arts campuses and say, "That is where second-rate talent leads a man?" Apparently, for some, there are few worse places to be. I was told by one of my graduate school professors that, although a good starting position, a teaching position at my college would be one that I would want to leave as soon as possible. His perspective served as a warning not to like the place too much and fall prey to a love that *dare not speak its name: (gasp!)* the love of the liberal arts. A fate worse than death? Fortunately, I had a graduate supervisor, Robert Stangeland, who thought otherwise. He encouraged me to apply for a position in 1985 at the then church-owned liberal arts institution called Camrose Lutheran College (which would become the publicly owned Augustana Campus of the University of Alberta in 2004).

As someone who feels that he has thrived in his career at a liberal arts institution—yes, I use the word *thrive* to anyone I chat with—I cannot imagine a better place to be at every stage of a professorial career. My view today of the *unspeakable* type of career not only being spoken, but *preferred*, is one that defies much conventional thinking, including that sometimes found at research-intensive universities and offered to its graduates seeking employment. My perspective is one shared by others and it presents a paradox that was articulated by Oscar Wilde on more than one occasion, including in his writings from prison published under the title *De Profundis*—namely, that looks can be and usually are deceiving.

In 1991, one of America's leading piano composers of the past century, Frederic Rzewski, composed a work for solo pianist based on Wilde's incarceration titled *De Profundis*. A piece that I have performed and recorded, it requires me to play and, at the same time, speak selected parts of the letter Oscar Wilde wrote from prison. In addition, I sing, hum, grunt, slap myself for body percussion effects, and imitate musical instruments and animals. The piece is transgressive in many ways; after all, classical pianists are trained *not* to make weird noises in public, let alone assume the identity of someone charged with *sodomy*. In addition, the work challenges normative views of what constitutes success, exposing the hypocrisy of Victorian society on key social issues.

With these transgressive and critical qualities in mind, picture me performing *De Profundis* in a chapel, in politically right-of-center Alberta, in 1995, after the firing of a gay instructor at another Alberta Christian liberal arts college, and before the provincial government was forced to protect gay rights by the Supreme Court of Canada. Now, imagine me speaking at one point the words of Wilde where he opines on the various twists and turns of life that are part of a rich human journey: "People who desire self-realization never know where they are going. They can't know. To recognize that the soul of man is unknowable is the ultimate achievement of wisdom. The final mystery is oneself."[4] Looking back, I am not surprised that my first performance of this work would take place at a teaching-focused liberal arts campus. In quintessential interdisciplinary fashion, music and English literature commingled and jostled with issues of faith, religion, politics, law, and the role of the artist in society. One need only look to the members of the Evangelical Lutheran Women's organization that were in the audience to underscore the degree of diversity and liberal arts mayhem present. I doubt even Garrison Keillor could have dreamt up a more unlikely cast of characters for an episode of his *Prairie Home Companion.*

I am grateful for the way that, right from the very start of my career, quality teaching and interdisciplinary perspectives were emphasized. While I had had excellent teachers in my previous musical training, the training itself was geared toward that prized breed of student known as (to be said in *hushed, reverential tones*) "the bachelor of music student." Accepted by means of audition, this student is assumed to have had substantial previous background in music making and, consequently, is much sought after by university music programs. I am a product of this undergraduate training, and I pursued two more highly specialized graduate degrees in piano performance as well. If there ever was a musical orchid to be prized, it's me. Consequently, coming to teach at an institution *without* a bachelor of music program was a shock; a liberal arts campus presented a greater range of student experience than I was used to or, frankly, cared to know. Along with having to learn how *not* to put a needle down and scratch the entire width of an LP in front of an entire class of forty music appreciation students, I had to learn how to speak about music and its various practices to students with minimal or no background in classical music. At times, it felt like a fate worse than death.

A particular course helped to reorient my rather narrowly focused academic perspectives. The course was one I had inherited from another professor, and its purpose was to introduce key concepts in music theory from a listening perspective. In this class, advanced and non-advanced musicians learned side-by-side on how to hear music and describe its inner workings without resorting to cliché or jargon. Together with my students, I learned how, in the words of so many grant applications I have since filled out, to "describe key questions, issues, and ideas to non-specialists." As I realize now, the course was significant in helping me *think through* the meaningfulness of my discipline to others, including researchers and students from other disciplines. Importantly, it was a liberal arts strategy that I learned through the *ears* of students.

Let's face it: the liberal arts are dangerous to your disciplinary health if you are intent on *not changing.* No sooner do you start recognizing the limits of your academic field—indeed, the blind spots that are inherent to all disciplinary perspectives—than you find you have proceeded down a slippery slope and are questioning all of the beliefs you have inherited. Proceeding into doctoral studies at the time of my first sabbatical, I chose an institution that would allow me to challenge many assumptions, including the premise that a person can't be both a performer and an academic. Having learned from my liberal arts colleagues in disciplines such as English and sociology that university music studies were about thirty years behind the times in cultural analysis, I knew that I wanted to teach the basic music lecture courses differently. I convinced my graduate committee to allow me to take challenging academic courses that introduced me to the world of critical theory, queer theory, feminist theory, and popular music analysis. I must admit that it did feel like I was trashing Mozart on occasion. My motives were questioned on my liberal arts campus; a well-meaning psychology professor expressed concern to me that I had turned my back on the composers he loved.

Ironically—and this is what I am sure to alert my current students to—if anything, my devotion to Mozart and to performing his music is stronger than ever. It is a love that embraces paradox, allows for irony, strips of mythology, and, when I embrace certain myths, I do so with awareness. These are the narrative strategies of the best composers and artists. These are the best strategies of concert pianists as well, for without them we become constrained by current professional notions that defy the long, unruly history of music making at the keyboard. Music benefits from the liberal arts; this academic context broadens discussions to include more types of music and moves beyond professional training concerns that can so dominate music departments. Yet at the same time, given their propensity to question and approach issues from fresh perspectives, the liberal arts can help to appreciate classical music and instrumental training in ways that those within the tradition often fail to do.

Why don't classical pianists improvise anymore? If we teach in a single course the history of medieval and Renaissance music, which had both popular and high-art traditions, why don't we teach the music of other periods in similar fashion? Who says that musical meaning for undergraduates needs to be anchored in the analysis of chords and forms, often to the exclusion of other types of knowing? These are but some of the questions that continue to haunt me from a disciplinary angle. At times, I feel like I am echoing the words of musicologist Susan McClary who, from a feminist perspective, states that she is "no longer sure what MUSIC is."[5] For me, the doubt she expresses is at the heart of both academic and artistic inquiry. Within spiritual traditions, a questioning process is the portal through which one passes before greater insights are received. Call it by whatever name you choose, but *skepticism* is prized by the liberal arts. Rather than shutting down questions of meaning, the teaching and learning traditions in which liberal arts and sciences campuses are grounded have the potential to open up new discussions around musical practices—past, present, and future.

III. Livin' in the Sticks

> When my country choir improvised a music drama on the book of Jonah, I learned that original things can be produced in small places as well as capitals. When forty performers presented this work to a packed church in Maynooth, with an area population of about two hundred, I realized that the per capita involvement with its cultural endeavor was exceeding the national average—or, let us say, to be safe, that it was exceeding that of Stratford, which frequently this year was playing to 29 percent houses.[6]

What it means to be a music professor at a liberal arts institution is one thing. To work at a campus that is smaller sized, in a town on the rural prairie in right-of-center Alberta, and be gay is quite another. The vastness of Canadian geography and the sparseness of our population outside urban centers, similar to certain areas of the United States, raise some pressing questions for music professors. Is it possible to have a vibrant performing career and be located outside major cities in North America or is this the type of career suicide that my former professor alluded to when warning me about staying too long at a liberal arts campus? As a classical pianist, I have found it challenging at times not to live in a major city for very practical reasons. Given my rural location, I find it more difficult to work with other musicians and to attend cultural events in larger centers, particularly operas and symphony concerts. Beyond distance issues, the climate of the Canadian prairie can leave roads treacherous at times seven months of the year.

I am luckier than some in that I live only an hour away from a major city and an international airport. Nonetheless, I've had to adapt, given travelling distances, typical winter driving conditions, and the sheer lack of public transportation in my rural area that, if it were available, might help me connect to those opportunities of which a classical musician might want to take more advantage. Without even a Greyhound bus or passenger train to help me in this regard, I've focused more on recital projects that are easier to coordinate, such as solo piano recitals. When scheduling chamber music recitals, I plan them for times of the year when our northern climate is more amenable to travel.

For a classical musician to live in a rural area may seem counterintuitive. So much of what it means to be a classical musician involves taking the styles of past and current cultural centers—Vienna, Paris, London, Rome—to the margins and smaller places. Today, for North Americans, those artistic hubs include more recent cities such as New York, Toronto, and Mexico City. This view of culture, however, is problematic not only for me, but for many other Canadian artists. Too often, cultural critics and commentators assume that *nothing of consequence* happens in small towns or sparsely populated areas. They also presume that finite resources are the death knell of creativity. While I know that creativity does flow from quality resources—I think of all the benefits resulting from the purchase of a new nine-foot Steinway Model D for my campus, for instance—I know as well that many artists in the past were as resilient, if not more so, than I have had to be in my career. I trace my ability to deal with meager resources to my training as a classical musician. In particular, as a church musician and organist, I learned à la J. S. Bach to use what resources were available. "No tenors today in the choir? Well, let's sing it in three parts then—soprano, alto, bass!" Voilà! This type of creativity is one that is replicated by artists, who use what they have at hand. One need only look to the likes of internationally recognized Canadians like painter Mary Pratt and writer Alice Munro to see examples of those who reflect in their art appreciation of the simple, both in terms of resources used and subjects chosen.

The quotation that began this section, by noted Canadian composer R. Murray Schaefer, addresses a mind-set that many artists have toward rurality that typically catches them up short when they experience artistic life in a small community. Schaefer challenges what he sees as a chauvinism that misreads what actually takes place in smaller places. A vestige of colonialism, this attitude labels any place without a certain size of population as being culturally inferior or, in common parlance, *Hicksville*. Despite so-called globalism, this notion continues to surface on different occasions and in various guises. Fortunately, it is a perspective that is challenged by Indie pop artists who refuse to be controlled by major corporate labels, choosing to live wherever they want and overseeing most aspects of their cultural products. In this regard, these musicians legitimate what classical musicians like me have been doing most of their careers—namely, taking culture from the so-called margins to the center. With major budget cuts to the Canadian Broadcasting Corporation (CBC) over the past two decades, I will no longer be recorded in live broadcasts in rural Alberta, sadly. In this one regard, at least in terms of location, according to the CBC, I am just *too far out.*

Ironically, our current global economy with its attendant technologies is one that seems to be benefitting artistic voices regardless of location. Today, musicians have the ability to record and distribute music easily and affordably through the Internet, iTunes, YouTube, and the like. As a music professor in rural Canada, I take advantage of these technologies, appearing in various digital guises to access audiences nationally and internationally. I feel like I am channeling the late Canadian pianist Glenn Gould in my willingness to experiment with media. At times, I spend more time on developing media presence than practicing or performing. However, my investigations into the use of video cameras by pianists for learning purposes have shown me how distances can be erased and communities connected. Because of current technologies, my life as a concert pianist is no different in some respects than if I were living in a major urban center.

Big cities aren't all what they are cracked up to be. When I had Frederic Rzewski as a guest artist on our campus in 2008, over one hundred people attended a recital of him performing some of his own compositions. As Rzewski pointed out to me, this was exciting for him; in New York City, he would have had thirty friends attending, mostly out of obligation. In Camrose, a town of only seventeen thousand, and at Augustana, a campus with barely one thousand students, he had over one hundred persons present. He was amazed. More than that, he was touched by the personal interest people took in him. In a talk he gave about his works, local citizens with limited or no musical training asked questions. Because I had performed recitals of his works previously, many individuals knew at least something about him and his works. A small campus in a small town allows personal relationships to develop between community members and artists. My favorite cashier from Safeway, Brenda, tells me to remind her when I am performing next. Like liberal arts students who arrive on campus without jaded backgrounds and are curious, local citizens can be more open and more curious than you first expect.

Perhaps what I am alluding to here is that there is a greater sense of community on my campus than what others from research-intensive institutions tell me they experience. Feeling part of a community on a smaller campus comes about through lived experience where individuals both within and outside of the campus come together to be resourceful in a common effort. In a music program at a smaller institution, this type of bond often develops through the sheer number of roles that each music professor assumes. In a department of four full-time professors and a dozen part-time sessional instructors, my colleagues and I often feel that we wear so many hats that it's hard to focus on what really needs to be done at a given moment. We are constantly juggling teaching, research, and service expectations. However, a confession: I gave up on multitasking over a decade ago. After a stint as chair of the Department of Fine Arts in a particularly difficult financial time on our campus, I found myself unable to focus. Period. If I were going to continue to perform, in addition to my teaching duties, I realized that I had to make radical changes to my *state of mind*. Fortunately, through discovering the benefits of contemplation, yoga, and running, I developed the type of attentiveness to everyday tasks that has helped me at the same time to focus on larger, more long-term goals.

An ongoing duty to which I have had to become accustomed in the pursuit of building a vital keyboard program at a rural institution is that of being a part-time fund-raiser. Unlike most university professors, including those on my own liberal arts campus, I work closely with our administration and Development Office in acquiring resources in order to fund new pianos, guest artist series, master-class clinicians, and other offerings that benefit students. Sometimes this work has meant cajoling my administration for support and at other times, it has meant asking community members for theirs. What I have learned is that people who live in smaller communities are more prone to give, to build connections with me, to feel pride in what we offer, and to take ownership in our music program's offerings. To have learned this in Canada of all places, where there is less a culture of philanthropy than in the United States, is significant.

The distinctive connection that is built among the members of a small town, the rural surroundings, and a small campus prompts things to happen that rarely are matched in larger centers. Each year my piano students present a group recital, with funds raised through admission charges or donations benefitting a local charity of their choice. Because many community people get to know my piano students well through being taught by them or having them for pianists in their churches and choirs, class recital events always amaze me for the quality and sheer number of personal connections that are revealed. My students perform for more people at these types of events than at most urban campuses. As Frederic Rzewski and R. Murray Schaefer state, audiences in small communities often surpass in size and enthusiasm what would happen in larger centers. In the end, a rural liberal arts campus can actually outperform larger institutions in providing the size and enthusiasm of audiences from which students benefit most. I suspect that my piano students have a greater resilience than most young artists because of their rural education where, in a unique confluence between community and art, they discover people who care about them and, consequently, their art.

IV. True Confessions

> "Get the books, and read and study them," Abraham Lincoln told a law student seeking advice in 1855. It did not matter, he continued, whether the reading be done in a small town or a large city, by oneself or in the company of others. "The *books*, and your *capacity* for understanding them, are just the same in all places. . . . Always bear in mind that your own resolution to succeed, is more important than any other one thing."[7]

Mea culpa. Underneath my polite, smug Canadian exterior—please join me in reciting "the Canadian national health care system is so superior to the American one"—is someone who has fallen in love with the life and mind of the sixteenth president of the United States of America, Abraham Lincoln. In reading Doris Kearns Goodwin's *Team of Rivals*, I couldn't help but marvel at this self-made, tenacious, brilliant man and his ability to teach himself the world's greatest literature in places far humbler and isolated than those in which I have lived. Although I have made the argument that "location, location, location!" is important in terms of a campus experience and that it makes a qualitative difference in the type of teaching and learning that goes on there, I don't believe that it's the *sole* determinant in getting a quality education. If place were everything, urban universities would win every time; in the "location, location, location!" contest, they are the ones seen as being best situated by media sources, corporate interests, and cultural commentators. Lincoln's statement that a good education can take place anywhere as long as the "resolution to succeed" is there counters the prevailing logic that cedes all knowledge, all experience, and all creativity to those in larger centers.

For me, the resilience that is exemplified in the lives of larger-than-life figures such as Abraham Lincoln is cultivated in the lives of faculty and students on liberal arts campuses. It is a resilience that I have even caught myself exhibiting at times. Yes, it's time for me to address the big elephant in the room: what it has been like for me to be gay on a small campus in rural Alberta. Although I have touched upon it already, I have not made it the centerpiece of this essay, as I wanted to talk about other aspects of music and liberal arts education that are important too. At this juncture, however, I want to be clear that it's because of the liberal arts—its destabilizing tactics, its ability to challenge norms, its ability to build meaningful community—that I have been able to live in a small town as a gay man. As you have read, I live only one hour from a larger urban center in Canada. However, Paul and I were only able to live as openly gay men in a small community and raise two sons here because it is a liberal arts town, filled with university employees and others who are educated, proactive in human rights, and compassionate.

How tolerant is our small, right-of-center community? Paul and I are still not quite sure how to answer that question. However, because of the support we have cited above and our activities in churches and other local organizations where people have come to know us, we feel accepted in the places that count the most for us. At the beginning of our relationship in 1991, given the hostile climate in Alberta to homosexuals and the reality that we could have been fired at our then-private Christian liberal arts college, Paul and I did consult a human rights lawyer in Edmonton to find out what *not* to do in order to keep our jobs in small-town Alberta. According to the law, we found out that we could do anything but publicly announce our sexual orientation in print. However, knowing *that* does not constitute a happy existence.

Are we happy? I think we are. We have found community here, with people of all orientations and ethnicities and religious backgrounds. We are part of a queer demographic that researchers are finally acknowledging as having *by choice* decided to stay in rural areas because of enduring relationships with people and the land.[8] Given recent human rights laws, the legality of same-sex marriage across Canada, and the unambiguous support of our public institution, we know we will not be fired because of our orientation. With pride, we have seen our sons grow up to be strong, positive role models to others. Our gay friends in New York, Vancouver, and Toronto tell us that, at the least, we are as happy as they are and, at the most, we may be happier. To them, with the cost of living so much cheaper here, being gay on the Canadian prairie seems like a more affordable, and possibly more desirable, *lifestyle choice.*

Appearances, as Wilde asserted within his Victorian context, can be and usually are deceiving. Contrary to popular perceptions, life in a town in a rural area can be anything but a miserable homophobic and xenophobic affair. Sexual and ethnic minorities can find meaningful communities at all stages of their lives. Regardless of prejudices that favor large, urban universities and discipline-specific training, liberal arts and science campuses can be seen to offer refreshing approaches to teaching, research, and service that beneficially challenge disciplinary boundaries and assumptions. Despite some concerns about the viability of smaller-sized, publicly funded campuses given budget cutbacks and diminishing support for the arts, they are well suited to the future. Am I concerned about the future? I am, but there are other aspects that I *can't wait for*.

Most liberal arts music programs are ready for the future because, compared to those at most other universities, they already are in the future. Music professors like me are doing today what others like our current students will be doing in the years ahead. With regard to larger music departments, I believe that it's time for their walls to come crashing down, if not literally, then figuratively. Most of them tend to be characterized by contentious relationships between "academics" and "performers," a series of interactions marked by a false dichotomy perpetuated by narrow research demands and equally constricted graduate student specializations.

The history of music prior to the twentieth century provides us with another paradigm, however; people like Robert Schumann did not just compose music, but wrote, discussed, and played. Even J. S. Bach taught Latin and catechism. The past is, in many respects, the future. Liberal arts campuses encourage professors to teach both lecture- and performance-based courses. I point to the past to ensure that my current students understand that the type of job they will do in the future, even at a research-intensive institution, is one that they see me doing in the present—namely, being a performer, lecturer, recorder of CDs, writer of papers, administrator. The days of narrow specialization, where a piano professor just does piano-related courses, is one that will likely not exist in the future.

What else do I see on the road ahead? I envision former piano students with jobs because they have studied Asian languages. This background will give them an edge in securing positions, since the growing middle class in Asia has taken a deep interest in the music of the Western art tradition. With declining enrollments, more and more North American music institutions are recognizing the recruitment possibilities that exist in Asia. I suspect that some former students will have diverse jobs like I have had, teaching a wide variety of subjects. I know, given current trends, that some of these liberal arts–trained musicians will be situated within departments other than music ones or be part of multidisciplinary teams without particular disciplinary affiliations. The types of appointments and cross-appointments we have within liberal arts institutions will become more of the norm, not less.

In the future, I expect that most teaching positions will assume versatility in being able to move between the analyses of Western European classical music, popular music, and world music. Most liberal arts–based music curricula are already requiring such dexterity. With professorial positions at larger institutions not being replaced and with growing multicultural populations in both Canada and the United States, pianists and others from the classical tradition will no longer be able to plead ignorance about the totality of music in the world. For some, it will be a fate worse than death. They will view the recent past as the glory days of disciplinary clarity where men were men, women were women, and performers and academics confined themselves to their respective roles.

Others will point to this future and say enthusiastically, "That is where the artistic life leads a man." Those persons whose lives and careers have been shaped by the liberal arts will sense something familiar about it all. They will recognize that they have, in many respects, already encountered the future. What's on the horizon? A stunning blue sky that invites one to dream, if not proceed. From where I stand, the road ahead looks as *straight* as the one I have just been on—in other words, be prepared for some interesting twists and turns along the way.

Works Cited

Brett, Philip. "Musicality, Essentialism, and the Closet." In *Queering the Pitch: The New Gay and Lesbian Musicology*, edited by Philip Brett, Elizabeth Wood, and Gary C. Thomas, 9–26. New York: Routledge, 1994.

Goodwin, Doris Kearns. *Team of Rivals: The Political Genius of Abraham Lincoln*. New York: Simon and Schuster, 2005.

McClary, Susan. *Feminine Endings: Music, Gender, and Sexuality*. 2nd ed. Minneapolis: University of Minnesota Press, 2002.

Rzewski, Frederic. *De Profundis*. Complete score available at http://imslp.org/wiki/De_Profundis_(Rzewski,_Frederic).

Schaefer, R. Murray. "Canadian Culture: Colonial Culture." In *Canadian Music: Issues of Hegemony and Identity*, edited by Beverley Diamond and Robert Witmer, 221–37. Toronto: Canadian Scholars' Press and Women's Press, 1998.

Trentham, Barry. "Old Coyotes: Life Histories of Aging Gay Men in Rural Canada." PhD diss., University of Toronto, 2010. https://tspace.library.utoronto.ca/bitstream/1807/26436/1/Trentham_Barry_201009_PhD_thesis.pdf.

Weber, William. "The Contemporaneity of Eighteenth-Century Musical Taste." *Musical Quarterly* 70, no. 2 (Spring 1984): 175–94.

Notes

1. Weber, "Contemporaneity of Eighteenth-Century Musical Taste."

2. See, e.g., Brett, "Musicality, Essentialism, and the Closet," 11–12. Brett traces how music has been viewed with moral suspicion in the West from the time of Plato and Aristotle to the present day.

3. Oscar Wilde, quoted in Frederic Rzewski, *De Profundis* (1991), 3.

4. Ibid., 5–6.

5. McClary, *Feminine Endings,* 19.

6. Schaefer, "Canadian Culture: Colonial Culture," 234.

7. Goodwin, *Team of Rivals*, 54.

8. See, e.g., Trentham, "Old Coyotes: Life Histories of Aging Gay Men in Rural Canada." Trentham examines the lives of three gay men aging in rural spaces. He reveals the distinctive forces that have shaped these people and that have provided them with meaningful lives within a Canadian context.

10

What Have I Done?!
A Renaissance Art Historian
Finds Her Way in the Rural Midwest

Julia A. DeLancey

Art History, Truman State University

In her influential book *Not for Profit: Why Democracy Needs the Humanities*, Martha C. Nussbaum makes the observation that the human "tendency to segment the world into known and unknown probably lies very deep in our evolutionary heritage."[1] Nussbaum connects that notion to our ability to develop compassion for others, and ties that in turn and in part to the potential of the humanities to nurture better democracies. This idea about worlds known and unknown has stayed with me as I've considered this essay, as have the cultural, geographic, and economic worlds I have encountered in my life as a professor. In many ways, I am perhaps an atypical choice for this volume: my scholarship has involved exploring an in some ways unknowable time and place, five hundred years ago and almost five thousand miles away. I have been fortunate enough to live, or spend significant time in, three different countries. And for all of my life, save for research trips, I have been a resident in towns or cities defined by the universities that they host. Of all of them, the place most originally unknown to me when I arrived, the place that required the most adaptation, has been Kirksville, in the center of northeast Missouri, the town of seventeen thousand souls where I live, work, and

Acknowledgments: I am deeply grateful to Truman State University and especially to COPLAC for the opportunity to contribute to this volume. I also appreciate very much feedback from the editors and participants in the 2013 COPLAC Summer Institute, especially Roger Epp, Kathleen Fine-Dare, and Therese Seibert, as well as Heather Cianciola, Pete Kelly, Troy Paino, and Cole Woodcox at Truman State University. Of course, all errors of fact or interpretation are and remain my own.

care. That it was unknown is very much shaped by the first two places I knew for any extended period of time.

I was fortunate to be born and raised in Ann Arbor, Michigan. Despite trips to the rural Midwest to visit family, I always believed—naïvely, of course—that Ann Arbor was simply the way most places were. I thought cappuccinos were easily available in the early '90s, that all video stores had foreign film sections, that all schools had absence policies for holidays from a wide variety of religions including Islam, Judaism, Christianity, and Buddhism, and that most school classes had kids from around the world in them. I continue to love Ann Arbor. I also continue to cherish the ways in which growing up there affected my view of the world and the ways in which community allows for an integrated life.

That environment continued to shape me as I moved into college life as a history of art major at the University of Michigan. With a student population of around forty thousand, the campus became a whole new world to me, which led, when I was a junior, to a study abroad trip to Florence, Italy. Although this can be said by countless others, it is nonetheless true for me that the trip changed my life. It cemented my love of Italy and all things Italian, of travel, of the Renaissance, and of seeing its artworks as and where they were meant to be seen. The trip presented to me another way of living, of thinking about one's place in the world, of processing the world through language. It also presented one of the many ways in which the local can serve as an entry point to big questions about leading an integrated life.

That love for travel, for the history of art, and for Italy led me—ironically—to the east coast of Scotland and the University of St. Andrews for graduate study. That experience involved moving to a completely unknown world: I had never been to any country outside the United States other than Italy and Canada, and I had accepted the place at St. Andrews sight unseen, other than the few photographs in the admissions brochures. St. Andrews is a community roughly the same size as Kirksville, only much older. It was founded in the twelfth century and hosts a university that recently celebrated its six hundredth anniversary, started over 350 years before the signing of the Declaration of Independence.[2] In addition, it is one hour from Edinburgh, one of the great European capitals. In a short plane ride I could reach continental Europe, and more specifically Italy and Florence, which drove both my scholarly interests but also my love of beauty, and the way of living and connecting with others that I found there. It was from that known world and local environment that my path took me to Kirksville, founded only in 1848, and to Truman State University, and a risky step outside of what I had known up to that point.

I recently had the opportunity to reconnect with my PhD supervisor. We had been out of touch for an extended period of time. When I applied for my position at Truman, he had cautioned me specifically about positions at small American colleges in rural areas where one mainly focused on undergraduate teaching (indeed, this was one of the main pieces of job-search advice he gave me that circumstances forced me to ignore). In striving to update him in a few minutes' time about years of my life, I realized that essentially what I had to say to this busy man of considerable intellect, skill, and accomplishment was something like this: while all the things that you cautioned me against have turned out to be true—in one way or another—I have made a life for myself that I find fulfilling and meaningful, in which the personal and the professional have come together in community, through scholarship and through teaching but also through food and friendship. What's more, this has happened in this new-to-me small town where I have encountered a set of questions about how to live an integrated life. Those questions continue to fuel me.

I have a vivid memory of making one very distinct decision when applying for the position I still hold. I saw the job listing for a Renaissance specialist at a university then known as Northeast Missouri State University.[3] Two thoughts flitted in quick succession through my mind. First, "I don't want to live in northeast Missouri! I don't even know where that is!" And then second, "Listen, missy, you'd better let *them* make that decision—you're hardly in a position to say no to a job you don't even have yet but sorely need!" I did apply and became a finalist for the position. However, I had applied from and was then living in Scotland. One of the administration's conditions at the time in continuing with my candidacy was that I would not be offered an on-campus interview. As a result, I would need to be willing to take the job in an unknown world, sight unseen. When the offer came, I accepted it.

My arrival in Kirksville meant that I had a rather protracted introduction to this new local environment. I left St. Andrews on a Thursday in early August, arrived home in Michigan that night, on Friday packed my few worldly possessions into my sister's car, and left Ann Arbor Saturday morning. We stayed Saturday night in Illinois, and drove the last two hours to Kirksville on Sunday morning. New faculty orientation began Monday. I had lived at that point in Scotland for five years and was moving to a world I had never before seen. I will never forget the drive from Illinois to Kirksville. As we drove by endless fields of corn and lawns decorated with planters made from truck tires or old toilets, I kept thinking, "What have I done?" My sister gamely commented on charming marigolds and lovely cows in pastures. And I kept thinking, "What have I done?" This was not the entry point I would have chosen at the time, but it will likely be a common one for other authors in this volume as well.

I was certainly warmly welcomed into this unknown world and new community. But the honest truth of the matter was that I felt as if I had been picked up and dropped on Mars. Indeed, I've often said that the transition from my hometown to living in another country was far less dramatic for me than moving home to the States, but to rural Missouri.

But I stayed, and made the transition and the integration. Since 1995, I have lived in Kirksville. Our town serves as the county seat for Adair County and is home to a university, a community college, and an institution founded in the late nineteenth century to train osteopathic physicians. Kirksville is a remarkable place and world unto itself, although one that is in some ways very small and accessible. My commute to campus is seven minutes if I walk. By car it's two; I only go through one traffic light, and—daily and reliably— am able to park across from the building where I work.

The size and rural location here foster a remarkable community that facilitates connection and integration. Because it's possible to get from one end of town to the other in about ten minutes, we are that distance— and mostly less—from most of our friends. This means regularly making calls that go something like this: "Hi. We know it's 5:30 and you probably already have plans, but we made too much [fill in a delicious meal], so can you come over and share it with us?" In the summer, we run into each other on walks, at evening concerts on the town square, and trading plants for gardening. Indeed, this is the thing that friends who have left here for other jobs comment on the most—that crafting close, lasting friendships wherever they are now is much more difficult because of distance, but also because of the weariness that comes with commuting. This plays out even more so in times of trial when the community here often enfolds those in difficulty. People organize meals, hospital visits, and child care, and accompany friends to medical appointments and surgeries, creating a network of support that becomes self-sustaining and mutually reinforcing.

For me at least, the provision, preparation, and consumption of food has played a key role in defining this world and crafting a community in this new locale. There are some good places to eat out, and the excitement was palpable a few years ago when two—two!—new eateries opened up, one featuring Greek food and the other Japanese. But the truth of the matter is that on any given night, the best meal in town is at the home of a friend. The limited options for eating out mean that we and our friends are challenged to cook more frequently, to cook better, and to cook more interestingly. I have friends who routinely tackle dishes such as brain, beef ribs, or spicy Thai curry—and who prepare food from Delhi, London, Cairo, and beyond. In addition, because we are in a rural community, we have remarkable opportunities to engage with community-supported agriculture. We buy almost all our meat from local farmers, some of whom have become friends, and the summer produce is remarkable, plentiful, and beautiful, sold by many area growers. For those residents who fish and hunt, the bounty extends almost infinitely.

Northeast Missouri can also be a place of considerable beauty. For me, as an art historian, this aspect has been important. I crave visual interest (not necessarily beauty, but interest) and so look, keenly, for things that engage me visually. Certainly, we are surrounded here by natural beauty: vibrant bright green fields of winter wheat or clover or, later in the season, corn; towering limestone cliffs; meandering streams cutting steep-banked paths through fields filled with cows or sheep or horses; calm lakes lined by nothing more than oak trees standing shoulder-to-shoulder with beautiful redbuds and dogwoods. And our campus is lovely. Based largely on the redbrick and white-trimmed Georgian campus architectural style created and popularized in the late eighteenth century by Thomas Jefferson at the University of Virginia, it also features a beautiful quadrangle designed by Hare and Hare, the landscape architects for the Nelson-Atkins Museum of Art. This sense of design extends beyond campus too—there are some lovely homes, particularly the many bungalows that punctuate so many neighborhoods in town, but also stately brick residences, reliable two-story farmhouses, charming Cape Cods, and the like. And there are beautiful gardens. As I write, our own is filled with tulips, daffodils, and masses of colorful annuals, a little world of color unto itself. These things have drawn and sustained me here.

Thus far, I have been writing about geographic worlds, and have—largely—given a sanitized view of Kirksville, one granted to me as a faculty member who makes a good salary and feels as if she has created a solid

place in this world for herself. And in numerous aspects it has been familiar—a college campus, much smaller than the one I grew up on, but with
familiar language, spatial layout, and norms. However, perhaps the newest
world I've encountered since living here—the most unknown but also the
one that has affected me and changed my outlook the most—has been the
diverse economic world that surrounds me here.

Two blocks away from our home stands a house I have kept an eye on for
almost the entire time I've lived in Kirksville. I remember thinking when
I first moved here that it was quite lovely and might be a nice place to live
someday when I could afford a house. Painted a dark slate grayish blue, it
has good proportions, a wonderful wide front porch, and two spreading red-
bud trees in the front yard. It looked comfortable, attractive, like it could be
home. And yet as I have watched that house over the years, it has become
increasingly run-down to the point now at which—were I to encounter it
anew—I would not even notice it. I know nothing about the family or families that have lived under its roof during this time. I've sometimes greeted
someone there while walking by, and small signs suggest that it might be
the same family, but finding anything more out at this stage seems a bit too
intrusive. However, same family or no, that house stays in my mind and tugs
at me. Had I walked by the house in the condition it is in now, but with the
mind-set I had when I first moved here, I would doubtless have wondered
why people didn't either paint it or tear it down, why they didn't pick the toys
up from the front yard, didn't rake the leaves, or mow the lawn.

This has all been brought more clearly to me here than other places
I've lived because of the layout often typical in small towns, particularly
in the older, central areas. Yes, there are homogeneous neighborhoods
here, neighborhoods where everyone is from the same socioeconomic
background, and where the houses all look the same or similar, and where
everyone makes roughly the same amount as their neighbors. However,
in Kirksville if you want an older home within walking distance of campus (and we wanted both) you wind up in very blended neighborhoods.
In many ways, this choice to live not in the areas zoned on the periphery
for single families but rather in the mixed-use central part of town has
increased my experiences with heterogeneity and has placed me in areas
where habits, experiences, and budgets are not the same as those with
which I am familiar.

The local has brought this all to me. Prior to moving to Kirksville I wasn't aware of poverty or need in the ways I am now. Certainly in both Ann Arbor and in St. Andrews, I knew there were areas of greater economic need, but they were areas that were always "over there"; I either passed through them (walking through the St. Andrews council estate on my way to the grocery store that had better produce) or could choose not to engage with them. They were always worlds separate from my lived reality. Even and in some ways especially on the Truman campus, I can be sheltered from them in Kirksville.

If I'm truthful, my initial knee-jerk reaction—both arrogant and ignorant—when I first moved to Kirksville generally involved disturbing statements that started with words such as "Those people" or "Why do they...?" I remember complaining to a friend about indoor upholstered furniture on front porches. He stopped me in my tracks by simply asking, "So now you want to legislate taste? Why shouldn't someone put a couch there?" Occasions for such observations happen almost daily: in grocery store aisles ("Why is she speaking sharply to her child?"), while driving ("Why is that muffler so loud?"), and in numerous other settings. I have been humbled by the number of times, increasing the longer I live here, that my answer to my own question about why people did things related to education, experience, and money.

Here we confront the economic reality of the small town in which I live. Adair County has a per capita income of $17,997 and over a quarter of the population lives below the poverty line; the statistics are similar for Kirksville, the county seat.[4] In addition, 51 percent of elementary and secondary students are eligible for free or reduced school lunches, and 4,320 people or 17.1 percent of the population are classed as food insecure, meaning they do not know where their next meal will come from. The rate for children is higher.[5] Because of Kirksville's size, it is possible to come up against the realities of this situation much more often than in a bigger, more diverse community, or in a smaller community in which things are much more homogeneous.

I need to say before moving on that I continue to struggle with the relative isolation here, with the lack of visual interest, and with the way that economics plays out in daily life (indeed, while I was editing this sentence, someone drove by with a loud muffler and my teeth immediately went on edge). Thinking about and creating visual interest (and yes, beauty) and order can be, for many, a luxury. I still chafe against the monotony of houses all clad in the same vinyl siding, with any interesting or unique detail stripped away to make the siding process easier; against trees cut down simply because it's too complicated to mow around them; and against a kind of indifference to visual interest, much less beauty, that comes partly from a common expectation that those things do not matter as much as expediency and efficiency.

At the same time, I also have a fuller picture of the ways in which all of these issues about creating visual interest, about what is possible to do with a home, about how we live our lives, are powerfully affected by poverty and by need of all kinds. I struggle with the idea that it is presumptuous if not arrogant of a professor, a financial outsider, particularly one who is not an economist, an ethicist, or a social worker, to write anything about these kinds of issues. They have come to me through this intense local world in which I live, walk through, and think about each day. And while I continue to skirmish with them, it is also just these kinds of issues that have made me look at higher education in a different way, particularly at the state's only highly selective, public liberal arts institution, and to wonder how such an institution came to be here, what it might mean to teach at all—much less to teach the history of art—at such a place, and how a public liberal arts institution might bridge to the other communities into which it is integrated.

The history of our university has been well told by numerous other authors.[6] In brief, in 1867 the "pioneer educator" Joseph Baldwin chose to found what was to become Truman State University in Kirksville mainly on the advice of the mayor of St. Louis and of Baldwin's nephew, who was a local resident and knew of an available, suitable building. Baldwin was one of the passionate leaders in a movement to establish "normal" schools, named for their aim of setting norms for teaching, to train teachers. Although originally founded as private, his normal school became a public institution only three years after its founding. Since then, Baldwin's First District Normal School has undergone several changes in name and purpose. The most recent are the 1985 designation as Missouri's highly selective liberal arts and sciences institution, and the related name change in 1996 to Truman State University.

Our student body is an interesting blend, and—as is the case with many universities—what one faculty member experiences in one department is very different from others. Truman tends to emphasize the accomplishments of our students, and for very good reason. For the class of 2011, the average ACT score was twenty-five to thirty—in the range of some top private schools—and 93 percent of the members of the freshman class had a 3.25 GPA or higher. Our graduates have a 97 percent acceptance rate into law school and 70 percent into medical school. We rank in the top twenty-five master's-level institutions for the percentage of students studying abroad, among the top twenty-five colleges and universities for producing Peace Corps volunteers, and are, nationally, one of the top three master's-level institutions whose students receive Fulbright grants. Some 60 percent of students come from counties in the Kansas City, St. Louis, or Springfield (Missouri) areas and so are urban, often from very well-respected high schools.

While all of those measures are true, there are others that we also need to take into account, because they suggest a more diverse set of students and adjustment challenges. For example, about 15 percent of our students are either from under-represented minorities or from outside North America, about 40 percent qualify for some sort of need-based financial aid, and about 40 percent come from rural areas. In addition, about 20 percent of our students are in the first generation in their family to attend college; if we add to that students who have only one parent who graduated from college, the percentage rises to something like 50 percent.[7]

Such statistics have prompted larger questions for me about the interaction between economics, education, understanding, and opportunity. On the one hand I do not believe, and do not want to believe, that any correlation exists between ability, accomplishment, and any of the statistics I outlined in the previous paragraphs. But some of those statistics mean that a student might not have the same level of support in navigating college life as a student whose parents are well versed in the way universities work. They will more likely be on their own in choosing courses. Some of them will need to work to pay for essentials. And then there's the cultural challenge of communicating with a professor who has two or three degrees, and perhaps herself or himself had two parents who themselves went to college—or even, as in my case, has never lived outside of a college town, so that that is the only world *she* has known. All of this has nothing to do with ability or motivation and everything to do with culture, access, and, to me, the public mission of the institution where I work.

When I think about it, I realize that my entire experience in higher education—both as a student and a teacher—has been in public institutions both in the United States and Scotland (where tuition is effectively free for domestic undergraduate and graduate students, regardless of need). Out of this experience, I have come to believe strongly that we have a responsibility to educate our children, to do it and see it done, especially for those for whom economics or experience or educational opportunity means it may not happen otherwise. These beliefs are at the heart of my intentionality in approaching integrating my life as a scholar, as a teacher at Truman, and as a citizen in Kirksville and beyond.

I wish that I could say I live this out consistently. I wish that I could say that each day I think about myself as a public servant, that I am mindful of the needs of my students and their economic situation—as well as that of the state of Missouri—when I stand in front of a class. Some days that happens. On other days, I simply wish that students had come to Truman with better (or any) experiences with art, that they were more visually literate, that they read more, thought more, wrote more. At times I'm simply overworked and tired, and revert to the attitudes that come from more familiar, comfortable worlds. On the good days, though, I hope that I act on the belief that engaging with the humanities—as a scholar, teacher, and citizen—matters to me and to students. In other words, I hope that we are better individuals and that all the places we live (campus, town, state, country, world) are better as a result of connecting with the work of creative minds considering powerful ideas. The trick has been how to do that. How does a specialist in Italian Renaissance painting, and in something as admittedly esoteric as color sellers, bridge such disparate worlds as sixteenth-century Venice and contemporary rural, northeast Missouri?

My scholarly work does, in some ways, connect with the ideas of local worlds and community. For the past eleven years my research, done mainly in the State Archives in Venice, has focused on a group of specialist men and women who imported, manufactured, exported, and sold a wide variety of coloring materials, in particular the pigments used to great effect by Venetian painters such as Titian and Veronese. Most recently, it has involved studies of color-seller shop locations within the fabric of the city and of one family that likely stood among the initiators and leading members of this relatively new trade specialty. Overall, my work has involved placing this particular group, central to Venetian art history, into the community, culture, and geography of the city.

But here I feel conflicted. As an art historian who specializes in archival work on the history of Italian Renaissance painting, it is difficult to do much of my scholarship in Kirksville. While archives are steadily digitizing more and more of their collections, the topics I work on are hardly at the forefront of historical inquiry and so are unlikely to be scanned for some time to come (and, in any case, there are lots of attendant problems with working with electronic versions of five-hundred-year-old paper documents). In addition, involving students in any meaningful way in this process means not only that they need to be able to read Italian (at a minimum), but also ideally that they are able to travel so that they can handle the documents and go through the challenging, exciting, and sometimes frustrating process of finding what one needs.

Another factor—true across many if not most small campuses—is that I am the only person on campus who works on my area. Here, I do not mean Italian Renaissance art history; rather, I am the only Italian Renaissance specialist on campus, period. We have someone in history who works on the same period in England, and Italian language specialists who work on contemporary Italy. But if I really want to "talk shop," to use the language, concepts, and approaches of my field, talk about my documents, "my people," "my objects"—in other words, to engage with that community—there is no one on my campus with whom I can truly connect.

Of course, it would be possible to change research subjects (and indeed, a good friend and colleague said that to me just the other day: "Well, when I moved here, I changed my research agenda. Why don't you do that?"). However, when I moved to Truman, I was just starting on a very new, exciting, and fruitful path of research, one I felt passionately about, not only for myself, but also for my field. The travel involved with it continues to sustain me on a variety of levels, some professional, and some personal. And I am, after all, trained as a Renaissance specialist. So my response has been a three-pronged approach: first, secure funding to support my scholarship so that I can continue it; second, foster contacts in my region; and third, engage with what it means to teach the humanities in this particular local environment.

On the first prong, I am happy to acknowledge the support of Truman State University and several external organizations. Three faculty research grants in my first three years at Truman allowed me to begin both a new project and archival work. Those grants enabled me to make the project competitive for external funding. We are fortunate in Renaissance studies to have a variety of grants, not only general, national ones such as those from the National Endowment for the Humanities, but also from more specific agencies such as the Gladys Krieble Delmas Foundation, which has grants for Venetian studies. These sources funded travel that was essential, not just for seeing the documents on which I work, but equally, given the relative isolation discussed above, for the building of a scholarly community in which

I was a member. Time in the archives tends to be intensive; however, there are also remarkable discussions over lunch, drinks after an archive day, and on day trips to see collections. This travel to other worlds also helps to make those worlds much more present, vibrant, and alive for students in the classroom.

This all leads to the second prong of the approach: fostering what can be fostered within the region and my home institution. Almost by coincidence, four of us who are friends from doing art historical and interdisciplinary research at the state archives in Florence have all ended up at universities in either Kansas or Missouri. We would often run into one another at national or international conferences and say, "We need to get together back in the States and make something of this connection!" Finally, one colleague took the initiative to invite us to Kansas to present short papers on our work. These now-annual gatherings have provided our campuses with a rotating crash course in innovative research in art history, but they have also sustained the four of us.

At Truman, faculty have been working over the last ten years or so to foster a more active scholarly community. At an institution that emphasizes teaching of undergraduates, research and creative work have, at times, been downplayed in favor of pedagogy. Slowly, though, the Caucus for Faculty Scholarship has formed to promote the teacher-scholar model and raise the profile of the excellent work being done by our colleagues. The caucus has advocated for funding and other forms of support. In addition, its focus has often been outward looking: how can we share our scholarship with the campus community—students, staff, other faculty members—as well as with area communities?

About the third prong, it's been a particularly interesting proposition to teach the humanities—art history in particular—in rural Missouri, especially since we are not surrounded by the kind of world-class art that dominates the survey courses. Numerous colleagues have done beautifully at that task. One has studied the remarkable architectural heritage we *do* have here. Another has worked to bring in what art we can from outside. While we have an outstanding University Art Gallery with a director who is keen to have as many art historical exhibitions as we can, we are continually challenged by not having a permanent collection. We have been fortunate, however, in having generous local and alumni collectors who have been willing to share their work with us. Two of the most recent art historical exhibitions, one of which featured Renaissance intaglio prints, and another that featured Chinese ceramics made for the European export market, were made up entirely of work owned by collectors who either live locally or are alumni or both.

Truman's students, of course, also play a vital role in all of this activity. The numbers cited above certainly suggest a high level of accomplishment. What they cannot convey is a sense of the vibrancy, the engagement, and the excitement that Truman students bring to the classroom and to life on campus. It is those things that have helped keep many faculty members at Truman. Our students tend to be curious, excited about learning and being at university, connected to the material, and—in many cases—connected equally to the local community around them. Many humble me in the paths that they have taken in life, the way they have met the struggles they face, and the passion they bring to learning and to working in the community and world in which they live.

This vibrancy also fuels what goes on in the classroom. As one example, in a recent semester I was fortunate enough to be able to teach a four-hundred-level course on the great Renaissance artist, Michelangelo Buonarroti. The students—artists, historians, psychologists, and others—had signed up to spend sixteen weeks reading the writing and studying the artwork of a man who lived and died in a very different world from theirs. It became clear through the course of the semester that one of the biggest challenges would be just imagining his life, his decisions, and their relation to the work that he made. How we could use Michelangelo's own sculptures, paintings, and buildings, his own poetry, his own words but also those of others about him, in order to understand his path and place in the world? While the course was about art history, it was also about compassion or, as Martha Nussbaum writes, developing "the ability to imagine the predicament of another person."[8] Especially in the humanities, the more we can have the travel experiences, the life experiences, the visual and material experiences that allow us to make other places, objects, and people be more vibrant and more present, the better. The more we can connect with the countries and colleagues and worlds that support us and help us to thrive, the more we can bring that awareness to our own students from wherever they come. And of course this helps in our own development, as we grow in and with the worlds we encounter.

In many ways, we are all engaged in bringing worlds together: for me, bringing the streets of sixteenth-century Venice or late nineteenth-century Paris alive in classrooms on a college campus in economically challenged, rural northeast Missouri. On one hand, one could argue that that is a fruitless exercise, a luxury: wouldn't it be better to take that time and effort and put it toward stocking the shelves of the local food bank? Indeed, in my lower moments, I wonder and will continue to wonder about that too. On the other hand, knowledge of these other worlds also matters. I am continually buoyed by the excitement of students when they learn about art made by men and women who died centuries ago, whose cultures held very different attitudes about class, gender, and sexuality, and about what art should be and do. Often enough, that encounter with the unknown changes them profoundly and is truly part of our evolution.

Works Cited

Nichols, David C. *Founding the Future: A History of Truman State University*. Kirksville, MO: Truman State University Press, 2007.

Nussbaum, Martha C. *Not for Profit: Why Democracy Needs the Humanities*. Princeton: Princeton University Press, 2010.

Violette, E. M. *History of the First Missouri State Normal School*. Kirksville, MO: Journal Printing Company, 1905.

Notes

1. Nussbaum, *Not for Profit*, 38. I am most grateful to John Garton both for bringing this volume to my attention and for encouraging me to write this essay.

2. In 2013, the University of St. Andrews celebrated its six hundredth anniversary, or its 602nd, depending on which foundation date for the University one accepts. For more detail on the various possibilities for the university's founding date, please see The University of St. Andrews, "600 Years: 1413–2013. History," accessed May 9, 2013, http://www.st-andrews.ac.uk/600/history/.

3. On July 1, 1996, Northeast Missouri State University became Truman State University, in recognition of the university's mission change in 1985 when it became the State of Missouri's only public liberal arts and sciences institution.

4. "State and County Quick Facts, Adair County, Missouri," United States Census Bureau, last modified June 27, 2013, http://quickfacts.census.gov/qfd/states/29/29001.html.

5. "Adair County," The Food Bank for Central and Northeast Missouri, accessed May 10, 2013, http://sharefoodbringhope.org/adair-county/, and "Map the Meal Gap," Feeding America, accessed May 10, 2013, http://feedingamerica.org/hunger-in-america/hunger-studies/map-the-meal-gap.aspx.

6. See Violette, *History of the First Missouri State Normal School*; and Nichols, *Founding the Future*.

7. I am deeply grateful to Gina Morin, associate vice president for enrollment management at Truman State University, for her assistance with the statistics in this and the previous paragraph.

8. Nussbaum, *Not for Profit*, 7.

11

How One Becomes
What One Is

Jonathan R. Cohen
Philosophy, University of Maine at Farmington

The invitation to contribute to this volume is welcome because it dovetails nicely with my current writing project. I am writing a philosophical travel memoir concerning my family's trip five years ago to visit Nietzsche's three favorite residences, Nice, Turin, and Sils-Maria (Switzerland). We dubbed the trip "In Nietzsche's Footsteps," and that is also the title of my memoir. The title has a double significance. On the one hand, we made it a point to walk on precisely those streets and footpaths that Nietzsche walked, which in many cases are known from his letters and his autobiography, and in a couple of cases are by now even named after him. But the deeper significance of the title is that, by way of considering Nietzsche's philosophy of individualism, the book is an opportunity for me to reflect on my own life as a scholar of Nietzsche and ask in what sense, if any, I can say I actually do follow in his footsteps when my life seems so very different from his: married, with children, a regular job, loyal to the religion of my parents, etc. So you see I am already busy reflecting on the road I've taken.

Part of that reflection, too, requires reflecting on the influence of place on someone living the life of the mind. Does the philosopher's location influence his/her thought? Or does a philosopher wander until he/she finds a place suitable to his/her work? Or neither? For a certain kind of thinker, the place where the thinking happens is irrelevant, and the person's writing seems to emanate from a disembodied, locationless mind. We are encouraged to write this way by our graduate training. One mind speaks to another and it doesn't really matter whether the minds are at Oxford or

Cambridge or Harvard or Stanford. Generally one has to look at the list of contributors at the back of the journal to find out where the author teaches, and the answer usually seems entirely arbitrary. One can even discover that an author one has read before has by this time relocated to a new university and be surprised by this, as the writing gave no hint that any change of location had taken place.[1]

The history of philosophy, however, gives the lie to this ideal of disembodied minds more often than not. While Kant could well have taken his famous walks in any town at all—and then it would have been the housewives of Farmington, not Königsberg, who set their clocks by his regularity—most of the greats betray their location in time and space quite clearly: Plato must necessarily have lived in the same Athens as Socrates, Aristotle must have known the Macedonian royal house, Hobbes must have been a royalist in the English Civil War, Locke must have traveled back to England in 1688 in the entourage of William of Orange, etc. Even apparently disembodied thinkers such as Descartes and Spinoza, whose very philosophies propound the idea of the mind being separated from the body, deeply reflect the (relatively) freethinking atmosphere of the seventeenth-century Holland in which they lived.[2] Or consider Hegel, an arch-academic philosopher who could move from Jena to Berlin without disrupting or altering his ambitious philosophical program—and yet when one reads the preface to *Phenomenology of Spirit*, written in Jena in October 1806, one cannot fail to hear Napoleon's guns thundering at the outskirts of town.

This point about the necessity of bearing in mind a philosopher's location in considering his/her work would seem to be too obvious to require mention in the case of Nietzsche, whose youthful enthusiasm for the cultural revival he expected to follow upon German reunification gave way to a strident rejection of German nationalism coinciding with his taking up a nomadic life outside of Germany in Switzerland, northern Italy, and southeastern France. Yet there is an argument against looking too closely at the places Nietzsche lived where one might least expect it, namely, the coffee-table book *The Good European*, a remarkable collection of photographs of the places Nietzsche lived and worked along with extensive biographical discussion and excerpts from published, unpublished, and epistolary writings that clearly reflect those places. This book was a major inspiration for my own project, yet its preface contains the following argument against considering the influence of place on thought:

[W]hat are we to make of it when Nietzsche tells us that he conceived the "Old and New Tablets" episode of *Thus Spoke Zarathustra* while climbing the path at Èzé, near Nice, or that the thought of eternal return overwhelmed him near a pyramidal boulder at Surlej? "Of Old and New Tablets" is a long and carefully composed text: it was not written on a hike. . . .

To push the question harder: Can one calculate the influence of Nietzsche's work sites on his principal ideas . . . ? Is eternal return a thought of Alpine lakes, will to power an effulgence of the northern Italian city-states, overman a dream of the mountains near Nice, genealogy a strategy for defeating the tourists at Sils-Maria? Such judgments could only be quirky, and this book has no desire to make them.

Well, excuse me, but I do. Quirky is as quirky does, I guess, and at any rate, having now been right there, I am quite sure that "On Old and New Tablets" *was* written on the mountain path at Èzé, and that the pyramidal boulder at Surlej (which is near Sils-Maria) did indeed influence Nietzsche's thought of eternal recurrence.[3]

The last paragraphs of "On Old and New Tablets" urge us to be tough, to not take the easy route, so that humanity will not stagnate into safe conformity but instead will continue to grow and innovate. Nietzsche's metaphor for this in *Zarathustra* is the overman, who in superhuman fashion overcomes every obstacle and lives his life in a continual state of personal growth. Though this vision is impossible to achieve,[4] it functions as a regulative ideal to direct the lives of actual humans to engage in activities that grow and strengthen themselves, their cultures, and the people around them. And thus the mountain path that Nietzsche climbed up from Èzé *la gare* (the train station at the bottom of the hill) to Èzé *la village* (the walled medieval village at the top of the hill, a busy tourist destination even in the 1880s), while all the other tourists were taking the easy route of riding the horse-drawn carriage to the top, seems to me the perfect place for Nietzsche to have conceived such an idea and to have written a first draft thereof in the pocket notebook he always carried. Here is the penultimate section of "On Old and New Tablets":

> "Why so hard?" the kitchen coal once said to the diamond. "After all, are we not close kin?"
>
> Why so soft? O my brothers, thus I ask you: are you not after all my brothers?
>
> Why so soft, so pliant and yielding? Why is there so much denial, self-denial, in your hearts? So little destiny in your eyes?

And if you do not want to be destinies and inexorable ones, how can you triumph with me?

And if your hardness does not wish to flash and cut and cut through, how can you one day create with me?

For creators are hard. And it must seem blessedness to you to impress your hand on millennia as on wax.

Blessedness to write on the will of millennia as on bronze—harder than bronze, nobler than bronze. Only the noblest is altogether hard.

This new tablet, O my brothers, I place over you: *become hard!*

Of course the passage was rewritten, expanded, and reshaped when Nietzsche was back at his desk, but still—this particular rough hillside and Nietzsche's exultant hike to its peak while the tourists took the easy way up speak unmistakably out of this particular text.

By the same token, a few minutes' rest taken near an odd-shaped boulder at the edge of an Alpine lake in the middle of a glacial gorge seems to me the perfect opportunity to reflect on the relation between the permanent and the impermanent, and on what it would mean to see both the quickly changing ripples on the water and the geologically changing shape of the mountainous landscape, though equally examples of pure becoming, as examples of pure, eternally affirmed, eternally recurring Being. Nietzsche's love for this landscape—and, again, I've been there and can affirm it to be breathtakingly beautiful—can easily be imagined to translate to a love of time, to the forces that brought the glacier down this valley, that left an odd-shaped erratic boulder by the shore of a lake full of Alpine melt off, that brought a chronically ill German expatriate philosopher to its shores to take his constitutional walks and then, in August 1881, this very day at this very minute, to need a rest precisely at this very place and start thinking (again) about the old Stoic idea of eternal recurrence. "[H]ow well disposed would you have to become to yourself and to life to *crave nothing more fervently* than this ultimate eternal confirmation and seal?"[5]

In short, while Nietzsche could of course have conceived of these ideas elsewhere, or could have thought of other things while at those two places, there seems to me a reasonable and instructive fit between what he thought and where he was, in those two cases and in many others.[6] And so—to return to the present essay—it is reasonable to ask what effect the little town of Farmington and its chronically underfunded public liberal arts college have had on the thought of that other philosopher, Cohen.

Well, I haven't had any original ideas of the caliber of overman or eternal recurrence, of course, but surely that can't be blamed on Farmington. And the fact that I, formerly a basketball guy from Philly, have taken up cross-country skiing since moving to the land of snow says nothing about my philosophical and academic career.

University of Maine at Farmington (UMF) began life as a normal school (the first public institution of higher learning in the state of Maine) in 1864, and a little over a hundred years later added a liberal arts program built from the content portions of the teacher education program. Little by little other disciplines were added—the first full-time philosopher was hired in 1985—and by now UMF's mission has been recast as Maine's public liberal arts college (though the education program is still big here—about half of our majors). We have an enrollment cap of two thousand FTE (full-time equivalency), and some 70 percent of our classes run with fewer than twenty students each. So we're small, and we excel in our attention and responsiveness to students. Both retention and graduation rates are well above the national averages. We've been named one of America's best colleges by *US News & World Report* for sixteen consecutive years (and counting).

So I'm proud of who we are and what we do, but, you know, truth be told, I think I probably could have fit in anywhere.[7] If I had been at a Research I institution, I would have written more (more scholarship, at least), been more of a specialist, and so on, and I think I would have been able to manage that reasonably well, although I must admit it was really nice to have relatively light publication expectations and thus be able to go for tenure and be an involved parent of four at the same time.

And yet, maybe we wind up where we're meant to wind up? I have titled this essay with Nietzsche's phrase for the process by which we move from potential to actual, thus discovering who we are in the very process of constructing ourselves. We approach life in a condition of (what we believe to be) freedom, yet we can look back at the road taken and realize there was something inevitable about it. People who knew me in high school who have found out much after the fact that I have become a philosophy professor have all said, yeah, right, of course he did. Nietzsche, by the same token, was already not such a good academic when he was an academic. His first book, *The Birth of Tragedy*, has no footnotes (horrors!) and ends with a long, embarrassing paean to Richard Wagner, thus embroiling Nietzsche deeply in the culture wars of the time rather than maintaining proper academic distance—so it's not surprising that he and the university parted ways by mutual agreement when his health began to deteriorate.

And when he left the University of Basel, he went south, not north, partly because of his revulsion at German nationalism and partly because he felt he needed a southern climate for his health. Thus began his nomadic life in southeastern France, northern Italy, and eastern Switzerland. It seems clear that in this case Nietzsche was the one who determined his place, not vice versa.

Similarly, when I was in graduate school and thinking about my upcoming career, I always thought I'd have to make a case for taking teaching seriously. I worked up all sorts of passionate arguments about the matter, making them in my head against the sort of research-only-and-damn-the-undergraduates trolls I knew among my graduate professors and expected to find among my future colleagues. But then I wound up at a teaching-first institution, where if anything we have to argue for research to be taken (and funded) seriously. So maybe that devotion to teaching I thought I'd have to defend was part of what made me suitable to UMF, rather than UMF's having that effect on me. It's the same with the idea of becoming a generalist because one is stationed at a small public liberal arts college. It's true that those conditions generally encourage that result, but really, I think I already was a generalist, already thought in terms of broad historical surveys suitable for undergraduates, already had interest in several areas of philosophy as well as many subjects outside of philosophy.

All the same, I believe my location at UMF has had an effect on me as a philosopher in (at least) three ways. One has to do with being in Maine, which has meant for me not just taking up skiing but getting to know Mainers, both students and neighbors, and becoming infected with their down-to-earth practicality. Years ago, a colleague in philosophy—a research-oriented, disembodied mind sort of philosopher, by the way, who sure enough made several attempts to escape and eventually did leave UMF a few years ago—told me with outrage that one of his students in his metaphysics class went to the college bookstore to buy his books for the course and was greeted by the clerk with, "Metaphysics! What do you want to take *that* for?" But you know what? I can't take metaphysics seriously now either (and indeed, now that my former colleague has left, we no longer offer the course). It may shock my philosophical colleagues at other schools, but frankly, I no longer care whether there could have been more tigers in the world than there are now, or whether Johnson is still Johnson if he loses an arm, or if he is now just a subset of Johnson. Honest, I really don't. Now when I do philosophy I have to see the connection with real life, and I get my students to do the same by having them write ethics journals about their own moral dilemmas, by having them read Italo Calvino's attempt (as Mr. Palomar) to look at the world in terms of Hegelian dialectic, by having them witness Rousseauvian participatory democracy in action by going to the Farmington town meeting, and so on.

A second effect has to do with being a generalist. I said above that I think I've always been a generalist, even before coming to UMF, but I do think that being at UMF has allowed that side of me to bear fruit in ways it would not have at a Research I institution. Thus I was able to write on both Nietzsche and ancient philosophy for my tenure rather than being limited to one specialization, as I might have been at a larger department. (And one of the papers on Nietzsche compared him with Martin Buber and Bruce Springsteen—this would surely have raised eyebrows in some prestigious quarters.) Over the years I have also written on John Locke and on Thomas Nagel, neither topic being anywhere close to what I studied in graduate school. I have also been enthusiastically encouraged in my current project, which will be aimed at the general public rather than specialists, to the point of being granted a sabbatical this year to write it. When, soon after arriving at UMF, I told our professor of poetry that I had an interest in creative writing, he was beside himself: "Oh, wow! So write your novel and we'll tenure you on the strength of the novel!" I didn't take him at his word, and it does seem to me appropriate for faculty hired in a discipline to show their ability within that discipline in order to earn tenure. But one of my colleagues in British literature is spending her post-tenure sabbatical on a novel, and my next-door-office neighbor, a professor of Spanish who won her tenure on the strength of her translations, has written nothing but plays (in English) for the last dozen or so years.

Yes, my next-door-office neighbor is in Spanish, not philosophy, and that sets me onto the third, and I think most important way UMF has shaped my career. Had I been hired at a large philosophy department, my primary peer group at that school would likely have been all philosophers. And I actually still thought that way when I first came. One day I had to move some heavy things around the house and yard, so I asked the other full-time philosopher (whom I mentioned above) to come help, and when we met with something that even we two could not budge, we said that what we needed was a third philosopher. Twenty years later, I can't believe I ever said that. By now I have been engaged primarily with non-philosophers, and while there surely is some sort of special commonality with the few of my colleagues who also teach philosophy, by now I am used to usually being the only philosopher in the room. I find this fun in two directions: I enjoy being the ambassador from philosophy, and I also enjoy being a tourist in other people's fields. I've always been a dilettante, but in my current situation that comes off as a virtue.

Engaging with non-philosophers has led to many of my most productive experiences as a professor, and here you must indulge me another personal story. Just months after receiving tenure, I ruptured my Achilles tendon playing basketball (thus becoming a mere subset of Cohen). I had been in the habit of walking to campus, but that was now too much to do on crutches. But since the rupture was in my right heel, I was unable to drive as well. So I put together a stable of friends who could drive me to and from campus. It was in the course of these drives that I talked general education with my friend the biologist, and sure enough I wound up serving as UMF's first director of general education.[8] On another of these drives with another of my chauffeurs, a music historian, I started comparing my thoughts about nineteenth-century philosophy with his thoughts about nineteenth-century music, and before long we were team-teaching (along with an art historian) a course called Philosophy, Music, and Art in the Nineteenth Century, and then the two of us offered a course on Nietzsche and Wagner, and another on philosophy and music (my friend titled it Music and Philosophy). And then I started writing on Nietzsche and music, and have published one piece, read another at a conference, and written most of a third, and the whole thing is going to become a book project when I finish the current one. It all followed from having a friend who wasn't a philosopher, which I'm sure was much more likely because I'm at a small public liberal arts college. I've also team-taught with two different literature professors, both of whom attend our occasional philosophy reading group, the population of which includes as well a psychologist, a political scientist, and a geographer. At a large philosophy department I might still be yawning my way through colloquia on whether it would be different if Johnson lost a leg rather than an arm.

The benefit I feel I've gotten from all this interdisciplinarity (well, it *should* be a word!) goes far beyond ticks on my C.V. I would argue that the very concept of general education is inherently philosophical, since it requires thinking at the highest, most transdisciplinary level about what education really is and what its purposes in undergraduate education really should be. Team-teaching with colleagues from different disciplines requires both learning about another field and responding to your partners' queries about yours, which in turn requires reflection on the very nature of your field and its differences from other fields. I'm sure this would happen less often, if at all, if I were at a larger institution.

On the other hand, my interdisciplinary and general education ventures have taken time away that I would have spent on my scholarship within the discipline, and sometimes I feel like I might have let down my graduate school professors by not staying more active in the field and not publishing more scholarly work. One of my peers from graduate school, also a Nietzsche scholar who worked with the same advisor I did, is now on the faculty at Stanford and serves as the president of the North American Nietzsche Society, and where am I? At some tiny, Podunk of a place with a pop-gun library and fewer than a dozen philosophy majors, spending my sabbatical on a project without footnotes.

I don't know if my professors actually feel that way about where I've wound up, but if they do, I would respond that Nietzsche didn't write with footnotes either, so maybe I'm actually following in his footsteps more faithfully than any of them. This is an issue that cuts to the soul of philosophy. Is what we're trained to do in graduate school—that careful, disembodied-mind kind of scholarship, rich with footnotes—really philosophy? Nietzsche would surely say not, would surely associate contemporary scholars of philosophy with "philosophical laborers and scientific men."[9] And there is no question that the way the discipline is carried on these days conforms quite closely to what Thomas Kuhn calls "normal science," with very little left of the divine *mania* Plato talks about, or the wonder at the universe Aristotle talks about.[10] So perhaps, like Nietzsche's being forced by his illnesses to resign from Basel—which he later considered lucky—I was lucky to have been cast aside, so far from civilization, lucky in the sense in which Garrison Keillor says, "Some luck lies in not getting what you thought you wanted but getting what you have, which once you have got it you may be smart enough to see is what you would have wanted had you known." Lucky because I think the situation of a philosopher at a public liberal arts college has allowed me to see things that would have remained hidden to me had I continued to live in the rarefied air of the institution at which I got my doctorate. Here's Nietzsche again (he seems to be on top of everything!):

> More and more it seems to me that the philosopher, being *of necessity* a man of tomorrow and the day after tomorrow, has always found himself, and *had* to find himself, in contradiction to his today: his enemy was ever the ideal of today. . . . [He had to find] the greatness of

[his] task, in being the bad conscience of [his] time.[11]

On the one hand, says Nietzsche, such untimely thinkers "expose how much hypocrisy, comfortableness, letting oneself go and letting oneself drop, how many lies [lie] hidden under the best honored type of their contemporary morality"—in our context, how the professoriate at Research I institutions in a way betrays the educational ideals it officially represents by ignoring its community, shortchanging undergraduates, and focusing on arcane research. And on the other, perhaps being the bad conscience of one's time allows a philosopher

> . . . to know of a *new* greatness of man, of a new untrodden way to his enhancement. . . . Facing a world of "modern ideas" that would banish everybody into a corner and "specialty," a philosopher—if today there could be philosophers—would be compelled to find the greatness of man, the concept of "greatness," precisely in his range and multiplicity, in his wholeness in manifoldness.

Perhaps in our day it is the generalist who is the true philosopher? Perhaps in our day it is engagement with non-philosophers and with non-academic life that makes one a better philosopher? Perhaps in our day it is teaching, not scholarly research, that constitutes the best arena for philosophical thinking? And perhaps it is at public liberal arts colleges, not Research I universities, where philosophy is hiding out for its own safety.

At any rate, the question of what philosophy is, is less to the point of this essay than the question of what I am, and so in closing I reach again for my friend Friedrich and that lovely phrase that serves as my title. Nietzsche expands on the idea of becoming who one is as follows:

> Learning changes us. . . . But at the bottom of us, really "deep down," there is, of course, something unteachable, some granite of spiritual *fatum*, of predetermined decision and answer to predetermined selected questions. Whenever a cardinal problem is at stake, there speaks an unchangeable "this is I"; . . . a thinker cannot relearn but only finish learning—only discover ultimately how this is "settled in him."[12]

Maybe the way to sum up what I've been saying in this essay is that coming to a public liberal arts college didn't change who I was deep down—I've always been a teaching-oriented, life-oriented generalist as a philosopher—but it did mean that I was asked certain fundamental questions rather than others. What will you do in this particular environment, so different from the one for which you were trained? What will you do as a generalist, as someone whose colleagues are mostly non-philosophers, teaching survey courses to first-generation undergraduates in the land of the snow? It is in my responses to those fundamental questions that I have become who I am.

Notes

1. Such writing often ignores the specificity of time too, against which we can deploy a wonderful passage from Kierkegaard's *Concluding Unscientific Postscript*, in which he makes fun of distinguished philosophers arguing that time is unreal and then, with no sense of irony, showing up promptly every two weeks to claim their paychecks.

2. I confess to having been surprised to learn this about Descartes: The *Meditations* are addressed to the Faculty of Theology at the University of Paris, and the subtle attempt to undermine Aristotle bespeaks the intellectual tension in Paris in the first half of the seventeenth century. Yet the *Meditations* were in fact written in Holland, and this helps explain how Descartes could write something so radical.

3. I am less sure about will to power and genealogy—though I can see strong cases being made in both cases—and so will leave those examples aside here.

4. The line from the preface to *Zarathustra*, "Man is a rope stretched between ape and overman," seems to me precisely to preclude anyone's actually being the overman, despite some people's—e.g., the Nazis'—attempt to interpret otherwise.

5. *The Gay Science*, trans. Kaufmann, sect. 341, in *The Portable Nietzsche* (New York: Penguin Books, 1954).

6. For example, Bismarckian Germany for his revulsion at German nationalism, cosmopolitan Nice for his idea of the "good European," etc.

7. My wife is always teasing me about my first reaction nearly every place we travel: "I could live here." I'm pretty sure too that I could even have done okay in some other career, but I'll leave those two lines of thought aside here.

8. And so far only, since the position was cancelled in 2008 because of our chronic financially strapped-ness, although there is a move afoot this year to bring it back.

9. *Beyond Good and Evil*, trans. Kaufmann, sect. 211.

10. Thomas Kuhn, *The Structure of Scientific Revolutions* (Chicago: University of Chicago Press, 1962), chaps. 2–4; Plato, *Phaedrus* 244ff; Aristotle, *Metaphysics* I.2 982b12. Look at all these footnotes!

11. This and the next two quotes are from *Beyond Good and Evil,* trans. Kaufmann, sect. 212.

12. Ibid., sect. 231.

12

Neither Here nor There
Testing the Boundaries
of Place and Pedagogy

Ellen Holmes Pearson
History, University of North Carolina Asheville

On a warm day, I sit with Josh Copus on his land in Madison County, in the mountains of western North Carolina. Josh is an alumnus of the University of North Carolina, Asheville, an art major and my former student. We occasionally see each other in Marshall, the 850-person town just north of Asheville that he and I both call home. Madison County is nestled in the heart of the Blue Ridge Mountains, an area known for spectacular views and rich music traditions. Josh has enjoyed considerable success as a potter and now owns land in Madison County, where he has three wood-fired kilns and a workshop. His academic training and studies of Asian, English, and North Carolina folk pottery, along with traditional apprenticeships in the Asheville area and across the nation, have helped him to develop his own unique style. We can see Josh's kilns as we converse about this place and how it influenced his work. We talk about his pottery and our love of Madison County, which nurtures so many talented creators of music, literature, and visual and performing arts.

Josh plays an important role in perpetuating traditional potting techniques, but he also understands the value of investing time and energy in twenty-first-century tools. Of course, as with most entrepreneurs these days, Josh has a website, and he relies on the Internet to market his products and cultivate clientele all over the world. Josh's tech-savvy is one of the reasons for his early success. He has put himself out to the world through the magic of digital technology, stretching, even breaching, traditional boundaries of place. Yet he is also firmly rooted in the same land that drew me in when I landed in western North Carolina a decade ago. Like me, Josh wants to share his love of this place with others. As we sit on his acreage, he talks of plans to open his land to tourists who would like to experience the arts in a natural setting. Agricultural tourism, ecotourism, and arts tourism are big businesses in western North Carolina. "We are," Josh boasts, "on the map for a lot of things. This is something else that will get people into Madison County, and we will get into their hearts." We strategize ways to attract people to our county and to take our county to them, knowing that these plans will require learning and relearning an ever-changing array of technological tools. Because of his liberal arts education, Josh knows how to learn, therefore he is uniquely equipped to cope with these changes. But as we reach beyond the boundaries of our campuses and draw the rest of the world into our communities, what parts of our identity will change or disappear? When we rely on the Internet and digital technology to show off our place, our products, and our projects, the fruits of our labor are neither here nor there, but rather they become part of that still-novel place called cyberspace. How will our sense of place shift with the increasing presence of technology?

In his keynote speech at a Phi Alpha Theta Carolinas conference, Clemson historian Paul Anderson talked about his sense of place and how, for him, weather provokes memory. He spoke of cold, wet days that revived memories of high school football games, and hot summer nights burning through the darkness on a country lane in his father's car.[1] I can say the same thing about my memories. Cold, heat, humidity, or sunshine can trigger vivid memories of places and events. For example, gray, cold, sleety weather transports me to February of 2003, when I braved an ice and snowstorm to travel to Asheville for my campus interview. It took me two days, several airplanes, and a rental car to get to UNC Asheville, where I was stuck for three days before I could return to my home in Connecticut. I have not forgotten the wintry weather through which I traveled, nor will I forget the warm welcome I received when I finally arrived late in the night. After delivering me to my hotel, two of my colleagues kept me company while I ate a warm bowl of soup. Southern hospitality. The next day, as another colleague gave me a tour of Asheville, he apologized for the barren look of the mountains, and he assured me that the city would green up in the space of another month. But for me, the winter landscape, barren of leaves and other vegetation, represented peaceful slumber and allowed me to see more of Asheville's stark beauty. As we traveled along Interstate 40 toward Black Mountain, I remember looking up at the ridgetops, where the skeletons of leaf-bare trees reached toward the gray sky, and whispering "beautiful."

Place has always been important to me. I came to academia a little later in life, and because I already had some mileage on me, I wanted to choose my place—both geographic and academic—carefully. My first career, as a sales manager for a luxury hotel, was great fun and allowed me to travel and work with a variety of people in a variety of professions. As I have told many of my students, the hospitality industry is an ideal career for a history major and a product of a liberal arts education. Tourism provides another way to think about place. I spent over a decade selling a particular place to others, and I was good at it. Although I thought about returning to graduate school to study history, I kept getting promoted. So I stuck around and eventually earned a post as director of sales for a luxury hotel. But graduate school continued to tug at me, and while still working full time I took my first graduate course at the University of New Orleans. Once I began there was no turning back. After three years of part-time graduate work, I received my master's degree, quit my job, and pursued a PhD at my dream school, Johns Hopkins University.

So there I was, letting go of a comfortable place with one hand while trying to grab the brass ring with the other. The faculty and my fellow graduate students at Hopkins challenged me intellectually and supported me emotionally. The history department's collegial atmosphere helped to set the tone for my expectations of life in academia. At times, however, the faculty's vision of academic life did not correspond with my own, and my dissertation director was not always comfortable with my professional goals. Although I made it clear from the beginning of my graduate career that I wanted to land in a place where I could *teach undergraduates*, UNC Asheville was not the kind of place that he envisioned for me. I insisted that an undergraduate-centered institution would not be a stepping-stone for me, but rather it was my destination. Eventually he gave me his blessing, and my perseverance has worked out well for me.

After I completed my PhD, I spent two years at a compass-point, comprehensive state university with large classes and little emphasis on student-centered teaching or close collegial relationships between students and professors. I used that time to develop my courses, to get a feel for life in academia, and to plot a strategy that would land me a better job— meaning, I thought, a position at a small to midsize private liberal arts school. Ironically, in the fall of 2002 I was invited to apply for a position at a

Research I institution, and since I had to update my C.V. anyway, I decided to apply for two other positions: one at a midsize Jesuit liberal arts school, and one at UNC Asheville. I still remember my preliminary interview at the American Historical Association with two of UNC Asheville's history faculty. They quickly understood that I was not daunted by the prospect of a heavy teaching load and the kind of time-consuming, student-centered teaching that their institution demanded. They were visibly impressed with the tactics I used to make sure that all 160 of my students received meaningful writing experiences each semester. And I was impressed by what they told me about UNC Asheville. I wanted this job. The attraction of Asheville and the concept of a public liberal arts experience seemed to be right up my alley. Apparently my colleagues thought so too, because they offered me the job. I have never regretted the decision to accept, but of course the road has not always been smooth.

I knew—sort of—what I was getting into by joining the faculty of a public liberal arts institution. I had received my bachelor's degree from a small Jesuit liberal arts school, so I knew what to expect with regard to rigor and culture. However, I did not grasp how steep the time commitment would be. I found it hard to schedule research and writing time, because my students demanded considerable attention. On the first day of class it has always been my practice to invite students to stop by my office and chat with me, just to say hello and to get to know them—but I never actually had anyone take me up on it until I started teaching at UNC Asheville. Imagine my surprise when one of my students popped in during my office hours, sat down, and said, "Well, you said to just come by and say hello, so I decided to do that!" We had a lovely chat, and I remember wondering how many other students I could expect just to drop in, and whether I could continue to rely on my office hours to get some reading or paperwork done. While I thrive on my interactions with students, it took me at least two years to get a routine down that could balance my students' needs with my own research and writing agenda.

Some faculty at liberal arts institutions consider scholarship an expendable luxury. Those of us in UNC Asheville's Department of History, on the other hand, believe in the integral relationship between an active scholarly life and excellence in teaching. One of the biggest advantages of a liberal arts institution is that we are not limited to the narrow research avenues that we pursued during graduate school. Moreover, because our liberal arts institution does not limit us to the narrow research avenues that we pursued during graduate school, we can spread our wings in a variety of directions. For example, my colleague Grant Hardy received his PhD in Chinese language and literature at Yale. He delights in telling our students that, although he never took a history course, he now teaches Asian history. While he still produces scholarship on pre-modern China, Grant has also published works in Mormon studies and he edited a collection of poetry on family relationships. Most of us keep our interests a bit closer to home, but Grant exemplifies one kind of creativity to which we can aspire.

Among the greatest joys of my career has been sharing my love of research and writing with students by teaching the senior thesis sequence of courses. In keeping with UNC Asheville's tradition of undergraduate research, each history student must complete a primary-source-driven research paper that represents original thinking and critical analysis of a particular topic. The very best of these papers are of publishable quality. This course is by far my most challenging—and at times the most frustrating—teaching experience, but it holds the potential for tremendous rewards. Students find the task daunting, as it should be. However, we try to lighten the load by easing them into research with a methods course, and they practice their research and writing skills in upper-division courses before they tackle their capstone project. My passion for research and writing is contagious, and because I can share my love of the historical conversation with my students, I see that same spark mirrored in their eyes when they talk about their own research passions. Research can be a solitary exercise, especially in a small department where there is only one person for each area of specialization. But some parts of the research process ought to be collaborative. As we help our students to connect with their own passions through scholarship, we also emphasize the importance of connecting with one another. I am an extrovert, therefore I actively seek out people at other colleges and universities who share my interests in order to cultivate an intellectual community. I try to cultivate these same habits in my students by placing them into support teams so that no one endures the research and writing process alone.

That same concept of teamwork and networking also applies to us faculty members as we strive to maintain our own research momentum, develop new courses, and contribute to the campus community through service. In my case, I may have contributed too much service too soon. I spent my first few years at UNC Asheville helping to implement a new core curriculum that we call Integrative Liberal Studies (ILS). As the first chair of the university's Diversity Intensive Committee for ILS, I was responsible for leading the effort to develop courses across the curriculum that placed diversity at their center. This was a trial-by-fire introduction into the campus culture—and campus politics—that in retrospect I should not have tackled at the beginning of my second year. As with any big curriculum change, this one had its avid supporters and its equally adamant detractors. Some faculty members chafed under what they considered to be unreasonably strict oversight of their teaching, and there I was, the new kid, trying to be a perky cheerleader for our new approach to delivering the curriculum. The time I invested in this initiative paid off, however. I learned a lot about university politics and I managed to escape my term of service intact and with my colleagues' respect. Most importantly, I was forced to articulate my own teaching philosophy, and it gave me a deeper understanding of the variety of pedagogical approaches one can take. Moreover, my early experience with diversity pedagogy led to other opportunities for service on committees dealing with diversity issues. I have learned a lot from my colleagues on these committees, and the respect I gained through this service has earned me considerable credibility among the faculty and administration.

Probably my biggest adjustment was a function of our identity as a public institution. All liberal arts schools are under scrutiny these days with regard to the value of education, and the faculty, staff and administration, students, and alumni of public liberal arts schools must expend considerable energy to keep the liberal arts mission alive. We must be on constant watch to resist the one-size-fits-all mentality that seems so popular among state legislators and central administrators. We are a unique place, with a unique mission and curriculum, and members of our faculty have stepped up to vigorously defend UNC Asheville's status as a liberal arts school. They have met with legislative committees and the UNC Board of Governors to explain the value of tenure and to justify UNC Asheville's singular mission. And, in some ways, this best-defense-is-a-good-offense attitude has shaped my pedagogy and service agendas for the next several years. While "traditional" learning is still central to my teaching, increasingly the realization that my students' classroom includes the larger community, and in fact the entire world, is taking me further afield and further outside of my comfort zone.

The faculty at my alma mater taught me the value of public service and social justice. I consider civic engagement an integral part of my professional and personal life; therefore I find it natural to incorporate service and civic engagement into my own classroom. From my first years at UNC Asheville, I involved students in service efforts that they could apply to their studies. These projects take their sense of community beyond campus and allow students to make important connections between course work and the "real world." Through service learning, students can reflect more deeply on their own beliefs and choices as they develop practical skills in areas such as project management and problem solving. For one of my classes, for example, I organize a cleanup day in the South Asheville Cemetery, a historically black cemetery in Asheville's Kenilworth neighborhood. During the workday, the students have lunch with members of the cemetery board to learn about the cemetery's history and race relations in Asheville before and during desegregation. Afterward, they write a reflection essay in which they relate experiences in the cemetery to assigned readings on the history of race relations in the United States. In one special service learning project a few years ago, my public history class participated in the planning and installation of the "Legacy of Byzantium" Orthodox Christian icon exhibit on campus. Public history students conducted oral history interviews of members of Asheville's Greek and Russian Orthodox communities, collected photographs and other images, and then helped to select images and quotations from their interviews to include in the exhibit. Our curator of Special Collections helped them to create Web exhibits based on their research. This project not only connected students to a previously unfamiliar part of Asheville's community, but it also helped them cultivate important interpersonal and technological skills that can be applied in a variety of professional settings.

Central to my teaching philosophy is a certain measure of trust that our students can handle the challenges of collaborative, hands-on learning. History, like all other disciplines, is a sustained conversation, conducted in an intellectual community that extends far beyond UNC Asheville. Whenever our students read, research, talk, or write about history, they engage in that conversation, alongside the most prominent and accomplished historians. I try to keep this image of a constant conversation alive among our students by fostering communities from the classroom outward. Community is often easy to build. Our small classes and liberal arts focus allow our students the freedom to play with a variety of intellectual tools. We are lucky, because UNC Asheville attracts the kinds of students who, once they have gained some foundational knowledge, are up to these challenges. My own pedagogical evolution has been a collaborative effort for which I thank many colleagues at UNC Asheville and elsewhere. Learning circles on pedagogy have helped me to cultivate my teaching philosophy and have made me realize how lucky I am to be at a place with so many fine teachers.

From my colleagues I have learned the value of "teaching with my mouth shut"—in other words, stepping aside and allowing students to take charge of their learning.[2] I have also learned that it is okay to take innovative risks in the classroom, even if those risks occasionally result in memorable failures.

In 2012, I celebrated two particularly notable achievements. I received the UNC Board of Governors Award for Excellence in Teaching, and I turned fifty. These milestones provoked me to take even more professional risks, and now that I have tasted life outside of my comfort zone, I have no intention of pulling myself back. My students and I were already creating community in the classroom, across classrooms in the university, and in the larger community. Now we are moving even further beyond the pale and into the digital world, which, although a community, really isn't a place. However, this un-place holds so many possibilities. We can, with this technology, invite a variety of communities into the classroom. At the same time, we can use technology to take ourselves beyond the boundaries of the university and community, thus helping our students to understand the significance of both local and global citizenship. In other words, in a contemporary, public liberal arts setting we cannot simply adjust once and comfortably settle into a new mode of teaching; rather, we must continuously adjust our teaching if we are responsive to our students and our mission.

I have been involved in digital history projects since graduate school, when I annotated history websites for The Center for History and New Media's *History Matters* gateway site. In the late 1990s, digital technology was in its infancy. These days, our students find an increasing number of primary sources and scholarly works available to them online. Blogs, wikis, tweets, videos, and TED Talks are the reality of the present, and who knows what innovations we will see in the future. While some academics complain about technology as a barrier to students' attention and success—and this is true in many instances—others have identified the advantages that technology can bring to the table. Yes, technology offers a distraction to our students, as they check e-mail and surf the Web when they should be engaged in class discussion or listening to the lecture.[3] They are not the only people on this campus who fall into that trap. How many times have we sat in a meeting and found it hard to resist the temptation to check our smart phones or navigate our laptops to our e-mail? And then there is the learning curve that technology presents to us. We tend to think of our students as far more tech-savvy than we but, in reality, many are techno-literate only when it comes to checking e-mail, tweeting, and using smart phone apps. They are generally unfamiliar with the programs that we use in academia and they are just as afraid as we are of learning how to use new forms of technology. How do we get students, and ourselves, beyond that fear and into exploring the new programs and processes that they, and we, need to learn?

Fortunately, at UNC Asheville we secured professional help. Jeffrey McClurken, chair of the University of Mary Washington's history department, was in on the ground floor of digital history. In the early 1990s he worked on the pathbreaking Valley of the Shadow project at the University of Virginia, and after earning his PhD from Johns Hopkins, Jeff embraced technology as part of his pedagogical toolkit. He quickly became a leader in the field of digital history and digital humanities. As one of the Prof-Hacker bloggers for the *Chronicle of Higher Education*, Jeff frequently reflects on the influence of technology in the classroom.[4] He has taught hundreds of historians and other scholars how to harness the power of digital technology for their teaching and scholarship. We enlisted Jeff's help to initiate a cross-campus Digital Liberal Arts Initiative that, we hope, will result in interdisciplinary efforts to incorporate more technology into the classroom. Jeff reassured us that we do not need to know how to use every tool out there, but rather our job is to teach our students to learn fearlessly. Today's digital tools will have changed significantly in the space of just a few years, therefore the most important skill they can learn is how to approach these tools with a sense of adventure, and to "play" with the technology until they master it. As a liberal arts university, we should be able to effect a sense of playfulness in learning more easily than at a larger comprehensive university. Jeff also cautioned us to take small steps, incorporating one technology-related assignment into our classes rather than immediately diving into all-digital course work. As Jeff likes to say, the best kind of learning happens when we step outside of our comfort zones and are forced to figure things out for ourselves. But learning doesn't happen when we are overwhelmed. Therefore we should aim for our students and ourselves to be "uncomfortable, not paralyzed" by the new tools we add to our classes.[5]

I am also learning to embrace (play the theme from *Jaws* here) distance learning. For years I resisted it, because I thought about it in only one way: impersonal, asynchronous communication between a faceless online instructor and a cast of hundreds, maybe even thousands, of faceless students. I was dismissive of that kind of learning, because I could not fathom how it could promote critical thinking and reflection. But then I started hearing about small-course distance learning opportunities offered at some of the Research I and elite private schools. Those stories, coupled with the conviction that pressure from North Carolina's General Assembly and General Administration would eventually force us to join the ranks of those providing distance learning experiences, provoked me to explore the possibilities. I contacted Greg Dillingham, our manager of Distance Learning Services. Fortunately for me (but maybe not so much for him), Greg greeted my inquiries enthusiastically. He introduced me to the technology and language of distance learning, and opened a world of possibilities for my students and me. Because UNC Asheville partners with North Carolina State University on engineering degree programs, it has access to sophisticated distance learning equipment and several teleclassrooms and teleconference rooms. The engineering program and a handful of other faculty across campus use the facilities for instructional purposes. Much of the time, however, the technology is used for administrative purposes, including meetings with administrators in Raleigh, Skype interviews with job candidates, and other individual and group meetings for which travel is not necessary. There is a general sentiment that the more these facilities can be used for instruction, the better, but that we must devise a way to offer distance learning experiences that will not undermine the liberal arts mission of the university. In fact, there may be ways that we can use distance learning to enhance the liberal arts mission.

Greg is not just a resource for technological knowledge, he is also a product of UNC Asheville's liberal arts tradition; therefore he is a creative and critical thinker. He helped me to concoct my own visions of how distance learning and other forms of technology can help us to become better educators and to forge and strengthen human relationships, rather than distance ourselves from one another. He told me a story about a teleconference in which a breast cancer survivor comforted a woman undergoing cancer treatment with a virtual hug. Although they could not physically feel that hug, the two women certainly felt one another's emotional support. These twenty-first-century exchanges force us to expand the possible ways that individuals interact with one another. This kind of intimacy at a distance brings humanity back into the world of technology. Shouldn't those of us in the community of liberal arts scholar-teachers and students be exploring the potential behind distance learning rather than dismissing it as contrary to our mission or damaging to students' intellectual and emotional growth? These inquiries should sit at the core of our liberal arts mission.

Digital liberal arts and distance learning opportunities open a world of possible interactions with larger communities as well. Locally, we could take our classrooms into the community by recording our humanities program's common lectures or by producing student TED Talks about specific aspects of the humanities courses, then sharing those talks with local high school teachers for use in their own classrooms. Thinking beyond the local, schools could partner with one another to offer small-class distance learning courses. For example, professors at two or three institutions could collaborate on an interdisciplinary, intercampus course. Students and professors would meet "together" in teleclassrooms on their respective campuses, which would allow participants to see and hear one another in real time. Students could use the teleconference or Skype technology to communicate with one another one-on-one, or within small groups, in order to share ideas, images, and presentations, and these collaborations could turn into projects involving digital technology. Yes, technology *can* fit into the liberal arts scheme—in fact, we can take control of these tools to foster better interpersonal relationships rather than simply dismiss the technology as a way to tear down personal bonds. Small-class, synchronous distance learning creates a virtual place that can be both here and there, thus broadening opportunities for learning while enhancing undergraduate research opportunities and giving students practice in team building across distances, among other valuable professional skills.

For me, one obstacle remains to embedding technology within the liberal arts culture: how to combine our goals of promoting digital literacy and active learning with critical thinking and reflection. At a liberal arts university where we emphasize creative solutions, we should be able to produce a remedy to the problem. My participation in an innovative learning circle has helped me to find possible solutions.

While it may seem at odds with my embrace of new technologies associated with speed, a desire to explore ways of incorporating a slower and more deliberate learning process into my kinetic teaching style provoked me to join UNC Asheville's Circle on Contemplative Practices. Before becoming part of this group, my experience with contemplative practices in the classroom was limited to occasionally allowing students a few minutes to write about a question or series of questions designed to foster in-class discussion. But then a humanities honors section *taught me* the importance of slowing down and allowing time to think before beginning a conversation. No matter what I tried, students simply would not talk until they were ready. At first I was frustrated by their deliberate approach to the readings. But after a while, my students wore me down, and I relaxed into their preferred pace. My experience with this exceptional group of students nudged me into the Circle.

The Circle's 2012–2013 theme of boundaries was well timed for my purposes, because of my pedagogical adventure into a digital liberal arts collaborative. With the help of the Circle participants, I have begun to realize the endless possibilities contemplative practices hold for stretching the boundaries of our classroom experiences. I want to take these contemplative practices beyond the classroom and see how we can apply them to our interactions with technology. How, for example, can we incorporate contemplative practices into interactive digital exhibits, both for the creators and for the audience? Taking it another step, how would contemplative practices benefit the students' experiences in a liberal arts–oriented, small-class distance learning setting? At this point I have more questions than answers, but I am not the only person who is thinking about these issues. I have already found a few kindred spirits among my colleagues here at UNC Asheville, and we hope to pursue these questions together.

I also learned much from Daniel Barbezat, executive director of the Center for Contemplative Mind in Society, who was the plenary speaker for the 2013 Creating a Mindful Campus conference at UNC Asheville. He emphasized that a professor's job is not to fill students with knowledge. Rather, students must be at the center of their education, and our job is to help them be mindful and to explore the process of educating themselves. Their education is about finding meaning and about learning to strategize and to navigate a variety of situations.[6] If we can cultivate reflection and active learning as a way of being, then the students themselves will be able to seek out and learn the techniques and skills that they need to perform well and to succeed.

During his plenary speech, Barbezat told a story of a physical chemistry professor who teaches by "having the students *behold*." Physical chemistry is a difficult subject, but if students are allowed the time to behold a cell model—to really examine it and to consider what they see—then they can recognize its characteristics. This time spent in deep consideration would allow them to recognize a cell model when they saw it again. He also talked about an elementary school teacher who told her students to look at their feet and pay attention to what their feet encountered as they walked. The children then observed the difference between how wood or cement or sand felt under their feet.[7] Applying this same practice of beholding to our purposes, instead of trying to wrest students' attention away from technology, it might be more beneficial to encourage them to pay more attention. If they are purposeful in their exploration and take the time to reflect on the information they collect, they may actually learn something—and they will be responsible for that learning.[8] They will have placed themselves at the center of their education.

Is technology the answer to everything? Well, no, of course not. Let's return to Josh Copus's home, which also is my home: Madison County, North Carolina. Nothing can replace being here, in this green space in the midst of the oldest mountain range in North America. The smells, the feel, the look of the place. The heat of kilns against the cool of a mountain spring. Face-to-face conversation with a young man who fills his former teacher with pride as he talks about his ambitions for this place. His ability to reflect on his situation in creative and practical ways is, in part, a result of his time at UNC Asheville, where he was able to practice his love of art while also getting a well-rounded education and developing the critical thinking and creative skills that helped him to become successful. Josh's plan to take his work out into the world, virtually, while attracting visitors to our place in the same manner, shows the potential to reach across boundaries, blending them so that the un-places of digital technology become centers for learning. We can be both here *and* there.

Works Cited

Finkel, Donald L. *Teaching with Your Mouth Shut*. Portsmouth, NH: Boynton/Cook Publishers, 2000.

Levy, David M. "No Time to Think: Reflections on Information Technology and Contemplative Scholarship." *Ethics and Information Technology* 9 (2007): 237–49.

McClurken, Jeffrey. "Digital Literacy and the Undergraduate Curriculum." In *Hacking the Academy*. Ann Arbor: University of Michigan Press, 2011. E-book, available online at http://www.digitalculture.org/hacking-the-academy/hacking-teaching/#teaching-mcclurken.

———. "Uncomfortable, Not Paralyzed." *Techist: A Blog about Technology, History, and Teaching,* posted January 22, 2008, http://mcclurken.blogspot.com/2008/01/uncomfortable-but-not-paralyzed.html.

———. "Waiting for Web 2.0: Archives and Teaching Undergraduates in a Digital Age." In *A Different Kind of Web: New Connections between Archives and Our Users*, edited by Kate Theimer, 243–54. Chicago: Society of American Archivists, 2011.

Perry, Marc. "You're Distracted. This Professor Can Help." *Chronicle of Higher Education,* March 24, 2013, http://chronicle.com/article/Youre-Distracted-This/138079/.

Notes

1. Paul Anderson, Keynote Address, Phi Alpha Theta Carolinas Conference, Furman University, Greenville, SC, March 23, 2013.

2. Here I refer to the concepts within Finkel, *Teaching with Your Mouth Shut*.

3. See, for example, Levy, "No Time to Think."

4. For examples of Jeff McClurken's blogs and other work, see McClurken, Prof-Hacker Posts at http://chronicle.com/blogAuthor/ProfHacker/27/Jeffrey-W-McClurken/238/; McClurken, "Digital Literacy and the Undergraduate Curriculum"; "Waiting for Web 2.0."

5. For more on this concept, see McClurken, "Uncomfortable, Not Paralyzed."

6. Barbezat, "Contemplative Higher Education," Address, Creating a Mindful Campus: Investigating Boundaries Conference, UNC Asheville, Asheville, NC, March 22, 2013.

7. Ibid.

8. For more specific techniques on how to get students to pay attention, see Perry, "You're Distracted. This Professor Can Help."

13

Finding the Road Back to the "Last Good Job in America"

Kathleen S. Fine-Dare
Anthropology & Gender/Women's Studies, Fort Lewis College

The Beauty of Uncertain Surprises

The road I took to a small, relatively unknown college located in a tourist destination in the American Southwest has been full of surprises. As I reflect on my career, I realize that one reason I have stayed put—this is the only academic job I have held, other than two brief teaching detours to New Mexico and Ecuador—is that nearly every day brings some new thing: an idea, an encounter, a challenge. Sometimes the surprises that have come to my workplace in particular and higher education in general have not been so welcome, leading me to ask, like Dorothy Parker, "What fresh hell is this?" Some of these I touch on below. But overwhelmingly the surprises have been delightful, instructive, and worth every moment of the journey. And usually, they involve students.

For instance, I recently received a Facebook message from a young Navajo woman who had been my student in Native American Gender Issues. This course counts toward degrees in the three programs in which I have faculty appointments: anthropology, gender and women's studies, and Native American and indigenous studies. The student was responding to a query I had posed regarding where I could send some literature I had picked up for her at the Library of Congress about a program for women veterans. I knew that she had left the army after three overseas deployments, two of which were to southwest Asian combat zones.

188

During the first few weeks of the course she rarely spoke up, instead tending to the baby son who was often in her arms. As the term progressed, however, she exhibited such strong qualities of self-possession and leadership that I asked her to be my teaching assistant for the same course the next year, in fulfillment of the catalogue description that says a Native American student will assist in designing and teaching the course whenever possible. As I hoped, she was an essential part of the success of the course, enriching the readings and class discussions with her experiences. A fluent speaker of Navajo, she had suffered such loss and violence in her family, her personal life, and on the battlefield that she was determined to obtain her bachelor's degree and devote her life to improving the world for her son, her family, and herself.

So when she responded in the affirmative to another query I had posed, that she serve one more time as my teaching assistant, I was thrilled and grateful for yet another unexpected gift during my career as a teacher-scholar. This description of my job was not in my vocabulary in graduate school, but it is one that has come to best characterize the work we do at public liberal arts institutions. Unfortunately, the existence of what is perhaps the best-kept secret of what higher education can offer is under growing threat.

There is a sizeable literature on the challenges posed to higher education as it is restructured following business models linked to global capitalism and informed by the anti-intellectual currents swirling ever wider, but particularly from the political Right. There are, however, few firsthand accounts from professors themselves that detail the quotidian and historical aspects of their jobs, as well as their responses to the threats posed to what the distinguished professor of sociology and urban education Stanley Aronowitz once called "the last good job in America." In his chapter in a 1998 book on the politics of work in today's managed university, Aronowitz adumbrated the threats to the institution of a tenured professoriate delivering higher education in a context of labor relations so humane and sensible that all Americans, not just professors, should enjoy them.[1]

In my essay I take up Aronowitz's challenge "to address [our] own future," and to celebrate "the idea of thinking as a full-time activity and the importance of producing what the system terms 'useless' knowledge."[2] This is why in this essay that otherwise, I hope, demonstrates why I continue to find much pleasure in my work at Fort Lewis College, I must also discuss my fears, hopes, and a few ideas for change.

Unforeseen Forks in the Road

Life, more often than not, is full of serendipity. What I envisioned I would do upon receiving my doctorate in anthropology from the University of Illinois half my life ago was to enter some kind of predictably stressful application process (a.k.a. the "meat market") for a tenure-track first job that would lead down the road to other applications and other positions until I arrived at something that looked vaguely like my graduate professors' careers. After a glorious undergraduate spring break road trip to Evergreen, a little town outside of Denver, I had fantasized about teaching at a college in Colorado, but was realistic enough to know that I shouldn't wish for a Rocky Mountain reward for long years of study in the Midwest. I had heard of the University of Colorado, Colorado State University, and Western State University, but I knew the chances would be slim to none that their need and my desire would ever converge.

Then, quite miraculously, I stumbled into a job at a college in—I could hardly believe it—Colorado, though I had not heard of Durango and certainly not of Fort Lewis College when I was hired as a temporary, full-time instructor to teach courses in anthropology, South American ethnology, and freshman writing. I learned about the job when the chair of the Department of Anthropology at Illinois—a man who had never spoken to me because our areas of interest were so different—actually came looking for me in my campus writing office, waving a piece of paper. "They are looking for a one-year replacement at a college in *Durango*," he gushed, in a way that made me think I should be thrilled about the opportunity. "Where?" was the only word I can remember coming out of my mouth, but curiosity put me on a plane headed to what was to become my scarcely hoped-for destiny. The experience of working at this small college would shape whom I would become as a teacher, of course, but also as a scholar, an intellectual, a colleague, a wife, a friend, an ethicist, and a human being. As I write from an upstairs office cooled by the fluttering green arms of white-barked aspen trees that hug my home, alongside which runs a river laden with brown trout, I shudder to think what might have happened to me had I not inexplicably gone to campus to write on a sweltering late July day in Urbana in 1983.

Writing is hard for all graduate students, but it is a particular kind of torture for cultural anthropologists, whose dissertation research is based on more than a year spent in often-distant places where one becomes transformed in ways linguistic, intellectual, and emotional. So when I agreed to interview for the replacement position at Fort Lewis College I saw it as a kind of temporary exercise that would get me back into "the field" and away from the torments of the writing desk, where I was trying to translate very rich personal experiences into academese. Because the job required that I teach four different courses per term, friends warned, "Don't do it; *you will never finish*"—the ultimate horror for an "ABD" (all but dissertation), quasi–human being. But I was too curious, too anxious to deal with the devil of the job hunt sooner rather than later, and too eager for an adventure west of the Continental Divide to pass up the one-year opportunity to step into someone else's shoes (that is, his office, his courses, the books he had already ordered, his network, his reputation), in a place that would not only be my idyll, but would prove to be physically reminiscent of the Ecuadorian Andes, for which I was quite homesick.

Nestled in the San Juan Mountains, part of the Western Rockies, Fort Lewis College is a four-year, undergraduate institution located near what is known as the Four Corners, formed by the states of Utah, Arizona, New Mexico, and Colorado. Tourists regularly travel to a marker west of here to have their photo taken with arms and legs simultaneously straddling different states. Fort Lewis College is described on the College Reality Check search engine as a "medium sized, minimally select, public, four-year" college.[3] Another website describes it as "situated on a mountainside perch" where "outdoor lovers" will find plenty to do. This site highlights the diversity of the college, whose students come from "forty-seven states, eighteen countries, and 122 American Indian tribes." The average class size is twenty-one. Throughout the course of one hundred academic programs, students can find plenty of opportunities for study abroad and experiential learning.[4] Freshmen are required to live on campus, but because the college is located on a high mesa and many faculty instructors must live far from town because of the high cost of living in Durango, it is difficult to return to campus for evening events, which at times gives the college a feel of being both residential and commuter.

Because of a long-standing agreement between the federal government and the State of Colorado, students from federally recognized Indian tribes who meet admission requirements attend the college tuition-free, a situation that exists in only one other college in the United States, the University of Minnesota, Morris. In 2011, 860 Native Americans were enrolled in an overall student body of close to four thousand (725 as residents from outside the state of Colorado), with the top five tribes in terms of student numbers being Navajo, Cherokee, Choctaw, Tlingit/Haida, and Chickasaw.[5]

This phenomenon creates another interesting neither-fish-nor-fowl characteristic of the college, as it is in many ways a Native American–serving institution without being an actual tribal college.

I had a hard first year, teaching eight courses and receiving very low pay ($16,500). Like many young women, I had never been instructed on how to negotiate salary. I was actually much more broke as a college professor than I had been as a graduate student and had to scrounge around for a roommate, cheap meals, and friends in this small town where for the first time in my life I knew absolutely no one. (Even in Ecuador there were archaeologists and others I had met before.) The salary didn't improve much when the guy I replaced found a position elsewhere and I was hired as a tenure-track instructor with the admonition that I complete my doctorate in three years, which I did, in 1986.[6]

Out of a sense of obligation to my original plan, one endorsed and practiced by my professors and graduate school peers, I applied to a few other jobs that would afford more time for research, a lighter teaching load, more prestige, and more pay than did this "first job." I believe I got one interview, but had so little to show for myself over the course of my first few years because I had only squeezed in enough time to finish my dissertation rather than publish or write more grants, that the verdict was pretty much in. Besides, I had decided that I wanted to stay, even if my conference badge now identified me as being "no one"—from, what is it, a military fort?—rather than "someone" from the top-ten-ranked University of Illinois anthropology powerhouse.

My experiences during the early years at Fort Lewis are not easily generalizable. The overriding common fact of life to which most of us at small colleges have had to adapt is that unlike our graduate school professors, we rarely have had a workload whereby we teach two or sometimes just one course per term so that we can focus on our research and professional lecturing; this, in fact, I expected. But some other things surprised me. First, I had always imagined a college job to be one where the faculty got together often to discuss each other's research and in general enjoy a life of the mind. This was a utopian ideal, as I found faculty members too busy and usually unwilling to talk about much of anything but the disappointments that consumed them and ways that I, as a new faculty member, might be enlisted to their particular cause.

Second, most faculty members—including all but one in my own department—were uninterested in and even seemed threatened by new colleagues' potential to undermine the grip of what many of us came to call the Old Fort culture of the institution, which had only recently been turned into a four-year college after being for many years a two-year institution and, before that, an Indian boarding school (and before that, an actual fort). Many faculty members had come to the college after a career in K through 12 schools, they often did not have a PhD, and they published little to nothing. With no faculty lounge, a Friday faculty assembly that eventually got axed, almost no money for team teaching (although I was thankfully able to do it twice), and precious few organized faculty exchanges, we could only get to know one another through committee and other largely bureaucratic activities.

Many things have changed for the better over the past three decades, as Fort Lewis College has tightened its admission standards, brought faculty salaries in line with those of national peers, incorporated an impressive amount of community-based learning throughout its curriculum, engaged students much more directly in faculty research, and received various infusions of federal grant funding, thanks to the persistence of the college grant writer and a few dedicated faculty members. Still, problems persist.

Many faculty members are inexplicably opposed to presenting their research on campus or on the college Web page, and there is relatively low attendance of faculty at colleagues' public lectures, music recitals, and art shows. Some professors hunker down into departmental bunkers, suspicious of each other and/or the administration, or just plain worn out. And despite the college's dedication to providing a humane, intellectual, and thoughtful context for understanding diverse ways of doing and being in the world, there has been a sense of helplessness over some persistent acts of hate expressed, for instance, in ugly graffiti and the literal torching of an Eritrean-born professor's office. Much of the hate speech has been aimed at gay and lesbian faculty members, who no longer fully trust in the safety of their workplace. While the college community, led by the president, has responded fairly quickly and energetically to these as yet unexplained and unidentified acts of aggression, a residue of fear, anger, and consternation has led many other people to mull everything over in silence, wondering if we can truly be the kind of model for tolerance and civility to which we aspire at this "campus in the sky," built on land many recognize as being on loan from Native Americans.

Although I am disturbed by the various ways we on campus can't always seem to get it together, I never fail to be cheered by the ways my colleagues address what ails us through lectures and discussions in the classroom, teach-in activities on campus, and encouragement for students to perform internships and other service at one of the many social justice agencies located in town or in one of the nearby Native American reservations. In some ways, by working on the periphery, my colleagues and I have had much freedom to design courses that address current concerns and to get them on the books quickly. Faculty members at major research universities can also have such freedom, but when they only teach two to three courses per year, the math can work against their ability to offer as many courses as they or their students might like.

One of the greatest challenges posed to me and to others who teach at COPLAC schools is how to span the classroom differences of student preparation, cultural background, social class, and widely divergent levels of basic skills without sending lectures and assignments to a bland middle ground. Because of its location, Fort Lewis College attracts many out-of-state students as well as those from the Denver suburbs who come here to study when they had already been accepted by much more prestigious schools. A central part of my job is finding ways to keep them on their toes while encouraging first-generation college students whose class and cultural backgrounds have not given them the same high quality academic grounding. One way to do this is by attending conferences where I make connections with faculty members at other universities. This kind of outreach has been indispensable, not only for the obvious reasons related to maintaining my scholarship, but also for the connections that are essential to my students' success.

When a Native Alaskan student, for example, came to my office, asking if I knew of any paid internships at museums, I could say, "Why, yes," thanks to the information I received from a former Illinois office-mate who is now a professor and curator at the University of Pennsylvania, about a National Science Foundation–funded program. The student applied for and received one of the NSF positions at the Penn's Museum of Archaeology and Anthropology, which led first to a job with her tribe in Alaska and a subsequent acceptance into the University of Pennsylvania's PhD anthropology program. I was in the room at the American Anthropological Association meetings when she gave a talk on her dissertation project on the ethics and biopolitics of taking blood and human tissue samples from Native peoples. This kind of work, which draws creatively on the Native American Graves Protection and Repatriation Act (NAGPRA) process, is on the cutting edge of communities' attempts to achieve justice by working both inside and outside the arena of federal law.

I have dozens of rich stories like this I could tell that demonstrate through individual inter-biographies the fruits that have resulted at the intersection of my job, my broader profession, and my sense of creativity and freedom that come from being tenured at a liberal arts school located on the periphery. My satisfaction from working at Fort Lewis College also stems from my having chosen a career in anthropology that, while not typically identified as one that leads directly to a specific job in the way a major in accountancy does, has opened many unanticipated doors for students and has kept me free of feeling burned out or bored.

Stacks of letters and strings of electronic messages received over three decades from former students indicate that they did not leave Fort Lewis College feeling bored either, and that they were able to find good jobs by employing their anthropology degrees in creative ways. One graduate is the Fulbright program advisor in Cyprus; another is a medical anthropologist for the U.S. Department of Veterans Affairs. Others work in cultural and environmental resource management. One of my former students, for example, is now regional coordinator of the Alaska Nanuuq Commission, which focuses on conserving a polar bear–centered arctic ecosystem.[7] But a rich college education in any field should bring satisfaction when done well, even, or especially, when information that is not directly applied to a job at a particular time and place rattles around in your brain, niggling at the obvious, until it is drawn forth to address some personal, intellectual, pragmatic, or visionary problem.

Interdisciplinary Liberal Arts Work at Fort Lewis College

Despite the challenges and frustrations, I have remained (usually) happily tethered to my job and willing to keep juggling several balls for many reasons, the first of which is my fascination with the ways the historical and cultural elements making up the place are reflected in the very diverse student body. Connected to this are the ways students, faculty, and staff have found creative ways to address human and environmental justice issues through various research and curricular projects that have become necessarily intertwined over the past three decades.

Participation in a variety of innovative, interdisciplinary programs where I could apply my anthropological training has been one of the highlights of my career at Fort Lewis College. One of them, the Human Heritage Program, allowed me to work with faculty and administrators from diverse disciplines on a common project designed to engage freshman students in a learning community. It brought rewards that went far beyond the moment. Perhaps most unexpected was that the experience allowed me to bring the glorious diversity of anthropology—which I have always considered the quintessential liberal art because of the ways it spans and integrates the natural and human sciences and humanities—into the consciousness of faculty, administrators, and students. The workshops, bull sessions, and co-teaching experiences that were part of the program were excellent opportunities to get to know colleagues and their disciplines, training, and scholarship.

The Human Heritage Program was designed initially to be a requirement for all freshmen, although this never transpired. Its goal was to introduce students to the grand trajectory of global history within a format that would feel more like a senior capstone than an ordinary freshman-level course, and as a result build confidence, intellectual curiosity, and skills. The idea for the course had come from a visionary dean of the School of Arts and Sciences who had obtained a major National Endowment for the Humanities (NEH) grant to make it a reality. The course required students to read original works, write profusely and in diverse formats, and study in a seminar-style format designed neither to patronize them nor to turn them off intellectually. I believe I put more energy and preparation into these courses than I did for any others, as I had to get up to speed on areas about which I previously only had a rudimentary grasp, such as ancient Greek theater, the American Revolution, the history of Western science, Mayan cosmology, and Chinese philosophy. In the process, I learned how to teach anthropology better, as these experiences helped me situate all university knowledge, including anthropology, within a much deeper and interconnected historical context. I also learned how to incorporate extra-academic but deeply intellectual and spiritual knowledge and experiences, to which I was introduced by Native American students, into my Southwest, gender studies, anthropology, and composition courses.

These rich initiatives ended when the NEH grant expired. But the courses were already struggling for internal reasons, because no clear rewards had been established for professors dedicated to working on this integrated liberal arts experience. Junior faculty members were afraid, not without reason, that their departmental seniors would not only ignore their participation in something outside the major, but also even punish them for it. Other professors were either uninterested in stepping outside their disciplinarily defined comfort zones, dismissive and disparaging of those who did, or outright disrespectful and hostile to the administration and faculty involved. The course sequence was increasingly staffed by adjunct faculty members seeking to do something other than work in the composition stable. What emerged from the conflict was the realization that the college was not structured in a manner that would effectively support a liberal arts mission based on interdisciplinarity that was not departmental.

Still, many faculty members refused to give up the ghost. After the college received an admonition from the North Central accreditation body to change general education from an unmonitored grab bag of distributed courses, they tried in earnest to design and deliver a distinctive general education program that would span all four years of a degree program. The new thematic studies program required students to take disciplinary-based courses at the lower division level and then specially designed, interdisciplinary courses during their junior and senior years that immersed them in four interconnected themes: systems, culture, technology, and environment. Human Heritage offerings were incorporated as fulfilling lower division "systems" and "culture" requirements, but they diminished to the point where they eventually disappeared. Finally, when a new president summarily and inexplicably fired the dean who had been supportive of interdisciplinarity, Fort Lewis College, in the minds of many faculty members to this day, began a slide away from being a true liberal arts college.[8] It bears remembering that honest and dedicated academic administrators who can demonstrate their own ongoing engagement with scholarly production and pedagogy are just as important to institutional success as good professors.

Teacher-Scholar-Administrator

One way I have addressed the ontological impossibility of being three different people to do the teaching, scholarship, and service that my job demands (not to mention the need for a fourth self to carry out my personal life) is to find ways to combine all faces of Eve. For example, during the first of two terms I served as anthropology department chair it fell to me quite suddenly to get our college into compliance with the federal NAGPRA legislation. Because Fort Lewis College had received federal funding in the past, and because the Department of Anthropology and the Center of Southwest Studies was in possession of human remains, associated funerary objects, and other objects of sacred and quotidian Native American cultural patrimony, I had to convince the college to respond to the legislative mandate to consult with representatives of all twenty-six tribes that might be culturally affiliated with our inventory. To comply with the law, I co-wrote a grant with an archaeologist colleague to the National Park Service to finance the travel, per diem, and consultation fees for Native American tribal representatives.

The overall experience of hosting two separate, two-day sessions with Native American consultants (combined with previously coauthoring the NAGPRA cultural affiliation report for Mesa Verde National Park)[9] led to a flurry of writing and conference presentations, including the organization of a professional panel on the repatriation process that included two Fort Lewis College Navajo graduates. I eventually published two articles, a book chapter, several book reviews, and a monograph on repatriation that continues to be used in U.S., U.K., and Canadian courses, much of which was based on a case study of Fort Lewis College.[10] While I am perhaps more known for this work, ironically, than I am for the scholarship on Ecuador on which my dissertation was based,[11] I am convinced that my career would not have incorporated this new direction had I been working at any other place.

The story does not end there. Since teaching about the Andes in a college in Colorado to Native North American students had enriched what I was writing about human rights and cultural revitalization and gender experiences in both North and South America, I decided in 2003 to organize an American Anthropological Association session to which I invited scholars who had worked on both sides of the Rio Grande (or with migrants who had traveled on both sides). The purpose was to discuss the cross-fertilization of ideas and experiences across the Americas. The panel resulted in a work co-edited with the late Steven L. Rubenstein, *Border Crossings: Transnational Americanist Anthropology*. The final chapter of the book was written in counterpoint with Steve, who envisioned a piece that would give students a firsthand, comparative account of what the trail from undergraduate education to a career in academia was like. In a piece we came to call the "Lizard's Dream," evoking the eyes-wide-open American experience, we went back and forth comparing our very different life, educational, and research experiences that eventually converged as we became researchers working in Ecuador, professors of anthropology, scholars of repatriation and museums, and co-editors of a book about the role of crossing borders in producing symmetrical knowledge.

World in Changes

Although my career as a scholar-educator has been and continues to be very rewarding, I have observed and experienced some recent developments in higher education that deeply concern me, even though I am a person who throughout her life has embraced change in everything from music to social media to technology with much enthusiasm and even a sense of adventure. This attitude is due in part to my feminist convictions, which have kept me wary of celebrating tradition and culture in ways that cover up social arrangements of injustice and inequality. I therefore read with interest articles and books that discuss emerging generational cultures, technologies, and industrial models, especially as they apply to higher education.[12] For example, a recent article in the *Chronicle of Higher Education* describes the current interest in measuring teaching and learning using "competencies" rather than credit hours, in internships and externships, in massive open online courses (MOOCs), and other modalities.[13] These modes are not unfamiliar to me, and have even been incorporated into my teaching both in the United States and in Ecuador. But they are increasingly being defined within and in relation to an "already always happening" world that is threatening to do away not only with academic tenure (which is enjoyed by less than 25 percent of the total professoriate today),[14] but also with face-to-face flows of knowledge and experience that loop dialectically in unpredictably rich ways from professor to student.

The fear of tenure's disappearing is related to more than anxiety about losing my job if I do not please administrators. It has to do with the necessity of teaching students not only about subject matters and skills, but also about the deeply human rewards of work itself. Whether one views this in Marxist or evolutionary psychological terms, it is certain that the labor we do in the world makes us human, gives us purpose, and allows us to help others find their own purpose. If the terms of that labor are unsatisfactory, partially realized, truncated, or under-remunerated, we and those to whom we connect suffer. This is why getting laid off, not finding work at all, not working at something satisfactory, or having a once-satisfactory job change drastically has such deep psychological and sociological consequences.

I could respond to these changes as my dad did when he took early retirement in the 1980s from his position as a high school athletic director. His job was so transformed by federal and state demands that he felt like an undervalued puppet of a system that had once given him a sense of purpose and self-esteem, but now seemed to ignore him completely. He felt as if everything he had done over the course of his career was delegitimized and worse, completely forgotten. I sometimes also feel like retiring, not only to escape the indignities of being viewed as the "old guard" and to explore teaching and writing in new contexts, but also to help out a money-strapped system that would perhaps like to absorb my salary by cutting my budget line.[15] I have, however, recently decided that I will continue to be a professor as long as it makes sense for me and for Fort Lewis College. I have also realized that tenure not only gives me freedom of speech, but also the responsibility to speak out.

So in bringing this essay to a close I must offer a caveat: If one goal of this book is to "show new and potential faculty what kind of careers are possible at places they haven't necessarily imagined for themselves," these new professors must realize that the differences in experience I describe are not merely those between the research-based institution where I received my PhD and the small undergraduate college where I came to work, but are also a result of cultural and economic changes affecting higher education in general. There are good reasons—essential ones—to protect and preserve liberal arts colleges,[16] but I suggest we do so by looking at the bigger picture in which all education, from pre-kindergarten to post-doctoral study, is contextualized.

Among the many factors adumbrated by Aronowitz that have changed my job have been poor and often confusing funding from the State of Colorado, institutional uncertainty regarding our purported liberal arts mission; the specter of the bottom line ("butts in seats") driving away innovative curricula and attracting quick fixes that take the college budget away from faculty lines and into centers linked to Student Affairs; faculty diffidence regarding their institution and their colleagues' programs of research; standards for promotion, tenure, and merit that are inconsistently applied; and an overall inability until somewhat recently to deal with deep-seated bullying, sexism, and old-boy-ism.[17]

Another problem is constant academic administrative turnover, which more often than not has gutted programs to which thousands of faculty work hours were donated and for which many wheels were reinvented. To return for a moment to the factors that brought an end to the Human Heritage and Thematic Studies Programs, I cannot fully describe how demoralizing it was to me and many others to have worked under a faculty- and curriculum-oriented administrator only to have the rug pulled out by new people rotating in who didn't know who we were or what we had done. During my tenure at Fort Lewis College, I have worked with no fewer than nine different presidents and eight deans.[18]

Other problems fester and divide on campus. Culture wars regarding the purpose of a liberal arts education rage alongside "labor wars," whereby the lab scientists insist they work much harder than their colleagues in arts, humanities, business, and social science. Business professors insist that their higher salaries are justified because of market factors. Some older faculty members resent those who are junior because of the administration's relatively new retention-oriented policy of giving new faculty members course release time (sometimes for multiple years), extra start-up funding for research, and freedom from college service work until they approach tenure. While this treatment of junior faculty is laudable, it has ironically contributed to some serious ship-jumping by excellent faculty members who have gone elsewhere, often after receiving outstanding teaching and featured scholar recognitions.[19] Some tenured faculty members have responded by cutting back all but absolutely necessary teaching responsibilities, which causes a yawning rift in the upper ranks as the jobs they vacate have to be taken up by the handful of full professors who still maintain a robust teaching-service-scholarship profile.

In general, present panics are rarely addressed with historical knowledge. This is because very little institutional history was written down, faculty members and administrators who knew it by heart have left or died, and those for whom historical amnesia is an advantage (oftentimes the bullies, but mostly those in a hurry) declare that mention of the past is irrelevant. To get some historical sense of my own in order to write this essay, I engaged in long conversations (and recalled previous conversations over the years) with a variety of colleagues, students, and a few administrators to get their take on what has gone wrong and what has yet to be done.[20]

As Aronowitz noted in 1998, the deeper meaning of tenure is gone. Most of the faculty know neither why it was created nor what they stand to lose if it disappears.[21] What may be the most daunting change to our workplace culture are the transformations exhibited by students entering college, many of whom are worse prepared than ever to read, analyze, identify, create, or sustain an argument. Many students also believe with unrecognized cynicism that, while it is crucial to possess a diploma to get decent pay in a decent job, the work it took to earn the diploma should be based on payments of time and money and not on the quality of the work performed. Others sincerely want to change their world for the better, but harbor the illusion that effective action cannot wait for informed and deep thinking. These changes relate not only to the advent of quick-response social media forms of communication that require quick assessment of sound bites and keyboard texting, but more profoundly to anxieties generated by a global recession, a shrinking middle class, labor uncertainty, and a series of catastrophic events beginning with the 9/11 attacks. These phenomena have resulted, for many, in a disconnection "from a sense of history and purpose" that creates instead an information-saturated ethos of radical presentism; an obsession with the "zombie apocalypse"; a misunderstanding of the differences between "voluntourism," poverty tourism, and critical social development work; and an impatience with the kind of measured research and reflection needed to write a research paper, disengage from social media, and plan for the future.[22]

In Support of Socioculturally and Historically Grounded Hope

I conclude by returning to the story that opened this essay. As I think about suggestions that higher education can be delivered online, purchased from competitive providers, or otherwise removed completely from a place called the classroom, I reflect on the richest courses I teach, ones that always produce unpredictable responses. In many respects, a course like Native American Gender Issues could be taught online; it is well organized and there are many readings and videos in which students must immerse themselves, providing feedback to me and to each other via online discussion groups. But I am certain that I would never have gotten to know my teaching assistant as I did, or had her reveal to the class, in a personal mapping session devised by my previous Tlingit/Athabaskan teaching assistant, what it felt like to look down from the plane onto Afghanistan terrain that looked like her Arizona reservation and contemplate the consequences of doing harm to its residents. This is something she had never spoken out loud, and likely never would have without weeks of face-to-face interaction with other students in a classroom context she had come to trust. We might be communicating now by means of e-mails and Facebook posts, but these would not be infused with the mutual trust and respect that they have had we not shared profound experiences in the classroom.

I hope that future educators resist the global economy–fueled, utilitarian reduction of higher education that aligns curriculum with the job market, transforms the humanities and social sciences into service for businesses, and creates what Aronowitz called an "industrial atmosphere" for the liberal arts. I hope they love their multifaceted, kaleidoscopic jobs as much as I have and fight to retain sabbatical leaves, faculty-controlled curricula, and the freedom of expression embodied in tenure. I hope they realize that the professoriate is in danger and needs to be protected, even as it encounters and embraces aspects of MOOCs, the "ministry" of service learning, and the fog of best-practice rhetoric. Most importantly, today's professoriate needs to learn as much as it can about a conservative American climate that pays lip service to the importance of education as it refuses to publicly fund it. If we don't, we'll have no power to change a culture that sees no connection between education and civic democratic life. Both my extraordinary Native American teaching assistants and many other students and faculty know firsthand the devastation that happens when culture and history are ignored in the name of quick, and sometimes irrevocably and devastatingly final, solutions.

I have been privileged to teach at an interesting, state-funded, liberal-arts-with-benefits college (in other words, it offers opportunities to learn plenty of skills and strategies to approach a world of jobs and civic engagement after graduation) located on a beautiful mesa rising above the Animas River of southwestern Colorado. What holds the educational mission together is a dedication to freedom that is bound up in the notion of the liberal arts—a knowledge magisterium that explores liberally, that is, freely, with intellectual curiosity and the very human drive to learn to do new things with our minds, spirits, and bodies—as well as in the practice of academic tenure, which gives instructors the freedom to express their convictions and, more importantly, to train their students how to arrive at well-considered convictions and to express them publicly.

These freedoms, however, are at risk. Just as the natural and social environments of southwestern Colorado have changed since I began my job (with gentrification, resource extraction, and worsening drought conditions posing significant threats to diverse human livelihoods and natural systems), so has the college environment changed, with internal contradictions and an increasingly hostile civic attitude toward education in general, and taxpayer-funded education in particular, looming large. Quality education filled with art, music, science, language learning, literature, and philosophy seems increasingly to be available only to those who have the wherewithal to pay for it. Publicly funded education from preschool onward confronts an odd combination of demands for (expensive) assessment, oversight, testing, and report writing at the same time as funds are pulled that create double and often triple duty for teachers and professors. The morality of volunteerism also provides an unexpected challenge, as demands to provide service opportunities for students often compete with intellectual and scholarly dedication. A democracy should have a high-quality education available to everyone, which is why publicly funded colleges must continue to exist, staffed by dedicated educators who are ensured the freedom to think, write, and profess their knowledge and skills to others.

Works Cited

Acevedo, Alma. "Gray Matters." *Chronicle of Higher Education*, March 18, 2012. http://chronicle.com/article/Gray-Matters/131228/?sid=at&utm_medium=en.

Aronowitz, Stanley. "The Last Good Job in America." In *Chalk Lines: The Politics of Work in the Managed University*, edited by Randy Martin, 202–21. Durham, NC: Duke University Press, 1998.

Cronon, William. "'Only Connect . . .': The Goals of a Liberal Education." *The American Scholar* 67, no. 4. (Autumn 1998): 73–80.

Dare, Byron. "Assessment as Ideology: Reagan's Revenge." *Newsletter of FOSAP* 7, no. 1 (Spring 1998): 19–25.

Edmundson, Mark. "The Trouble with Online Education." *New York Times*, July 20, 2012, A19.

Ehrenberg, Ronald. *What's Happening to Public Higher Education? The Shifting Financial Burden*. Baltimore: Johns Hopkins University Press, 2007.

Field, Kelly. "Colleges Ask Government to Clarify Rules for Credit Based on Competency." *Chronicle of Higher Education*, February 13, 2013, A6.

Fine, Kathleen Sue. *Cotocollao: Ideología, Historia, y Acción en un barrio de Quito*. Quito: Abya-Yala Press, 1991.

Fine-Dare, Kathleen S. *Grave Injustice: The American Indian Repatriation Movement and NAGPRA*. Lincoln: University of Nebraska Press, 2002.

———. "Truth, Postmodernism, and the Liberal Arts." Commencement Address, Fort Lewis College, Durango, CO, December 16, 1995.

———, and W. James Judge. "Anthropological Frameworks for Establishing Cultural Affiliation, Final Report: A Document to Accompany the Inventory of Native American Human Remains and Associated Funerary Objects in the Possession or Control of Mesa Verde National Park." Prepared for Mesa Verde National Park and Research Management Division in Partial Fulfillment of Contract #MEVE-R-94-0436, 1995.

Fischman, Josh. "Exploding the Myth of the Aging, Unproductive Professor." *Chronicle of Higher Education*, March 18, 2012. http://chronicle.com/article/Exploding-the-Myth-of-the/131225/?sid=at&utm_source=at&utm_medium=en.

Ginsberg, Benjamin. *The Fall of the Faculty: The Rise of the All-Administrative University and Why It Matters*. New York: Oxford University Press, 2011.

Harkin, Michael E. "Crisis in Higher Ed, Part 1." *Anthropology News* 54, no. 5 (March/April 2013): 3–4.

Honan, William H. "Small Liberal Arts Colleges Facing Questions on Focus." *New York Times*, March 10, 1999, A16.

Johnsrud, Linda K., and Vicki J. Rosser. "Faculty Members' Morale and Their Intention to Leave." *Journal of Higher Education* 73, no. 4 (July/August 2002): 518–42.

June, Audrey Williams. "Aging Professors Create a Faculty Bottleneck: At Some Universities, 1 in 3 Academics Are Now 60 or Older." *Chronicle of Higher Education*, March 2012. http://chronicle.com/article/Professors-Are-Graying-and/131226/?sid=at&utm_source=at&utm_medium=en.

Kean, Patricia. "Building a Better Beowulf: The New Assault on the Liberal Arts." *Lingua Franca* 3, no. 4 (May/June 1993): 22–28.

Martin, Randy. *Under New Management: Universities, Administrative Labor, and the Professional Turn*. Philadelphia: Temple University Press, 2011.

Newfield, Christopher. *Unmaking the Public University: The Forty-Year Assault on the Middle Class*. Cambridge, MA: Harvard University Press, 2011.

Rubenstein, Steven L., and Kathleen S. Fine-Dare. "The Lizard's Dream." In *Border Crossings: Transnational Americanist Anthropology*, edited by Kathleen S. Fine-Dare and Steven L. Rubenstein, 289–330. Nebraska: University of Nebraska Press, 2009.

Rushkoff, Douglas. *Present Shock: When Everything Happens Now*. New York: Current, 2013.

Schneider, Carol Geary, and Robert Shoenberg. "Habits Hard to Break: How Persistent Features of Campus Life Frustrate Curricular Reform." *Change* 31, no. 2 (1999): 30–35.

Sutton, Robert I. *The No Asshole Rule: Building a Civilized Workplace and Surviving One That Isn't*. New York: Warner Business Books, 2007.

Tuchman, Gaye. *Wannabe U: Inside the Corporate University*. Chicago: University of Chicago Press, 2011.

Wilson, Robin. "The New Faculty Minority: Tenured Professors Fight to Retain Control as Their Numbers Shrink." *Chronicle of Higher Education*, March 22, 2013, A25–26.

Notes

1. "Now there are some who view my teaching and writing as a luxury that should be ended at the earliest possible convenience and, indeed, are waiting for me to retire or leave by any other possible circumstance. . . . According to some . . . I have too many privileges. I offer another perspective on this position. I am a radical because I believe that people work too hard for too little and that their work is more like labor, not under their control. The situation of the few holding the last good job should be universalized, not suppressed"; Aronowitz, "Last Good Job in America," 210.

2. Ibid., 220–21.

3. http://collegerealitycheck.com.

4. http://collegeapps.about.com/od/collegeprofiles/p/fort-lewis-college.htm. The website CollegeData.com characterizes Fort Lewis College as having "moderately difficult" entrance requirements: More than 75 percent of freshmen were in the top 50 percent of their high school class and scored over 1010 on the SAT I or over 18 on the ACT; about 85 percent or fewer of all applicants accepted. Cappex.com reported that in 2012 enrollment was 3,853 and that in-state tuition was $4,048 with a 71 percent acceptance rate.

5. A bill has been introduced in Congress to provide federal funding for the tuition waiver, which will relieve the State of Colorado from this obligation. See http://durango-herald.com/article/20130427/NEWS01/130429583/0/SEARCH/Lawmakers-reintroduce-tuition-waiver-measure.

6. Six of us were hired ABD that year. Although the "rules" stated that the title of assistant professor could only be conferred upon those who had their PhDs in hand, the three of the six who were male were hired as assistant professors while the three of us who were female came in as "instructor." It took many years for the salary differential to be erased through equity adjustments and merit pay raises.

7. http://thealaskananuuqcommission.org/staff.html.

8. Fine-Dare, "Truth, Postmodernism, and the Liberal Arts."

9. Fine-Dare and Judge, "Anthropological Frameworks for Establishing Cultural Affiliation, Final Report."

10. See Fine-Dare, *Grave Injustice.*

11. For instance, Fine, *Cotocollao.*

12. One recent and very interesting book that, while somewhat flawed, nonetheless has much to say of relevance in understanding the world of our students, is Douglas Rushkoff's, *Present Shock: When Everything Happens Now.*

13. See Field, "Colleges Ask Government to Clarify Rules for Credit Based on Competency"; and Edmundson, "The Trouble with Online Education."

14. Wilson, "The New Faculty Minority."

15. See Acevedo, "Gray Matters"; Fischman, "Exploding the Myth of the Aging, Unproductive Professor"; and June, "Aging Professors Create a Faculty Bottleneck."

16. See Cronon, "'Only Connect . . .'"; Ehrenberg, *What's Happening to Public Higher Education?*; Harkin, "Crisis in Higher Ed, Part 1"; Honan, "Small Liberal Arts Colleges Facing Questions on Focus"; Kean, "Building a Better Beowulf"; and Schneider and Shoenberg, "Habits Hard to Break."

17. See Sutton, *The No Asshole Rule,* for an excellent treatment of the ever growing but increasingly subtle phenomenon of bullying and harassment in the workplace.

18. Tuchman, *Wannabe U,* 78. See also Martin, *Under New Management*; and Newfield, *Unmaking the Public University.*

19. See Johnsrud and Rosser, "Faculty Members' Morale and Their Intention to Leave."

20. I must first thank some of my former students who were particularly important as I contemplated the relationship of teaching to living: Jenny Brown, Kelli Ford Brush, Merlyna Crank, Bryanna Durkee, Stacy Falk, Kate Freeman, Royce Freeman, Teahonna James, Chris Kyle, Samantha Solimeo, and Jon Wolseth. I am grateful to the following Fort Lewis College colleagues (current and former) for helping me conceptualize what sorts of issues might be addressed in this paper: Barbara Burton, Shere Byrd, Beverly Chew, Philip Duke, Larry Hartsfield, Kelly Jenks, Marcy Jung, Page Lindsey, Michael Martin, Pete McCormick, Susan Moss, Chuck Riggs, Faron Scott, Amy Sellin, Karen Spear, Jennifer Stollman, Gene Taylor, and Yohannes Woldemariam. I am particularly grateful to Rebecca Austin and Byron Dare for providing detailed commentary on an early draft of this paper that helped me improve it significantly. Byron Dare's article "Assessment as Ideology" has informed much of my understanding of the negative role Reaganomics has had on higher education from the late twentieth century forward. Finally, excellent comments received from members of the 2013 COPLAC Faculty Institute held June 6–9, 2013, at the University of North Carolina Asheville campus were essential to my being able to make serious and meaningful revisions to this piece. I am particularly grateful to Julia DeLancey and Roger Epp for the careful and very helpful critiques and edits they gave to this essay. Finally, my sincere thanks go to Carol Smith and other members of the Dean's Council of Fort Lewis College for nominating me to COPLAC for this project, and to my dean, Maureen Brandon, whose office financed my trip to Asheville.

21. Aronowitz, "Last Good Job in America," 208; Ginsberg, *Fall of the Faculty,* 131–48.

22. Rushkoff, *Present Shock,* 17–18, 47.

14

The Liberal Arts
Leave the Ivory Tower
and Enter the Trenches

Robin Bates
English, St. Mary's College of Maryland

Public liberal arts colleges seek to address, in their own small way, the threat to democracy posed by the widening income disparity between the wealthiest Americans and everyone else. This gap, which has been growing steadily since the 1980s, has impacted education in addition to other areas of life. In a June 16, 2013, column in the *New York Times*, Rebecca Strauss, associate director of publications of the Renewing America initiative at the Council on Foreign Relations, wrote that America is increasingly becoming a country of two educational systems.

> The truth is that there are two very different education stories in America. The children of the wealthiest 10 percent or so do receive some of the best education in the world, and the quality keeps getting better. For most everyone else, this is not the case. America's average standing in global education rankings has tumbled not because everyone is falling, but because of the country's deep, still-widening achievement gap between socioeconomic groups.[1]

Strauss notes that the distinction manifests itself at all levels of education. At the college level, it can be seen as the difference between, on the one hand, highly selective private colleges and elite public universities and, on the other, community colleges and lower-tier public universities. Strauss reports that per-pupil spending at the former has been increasing at twice the rate of the latter so that the selective-college advantage is now six times larger than it was in the late 1960s. Students from families in the upper quintile of income level, meanwhile, are eight times more likely to enroll in highly selective colleges than are students in the bottom quintile. The education they receive ensures them an enviable rate of success.

> Those who get in are doing better than ever. The best colleges are see-
> ing their dropout rates fall to near-zero levels, especially for women.
> The education they offer is generally better than what students get
> at less selective schools, too. One very revealing fact is that even for
> equally qualified students, academic outcomes at selective colleges are
> better across the board and their graduates earn more and are more
> likely to progress toward an advanced degree.[2]

Public liberal arts colleges seek to bridge the divide by offering an education that, while featuring a curriculum similar to that at the best colleges, is available to students who cannot gain admission into or afford those schools. With their public mission, public liberal arts colleges target lower-income students who have the potential to succeed, even if they don't have the requisite test scores or high school credentials. These students receive, at state prices, the liberal arts education that will always be expensive because its delivery requires small seminars, individualized instruction, a labor-intensive emphasis on writing, reading, research, oral presentation, and critical thinking, and a small and nurturing residential campus experience that fosters student leadership skills.

In addition to negotiating a difficult financial terrain, public liberal arts colleges encounter another challenge not faced by their private peers: they have to persuade lower-income students of the value of a liberal arts education. Since students even at public colleges face significant debt loads upon graduation, they want assurance that majoring in music or philosophy will still land them a job. Lower-middle-class parents may regard college education as a ticket to the American dream, but they require an explanation as to how the liberal arts will get them there—a concern less likely to trouble upper-class parents, who are confident that field of study is not as important as college ranking. Public colleges, therefore, cannot assume that a liberal arts education speaks for itself. They cannot simply talk about how it deepens the soul or develops the whole person. They must make a practical case for it.

Nor is it only students and their parents who need convincing. State legislators can prove skeptical, sounding like the utilitarian Mr. Gradgrind from Charles Dickens's *Hard Times* as they insist on vocational payoffs for the money they allocate. Little wonder then that "public liberal arts college" sounds to some like an oxymoron.

In this essay I claim that public liberal arts colleges make one of their biggest contributions to liberal education when they are forced to explain its functional value. By having to articulate connections between the disciplines and the "real world," these colleges open up new research avenues and new teaching possibilities. What appears to be a problem, in other words, becomes a strength. For illustration, I focus primarily on my own teaching and scholarship as an English professor at St. Mary's College of Maryland, but I touch on other examples of outreach as well.

First, a word on St. Mary's, which has a history of inclusiveness going all the way back to the state's colonial roots. English Catholic gentry settled St. Mary's City at a fractious time—religious tensions were on the rise in 1634 England—and to ensure peace with the English Protestant immigrants and indentured servants that would quickly outnumber them, the Catholic leaders instituted an Act of Tolerance. This legal gesture proved effective for several decades and would later serve as the model for the First Amendment in America's Bill of Rights.

In 1840 Maryland remembered her colonial Act of Tolerance and honored it by establishing a "monument school to the people." St. Mary's Seminary, a nondenominational women's high school, was designed to celebrate the values of inclusiveness, tolerance, and affordability. These values have been woven into the school's fabric ever since as St. Mary's became Maryland's first junior college in 1927 and a four-year residential liberal arts college in 1964. The state legislature designated it as Maryland's public honors college in 1992. St. Mary's is strictly undergraduate with the exception of a master of arts in teaching program. Most of its two thousand students live on campus.

Looking back at my own history, I can see why the school resonated with me when I interviewed for a job in 1981. I grew up in segregated Tennessee and therefore saw up close the corrosive influence of exclusion. In 1961, when I was eleven, I was the oldest child plaintiff in a landmark civil rights case where four white families and four black families joined together to sue the Franklin County Board of Education for failing to comply with the Supreme Court's *Brown v. Board of Education* ruling. In the case we argued that the other children and I were being denied our right to attend integrated schools.

I remember during this time visiting the two-room African American school in Sewanee to donate books designed to instill black pride in the students, such as biographies of George Washington Carver and Harriet Tubman. I also became vaguely aware of how alien the *Dick and Jane* books appeared to African American children.

When I reached college age, I headed north to escape the ugliness of racism. Carleton College in Northfield, Minnesota, was doing its best to be inclusive, bringing in African American students from inner-city Chicago and a few farm kids from the rural Midwest, including the woman I would later marry. But private liberal arts schools, to pay the bills, can serve only so many lower-income students. Many of us sensed the large divide between the smattering of first-generation college students and the preponderance of sons and daughters of professionals for whom attending college was no more momentous than attending high school.

There was also a second divide I experienced, this one academic. Although I loved literature, English at that time was not taught in a way that acknowledged deep social divisions or, for that matter, any history at all. Although I had been caught up in the civil rights movement as a child and I was now threatened with the Vietnam draft once I graduated, formalist criticism predominated in English departments. Literature was presented as something that transcended history. If college was an ivory tower, literary studies was a tower within that tower.

Almost against my will, I was driven to major in history, which lacked the poetry I hungered for but at least spoke to my social justice concerns. I was especially taken with the writing of Antonio Gramsci, the Italian Marxist who in the 1930s argued that isolated theory and untutored praxis could be joined and made effective through the figure of the educated workingman, whom Gramsci referred to as the organic intellectual.[3] Inspired by Gramsci and also by social philosophers Herbert Marcuse and Walter Benjamin from the Frankfurt School, who examined the relationship between culture and history, I looked for ways to connect my academic work with my desire for justice. I would recall Gramsci's formulation later when I started teaching first-generation college students at St. Mary's.

I switched to English in graduate school, and although formalism still held sway, I discovered the reception theory of Hans Robert Jauss, which gave me a framework for analyzing interactions between readers and literary works. Suddenly I had a way of charting literature's impact on history. I was especially drawn to the notion that literature can change our "horizon of expectations," causing reality itself—or what we experience as reality—to change.[4] Literature, I came to understand, need no longer be viewed as isolated, but could be seen as integrally bound up with the world.

This approach proved to be invaluable at St. Mary's because many of my students didn't hold literature in the high regard that I did. A fair number had little prior experience either with literature or the liberal arts and regarded them as peripheral to their lives. These students included farm kids from southern Maryland and Maryland's Eastern Shore and students of color from inner-city Baltimore and Washington. Most were vocationally oriented and, in my early days there, they saw St. Mary's as a safe small school that one attended before transferring to pre-professional programs at the University of Maryland. To address their concerns and persuade them to stay, I had to listen closely and see literature through their eyes. Reception theory proved very useful.

In the thirty-two years that I have been teaching at St. Mary's, I have encountered hundreds of what I call student-reading stories. Because our classes are small—capped at twenty-two for surveys, sixteen for upper-level classes, and twelve for senior seminars—I have been able to scrutinize student responses to the works that I assign and figure out how the students arrive at their interpretations. Even off-the-wall student analysis contains kernels of insight, which can be developed once one knows the student's story and how he or she arrived there. With my wealth of experience I can now reach practically any student, however poorly prepared or alienated he or she is. In return, the students, through their wide-ranging responses, have revealed that literature illuminates many more dimensions of life than I ever could have imagined. I have used student insights to design courses, conduct seminar discussions, coach individuals, and develop my own scholarship.

Out of these many reading stories, I recount one by an exceptional student who wrote her two-semester senior project on "Reading in Jane Austen." Reading plays a significant thematic role in four of Austen's six major novels—*Northanger Abbey, Sense and Sensibility, Mansfield Park,* and *Persuasion*—and Errin was particularly interested in *Mansfield Park,* her favorite Austen work. I describe the project in detail because it captures how momentous a liberal arts experience within an intimate setting can be for a student.

I start with some background information. Errin was born two months prematurely and has a number of physical defects, including some general coordination and fine motor issues, and a paralyzed larynx that causes her to speak with a raspy voice that is hard to understand. As Errin explored Austen's novels, I came to understand why she was drawn to her topic. Ridiculed as a child for her birth defects, she retreated into a world of books. She therefore identified with the ways that some of Austen's characters, especially Catherine Morland in *Northanger Abbey*, find solace in reading.

Errin chose the topic for her senior project in part because she was facing a fresh anxiety: having found a home at St. Mary's, which excels at welcoming students who are different, she was worried more than most students about graduating. Would separation from this protected environment plunge her back into the harsh world she remembered from her earlier schooling? She therefore grappled with Catherine Morland's dependence on Gothic fiction and the heroine's need to move beyond it. As she developed her ideas, she began to describe reading in Austen's novels as a mixed blessing. While reading provides a refuge for Catherine—and also Marianne Dashwood in *Sense and Sensibility*, Fanny Price in *Mansfield Park*, and Captain Benwick in *Persuasion*—it can also be a trap. Eventually one has to find other resources than books for help on life's path. It took all of Errin's courage to arrive at this conclusion, and her resistance took the form of many false starts.

Yet despite having come so far, Errin's project still wasn't entirely jelling and we couldn't figure out why. She kept on talking about the importance of mentors and I, trying to keep an unwieldy project focused on the theme of reading, didn't understand how this other concern fit her thesis. The St. Mary's Project experience is an intense one, with weekly and sometimes biweekly meetings between student and mentor, and for a good part of the final six weeks we felt we were pounding our heads against a wall.

The light dawned about two weeks before the project was due. We realized that Errin wasn't only interested in the mixed blessing of reading but also in the mixed blessing of mentorship. The two are related as we see mentor figures teaching their pupils how to read wisely. *Mansfield Park* is a central work in this sense because the young Fanny is guided in her early reading by her older cousin Edmund Bertram, with whom she will later fall in love. When Fanny is torn from her home as a child, Edward functions as a surrogate father and helps shape her values.

Later, however, Edmund proves an unreliable guide. He becomes infatuated with the facile Mary Crawford, forgets his moral code, and agrees to perform in a scandalous drawing room play. Now it is shy and demure Fanny, left alone as the conscience of the family and facing fierce pressure from the Bertram siblings, who must apply the moral standards she has been taught. The student must stand strong, even though it means breaking with the teacher.

Errin, in other words, was grappling with moving beyond not only her books but also her mentors, especially her mother, who had fought to keep her out of special education when she was a child and who had always been her biggest supporter. A deep part of Errin's essay was facing up to the fact that she would soon be confronting life's challenges on her own. Although I don't recall Errin writing explicitly about her own journey in her senior project, nevertheless, as her mentor, I could see and appreciate what it required of her to take the next step. Austen can't entirely be given credit for the fact that Errin has gone on to become a successful librarian and is now doing well in law school. But at a time in her life when she was facing a daunting challenge, Errin found in literature a way to name her fears and imagine a way through them.

Of course, most student experiences in my literature classes are not this drawn out. Every year, however, I can point to smaller-scale versions of students tackling major issues. To cite some random examples, I have seen students wrestle with debilitating perfectionism through *Sir Gawain and the Green Knight*, with past partner abuse through Chaucer's *Wife of Bath's Tale*, with faith and doubt through Christopher Marlowe's *Doctor Faustus*, with gender identity confusion through Shakespeare's *Twelfth Night*, with the consequences of irresponsible behavior through Coleridge's *Rime of the Ancient Mariner*, and on and on.

The thousands of hours I have spent over the past thirty years listening to students and striving to convince them of literature's importance has in turn shaped my professional work. Although early in my career I wrote traditional articles for academic publications, in recent years I have begun directing my works toward a more general audience. For instance, I recently self-published a book entitled *How* Beowulf *Can Save America: An Epic Hero's Guide to Defeating the Politics of Rage* (2012), bringing it out quickly to coincide with the presidential election season. In it I argue that the deep anger that has torn apart American politics in recent years is not unlike the anger that confronted medieval Anglo-Saxon society and that we have our own versions of the trolls and the dragons that rampage through the poem.[5] Walter Benjamin has written that there are times when the present and the past align, providing "historical holes" that allow moments in the past to speak with particular urgency.[6] In my book I argue that the anxieties that the Anglo-Saxons experienced over unequal wealth distribution are not unlike present-day anxieties, with its talk of "makers vs. takers" and "the one percent." As I see it, it is no accident that a new translation of *Beowulf* made its way to the *New York Times* best-seller list in 2000 and that two *Beowulf* films have been made since then. We have our own jealous warriors and hoarding kings that we are called upon to heroically resist.

There are many in literary studies who would take exception to my approach. Certainly I can hear Stanley Fish, an occasional blogger for the *New York Times*, grumbling that I am trying to justify literature's existence on utilitarian grounds. In his column Fish has asserted that literary works "cannot be justified except in relation to the pleasure they give to those who enjoy them" and that the humanities "are their own good."[7] But just as liberal arts colleges have to take the pragmatic concerns of parents into account as they advocate for the liberal arts, so looking for a pragmatic dimension to literature opens up new insights. Indeed, it is the very tension between the pragmatic and the aesthetic-contemplative that defines both public liberal arts colleges and my writing.

I hasten to add that my own approach to literature is far from the only one that a public liberal arts environment has fostered. My departmental colleagues have found their own ways to convey the urgency of literature to their students and the general public. Our Shakespearean, for instance, works with a prison performing arts workshop that takes Shakespeare into prisons, dramatically lowering recidivism rates. Our contemporary Americanist, who regularly teaches courses in civil rights literature, published an anthology of civil rights poetry with Duke University Press and now travels around the state for the Maryland Humanities Council talking about the importance of that poetry in the battle against segregation. Our Mark Twain specialist fills our gym each year with humorists and writers (Peter Sagal, Larry Wilmore, David Rakoff, John Hodgman) who talk about the importance Mark Twain holds for them and who, in turn, feed my colleague's own understanding of Twain's role in shaping American society. (The same colleague also sponsors a Mark Twain humor-writing contest.) A former creative writing teacher, now retired, was so assiduous about taking poetry into the public schools that, partly in recognition of his efforts, he was named Maryland's poet laureate so that he could extend that effort around the state.

Nor is it only the English department that feels driven to find ways to share its ideas with the public. An art professor is having her students paint public murals around the county, biology faculty are working with state agencies and a local aquaculture company to develop and test new oyster setting methods, and an economist has been delving into archival records from the St. Mary's Historical Commission to figure out how tobacco functioned as currency in colonial Maryland. In one extended project that has resulted in a number of articles copublished with students and sent many students on to graduate school, a psychology professor has been working with families to study developmental differences between special needs children who have been adopted and those who have been raised by their birth parents.

To be sure, not every faculty member is interested in reaching out to the community, and there are many faculty at St. Mary's who focus only on traditional scholarship. This, of course, is entirely appropriate; there is always the danger that rigor will be lost when one begins directing one's efforts toward non-academic audiences or pursuing issues that do not have a history of academic inquiry. The advantage of such public ventures, on the other hand, is that they can breathe new life into disciplines that have become insular and moribund, as was the case with literary formalism in the 1960s. The tension between the academic and the experiential can be a dynamic one. Public liberal arts colleges, because of their unique positioning between the public and the academic, can function as hothouses for new approaches to academic study.

Working within such an environment gave me the confidence five years ago to lobby for a new community outreach requirement when the college was revising its core curriculum. The faculty proved receptive and we now require all students to have some experience outside a conventional classroom. The requirement is called Experiencing the Liberal Arts in the World (ELAW). It is designed to help students connect liberal arts education with practical problem solving. About half of the students fulfill the ELAW requirement by studying abroad. The other half either undertake internships coupled with academic projects or enroll in courses with a civic engagement component. Whichever option they take, the students must write a reflective essay exploring "possible connections between concepts, ideas, facts, or skills learned in class and those learned through experience." These essays describe experiences as various as spending a summer researching leeches, studying Buddhism in the Himalayas, taking notes for doctors in public hospitals, and setting up special learning projects for low-performing children in local schools. More often than not, the students describe their experiences as life changing.

The least developed ELAW option is the category of courses with a civic engagement component. While the educational studies department regularly requires students in its classes to assist in schools, other departments offer relatively few such courses. And yet, as the English department noted while proposing a Word in the World course, "Our purpose in teaching this class is to allow students to explore the rich connections possible between the study of literature or writing and the larger world in which they live; to put to rest the misconception that the life of the mind, and of books, is somehow opposed to and apart from the life we live, and the world we live it in."

To encourage other faculty to develop such courses, the college applied for and received an Andrew W. Mellon Foundation planning grant, which was followed up by a second implementation grant. Much of the money is intended to enable faculty to look for curricular opportunities to bridge the gap between the classroom and the broader world. Among the courses that have been funded are Spanish in the Community, where students help tutor Spanish-speaking children in the public schools, and a religious studies research colloquium in which students survey local community agencies and corporations (including the Navy base and local defense contractors) to determine the needs for workshops, seminars, and instructional material that can help people develop interreligious competency. Because the college is an active archaeological site, faculty are also developing a multidisciplinary course that involves students both in the methodology of the archeological analysis and in the relationships between museums, historical preservation agencies, and landowners affected by digs and excavations.

If the Mellon project proves successful, faculty will discover new ways to engage their students in course content. In addition to motivating students, the new classes may also open up new research areas for faculty, including joint research projects they can undertake with students. The courses will also give students ideas for possible careers or point the way to further schooling.

In addition to bridging gaps with the external community, faculty have also applied their scholarship within the college community. Philosopher Sybol Anderson, for example, has made practical connections between her writing on Hegel, especially on recognition,[8] and the college's minority population. She now heads a program critical to supporting them. The DeSousa-Brent Scholars Program is designed to support students from historically marginalized groups. The program's name is derived from two of the early seventeenth-century colonial settlers, the "molato" Mathias DeSousa, perhaps of African descent, and Margaret Brent, a landowner who agitated for the right to vote, which the 1648 General Assembly denied her because she was a woman. The program began as a summer bridge program with thirty students. In the spring of 2013, the State of Maryland provided a $300,000 challenge grant to increase participation in the program (it is now at forty-five) and extend it to all four years. The funding will increase annually for several years provided that certain performance objectives and metrics are reached.

For Anderson, a woman of color, issues of recognition are critical to historically marginalized groups. Speaking of the DeSousa-Brent scholars, she notes that students from groups traditionally underrepresented in higher education require two kinds of recognition. The first is to be recognized as full members of the college community, which is to say, to be seen as intelligent individuals rather than as stereotypes. The second kind is self-recognition so that the students have a clear sense of their strengths. This self-acknowledgment proves difficult, Anderson believes, because students lose confidence when they perceive themselves to be seen through the lens of stereotypes.

One consultant to the program is Dr. Angela Johnson, a member of the educational studies department who has published articles in a wide range of scholarly journals about why minority women, including very smart women, often underperform in college science classes. Johnson has concluded that although the DeSousa-Brent scholars enter St. Mary's at a disadvantage, eventually they do catch up to the rest of their class. Confirming Johnson's perception, Anderson points out that, while the DeSousa-Brent scholars often enter St. Mary's with SAT scores below 1000, roughly one-third go on to earn grade point averages of 3.0 or better, some as early as their first semester of college.[9]

To foster such success, however, the college has had to assemble faculty and staff who believe in the mission of the program. The summer bridge program has evolved so that now the students receive help in writing and in the sciences. A twelve-hour biology boot camp prepares students for a notoriously difficult introductory class. Students also work with the library staff to research topics in conjunction with the college's summer reading, receive coaching at the Writing Center in drafting an essay on the book, and meet with librarians and faculty across the disciplines to discuss the essay. When school begins, the Writing Center knows which classes the students are taking and works in conjunction with their professors to help them produce successful essays.

Whether it leads to new and imaginative ways of reaching out to the community or to students, the public liberal arts ideal is proving a rich and stimulating context for faculty. I can thank this environment for my own current project, a blog with daily posts that explore the intersections between literature and life.

To put my blog in a larger framework, I look back to the so-called culture wars of the late 1980s and early 1990s. I was distressed at the time by how such public figures as Secretary of Education Bill Bennett and National Endowment for the Humanities chair Lynn Cheney had conscripted literary classics as enemy combatants in the battle against multiculturalism, postmodernism, and popular culture. "Austen, Not Alice Walker" was a slogan that some bandied about, and leftie humanities professors were regarded as the barbarians at the gates—or rather, within the gates—threatening to overthrow Western civilization and Judeo-Christian values. But while I objected to the ways that literature was being reduced to right-wing talking points, and while I noted the rich multicultural dialogues occurring in literary classics such as, say, *Sir Gawain and the Green Knight*, I liked the way that literature had been elevated to a place in the national discourse. Better this than being relegated to dusty museum shelves. Thus began my decades-long project to raise literature's visibility and esteem in the public eye. I just needed to find imaginative ways to reach people who were not in college.

At one point I wrote a book with the self-help-sounding title, "Better Living through *Beowulf*: How the Early British Classics Can Guide You beyond Terrorism Fears, Relationship Anxieties, Consumer Emptiness, Racial Tension, Political Cynicism, and Other Contemporary Challenges." In the book I included chapters on *Beowulf*, *Sir Gawain*, Chaucer's *Wife of Bath*, Christopher Marlow's *Doctor Faustus*, Shakespeare's *Twelfth Night*, Aphra Behn's *Oroonoko*, Jonathan Swift's *Gulliver's Travels*, Alexander Pope's *Rape of the Lock*, and Jane Austen's *Pride and Prejudice*. In addition to showing how the works addressed issues that are still with us, I also included such tongue-in-cheek exercises as "The Faustus Guide for Soul-Selling," "Shakespeare's Travel Tips for Crossing the Great Gender Divide," and "Ask Jane: Advice for Lovers." English teachers will do anything to get students to engage with literature, and this was my attempt to get others to engage as well. A general hunger for substantive literary experience is what turned Seamus Heaney's translation of *Beowulf* into a best seller, and I thought of my book as a way to get readers to return to other classics. I also suspected that not everyone successfully read *Beowulf* after purchasing it and figured that a guide such as mine might help them with the elliptical language, the digressions, and the flashbacks.

"Better Living through *Beowulf*" (the manuscript's working title) was accepted by a small but elegant publisher and was due to come out in 2009, only to be put on indefinite hold by the recession. My son, who works in marketing, offered to design a blog where I could achieve some of the same ends. I borrowed my book's title, added "How Classic Literature Can Change Your Life," and took up the challenge.

Better Living through Beowulf has extended my teaching mission in ways I could not have dreamed. During the school year, the blog receives ten to twenty thousand different visitors a month. On Monday through Friday, the topic is open while on Saturday I apply literature to the world of sports. On Sunday I apply it to spiritual matters.

Sometimes I write about how I myself have used literature to negotiate life issues, whether facing up to racist bullying as a child (*Huckleberry Finn* was an important work), dealing with the death of loved ones, working with aging parents, experiencing the joy of grandchildren, attending reunions, or even handling small matters like the end-of-semester crunch or attending reunions. Sometimes I write about contemporary political controversies and debates. Sometimes I recount what various works of literature have meant to my students (always with their permission), and I must have a dozen posts on how different young people have responded to Jane Austen's novels. I also use posts to think through the preparation of courses and teaching difficulties. Often my students and former students read the blog and give me feedback.

Many of my readers are high school English teachers looking for inspiration and attempting to stay positive in the face of constant testing and Common Core State Standards. Other readers are people who felt alienated by English classes in college and are using the blog to find their way back to literature. I have readers from as far away as Uganda and Slovenia who regularly write in with comments.

On occasion, posts have been picked up by people who disseminate them to a wider audience, causing unexpected spikes in readership. Prior to the 2010 Super Bowl, the ESPN online magazine linked to a column about how Indianapolis Colts coach Jim Caldwell, a former English major, inspires his players through poetry (most notably William Ernest Henley's "Invictus"). When I criticized an article comparing conservative talk show host Laura Ingraham to Jonathan Swift (unlike Ingraham, I argued, Swift was willing to satirize himself), my post appeared in a compilation of articles about Ingraham. A post critiquing the artistic poverty of Ayn Rand's *Atlas Shrugged* found its way into an online libertarian newsletter.

Because of the blog, my classroom has expanded exponentially. It is as though I have been able to take literature from the ivory tower and out into the trenches. It may well be that I would feel moved to pursue this project even if I were not teaching at a public liberal arts college, but the blog feels like a natural extension of what I already do. If escalating costs in an era of growing income disparity mean that only the wealthy and a few scholarship students can afford a liberal arts education, then it is up to faculty to figure out new ways of reaching the general public. If, in the process, we find ourselves confronted with Gradgrindism and the belief that the humanities are superfluous, then we must become imaginative as we make our case. Fortunately, those teaching at public liberal arts colleges already have a lot of practice doing so.

Works Cited

Anderson, Sybol. *Hegel's Theory of Recognition: From Oppression to Ethical Liberal Modernity.* London: Continuum, 2009.

Bates, Robin. *How* Beowulf *Can Save America: An Epic Hero's Guide to Defeating the Politics of Rage.* New York: Discovering Oz Press, 2012.

Benjamin, Walter. "Theses on the Philosophy of History." In Benjamin, *Illuminations,* translated by Harry Zohn, 253–64. New York: Harcourt, Brace and World, 1968.

Fish, Stanley. "Will the Humanities Save Us?" *New York Times,* January 6, 2008, accessed July 1, 2013. opinionator.blogs.nytimes.com/2008/01/06/will-the-humanities-save-us.

Gramsci, Antonio. "The Formation of Intellectuals." In *The Modern Prince and Other Writings,* translated by Louis Marks, 118–25. New York: International Publishers, 1957.

Jauss, Hans Robert. "Literary History as a Challenge to Literary Theory." Translated by Elizabeth Benzinger. *New Literary History* 2, no. 1 (Autumn 1970): 7–37.

Strauss, Rebecca. "The Great Divide: Schooling Ourselves in an Unequal America." *New York Times,* June 16, 2013, accessed July 1, 2013. opinionator.blogs.nytimes .com/2013/06/16/schooling-ourselves-in-an-unequal-america/?hp.

Notes

1. Strauss, "The Great Divide."

2. Ibid.

3. Gramsci, "Formation of Intellectuals."

4. Jauss, "Literary History as a Challenge to Literary Theory," 13.

5. Bates, *How* Beowulf *Can Save America*, 18.

6. Benjamin, "Theses on the Philosophy of History," 257.

7. Fish, "Will the Humanities Save Us?"

8. Anderson, *Hegel's Theory of Recognition*.

9. These comments were made to the author in conversation.

Afterword
The Road Taken
and the Difference It Makes

Joseph Urgo

Senior Fellow, Association of American Colleges and
Universities, University of North Carolina Asheville

> Your work becomes your personal life. You are not much good
> until it does.
> —Willa Cather, *The Song of the Lark*

There is considerable angst in the essays in *Roads Taken*. There is considerable joy as well, expressions of pleasure for having lived what many characterize as an integrated life on the faculty of a public liberal arts college. My
epigraph is spoken by Cather's Thea Kronborg, an artist who emerges from
a small midwestern American town to achieve fame as an opera singer. Her
words speak twice to the testimonies in this volume. On the positive side,
they reflect the sense held by many of the professors that their careers at
public liberal arts colleges are perfectly balanced—with sufficient emphasis
on research to remain current in their fields and to model scholarly pursuit
to their students, and sufficient emphasis on undergraduate teaching to
make a real difference in the lives of the men and women who populate
their classrooms. On the other hand, the angst expressed in these testimonials, reflecting the claustrophobia that often comes to cosmopolitan
minds in small-town or rural settings, is equally articulated. The sense that
life—culture, the arts, professional currents—is happening elsewhere and
may not always be compensated for by the wholeness of a self-contained
professional experience. The struggle to make a full life in a small place is

what produces, for some, at times, an experience that is, in fact, "not much good." On balance, however, it's the struggle that makes these professors so effective and makes the colleges represented in this collection so vital to higher education in North America today. And as Cather has documented so thoroughly in her work, ambivalence toward remoteness fuels creative energies and often, through its struggle, serves as an incubator for future achievement.

The Council of Public Liberal Arts Colleges was established in 1987 and today it "advances the aims of its member institutions and drives awareness of the value of high-quality, public liberal arts education in a student-centered, residential environment." There are twenty-seven member colleges and universities that have earned a place with COPLAC. According to its mission statement, "COPLAC represents a distinguished sector in higher education. Some campuses have received designation from their state legislatures or public university systems as the state's public liberal arts college or the public honors college for the liberal arts. Others have carved out a less formal but no less visible role as such in their states or province" (http://www.coplac.org/about/mission.php).

The concept of a liberal arts education exists in the popular imagination in two diametrically opposed scenarios. One is as an expression of privilege, as the curriculum that informs selective, private liberal arts colleges. In this scenario, the liberal arts seem akin to wealth, as private property, the purview of privileged young people from equally well-educated families. Yes, everyone has heard about financial aid and the golden ring of a free ride—but to working-class families and first-generation college families, that's more like winning the lottery than something to be planned for and anticipated. The other scenario that showcases the liberal arts is in the general education portion of the university or community college curriculum. Academically passive or career-focused students often consider these courses to be hurdles, "required courses" that must be endured (and passed) in order to get to one's pre-professional major. Professors, themselves men and women of privilege, create the courses that make up these requirements and they are always explaining how good the content is for you in abstract language about being well-rounded and possessing breadth. If what you want most of all is a job, this material would seem, again, best suited for students of leisure.

But it is in no one's interest—perhaps least of all the wealthy classes—for the liberal arts to be considered private (and high-priced) property or to serve solely as some kind of gateway to the practical skills one needs to possess to find employment. As successful as the residential liberal arts college model has been in North American higher education (so much so that it has become an object of global emulation), its association with wealth and privilege has tarnished by association the liberal arts curriculum in the public imagination. Accusations that the liberal arts are "irrelevant," or that they are best seen as "luxury" studies, or that they do not "produce" or "work," are the same accusations that are leveled against the privileged few by working classes. In the public imagination the liberal arts and the wealthy classes exist within a rarefied continuum. It's this continuum that results in such vehement arguments against the liberal arts by politicians seeking populist credentials or by well-meaning educators who want to protect average students from falsely identifying with privilege or setting their sights too high.

It is the shared mission of COPLAC institutions to roll against this tide and to provide a liberal arts education—understood as the entryway to advanced study, graduate work, and positions of long-term influence and consequence—in a public setting. In short, these institutions are committed to class mobility. COPLAC institutions understand that they serve a small segment of the college-going population, but they also know that this segment will assume greater responsibilities in society because of skills and habits of mind that they will gather through a liberal arts and sciences curriculum. Some highly motivated students are simply put off by the idea of a private school education, but at the same time, they possess the capacity and the desire to be challenged by the rigor of an academic field of study in a residential liberal arts setting. These students will never be in the majority—the vast majority of students in North American colleges and universities are seeking credentials for work and see education as a means to an end. Students who pursue a liberal arts education are attracted to ideas and to abstract, cognitive challenges. They often enter into collaborative, academic partnerships with faculty and they seek research opportunities as undergraduates. And many of them will become, in numbers disproportionate to their share of the student population, leaders in their fields, often going on to graduate school for advanced study.

For this model to work, of course, we need faculty members willing to make careers at institutions off the main traveled road of higher education. The challenge is considerable. To begin with, very few graduate faculty will have had any experience in this sector of higher education. The prevailing system of academic status leads most graduate faculty to hold such institutions if not in contempt, then certainly in low regard. We see reflected in a number of the testimonials in this volume the fact that graduate training offers little or no preparation for careers at public liberal arts colleges. Most faculty members pursued graduate study and became professors because they wanted to emulate their mentors; likewise, graduate faculty pride themselves on producing PhDs who go on to careers in which they continue intellectual projects that had their start in graduate seminars and research laboratories. In this context, the road taken by the new PhD reflects directly the successes of the mentor. There's nothing wrong with this scenario until it bumps up against the affiliation biases of many graduate faculty.

If we put the needs of undergraduates first, the placement of our best faculty in teaching-intensive environments ought to be counted as a pedagogical achievement. A common thread in these essays is that, in the absence of graduate students, faculty look to undergraduates as research partners and intellectual collaborators. Graduate students at research institutions demand an enormous amount of time from faculty and have as their chief ambition to complete their own program of research. Undergraduates at these institutions are often taught by graduate assistants and compete for faculty mentorship with their graduate student instructors. At a liberal arts college, faculty expectations for undergraduate performance are raised exponentially, and it is not uncommon for juniors and seniors to be doing graduate-level work in labs, studios, and independent research projects. As all good teachers know, the best students will rise to the level of expectation, and students at liberal arts colleges are held to the highest standards because faculty need them to do so. As a result, a residential liberal arts college resembles what Joel Sipress at the University of Wisconsin–Superior calls "a common community of learners," without the exclusionary hierarchy of students (doctoral, master's, baccalaureate) characteristic of universities.

Because undergraduate students at liberal arts colleges are vital to the intellectual work of the faculty, the student experience will always be at the center of the mission of these institutions. And because the student experience forms the core of the mission, faculty members will be called upon, on a daily basis in and out of the classroom, to communicate complex ideas and concepts in language understandable to the world beyond that of their professional peers and colleagues. It is the constancy of this experience, for example, that undergirds the blog project taken on by Robin Bates at St. Mary's College of Maryland, *Better Living Through* Beowulf, explaining the practical value of the literary arts. It is seen as well throughout the numerous examples of student-faculty collaborations described in these essays, taking up faculty time and energy that, in another setting, would be called upon to meet graduate demands. The precocious students who are attracted to the life of the mind that so thoroughly informs a residential liberal arts college are in turn given opportunities for collaboration, leadership, and a role in institutional governance that rivals their classroom experiences for educational value.

Most of the faculty whose voices inform this volume have chosen (or landed in) career paths at variance from what they had envisioned and, in some cases, deeply desired. As Therese Seibert at Keene State reflects, education has a way of derailing (or, perhaps, jump-railing) the best-made plans of students—graduate and undergraduate alike. Such faculty experiences are, of course, of tremendous value in their role as undergraduate mentors, guiding students, many of whom are undergoing transformative experiences as they become immersed in the new worlds of ideas and opportunities. Nothing teaches so powerfully as empathy, with its complete distance from condescension or intimidation. Faculty at public liberal arts colleges can take their students into the unexpected because they've been there; in fact, many of them *are* there.

Furthermore, it is the very nature of their work with precocious undergraduates that has kept many of these faculty members intellectually vital—the daily work is, in a word, satisfying. The testimonies in this volume emerge from lives lived by some of the contemporary era's most dedicated educators. While some struggle with working conditions, insufficient resources, and remote locations, all share a commitment to collaborative undergraduate learning, and all share in the conviction that at its essence, life is a social, learning experience and education is its nutrient. A sense of a shared mission permeates these essays, a mission that is not alien to the work that one does day to day, in the classroom, in the lab, in the field, but that fully informs the spirit, the content, and the sense of purpose that move that mission from abstraction to execution. Too few in any profession today are fortunate enough to be able to say that their working life brings such personal satisfaction; too few students benefit by the inspiration that such lives are capable of providing. The blending of personal and professional satisfaction makes for good living—and good work.

Public liberal arts colleges are higher education's gems, pursuing a vital purpose as they provide the setting to fulfill the ambitions of some of our most promising young people. And by claiming the liberal arts and sciences for the public trust, the faculty at these institutions profess the centrality of deep learning and intellectual vitality to the health and well-being of our collective future. All of the COPLAC schools have strong civic engagement components and are guided by missions pledged to strengthening democratic structures and community organizations. Many have curricular requirements in the realm of service learning and other community-focused academic purposes. Again, contra-trend, these colleges are seeking to reestablish the obligation of an educated citizenry to engage in public affairs for progressive change. The testimonies in *Roads Taken* represent the power of the individual voice and the difference that can be made by individual effort and lives of integrated commitment. What is done effectively and with conviction on a small scale has the potential, over time, to move us forward in large, encompassing ways for the good of us all.

Notes on Contributors

Robin Bates teaches English at St. Mary's College of Maryland. He has twice received Fulbright awards to teach in Slovenia, has published articles on *Citizen Kane, Rules of the Game,* and *Jonah, Who Will Be 25 in the Year 2000,* and is the author of *How* Beowulf *Can Save America: An Epic Hero's Guide to Defeating the Politics of Rage* (2012). He also writes daily on his blog *Better Living through* Beowulf: *How Great Literature Can Change Your Life.*

After receiving degrees in philosophy from Harvard, Johns Hopkins, the Jewish Theological Seminary, and Penn, **Jonathan Cohen** was happy to find an academic position in a small town in west-central Maine, halfway between the coast and big ski resorts. Love for a small public liberal arts college called the University of Maine at Farmington, followed later. He has taught everything from Critical Thinking, to Consciousness and Existence, and has published/presented work on Plato, Aristotle, Rabbi Akiba, Locke, Nietzsche, Buber, the Beach Boys, Thomas Nagel, and Bruce Springsteen. His book *Science, Culture, and Free Spirits: A Study of Nietzsche's Human, All-Too-Human* was published in 2009.

Julia DeLancey is professor of art (art history) at Truman State University in Kirksville, Missouri. She earned her BA in the history of art (honors) from the University of Michigan, and her PhD, also in the history of art, from the University of St. Andrews in Scotland. At Truman, she has received the Educator of the Year award and an Allen Fellowship for Faculty Excellence. Her scholarship focuses on artists' materials in Renaissance Florence and Venice, although she is also working on a secondary project on Leonardo da Vinci's anatomical studies.

Roger Epp is professor of political science at the University of Alberta, Edmonton, Canada. During more than two decades at what is now the University's Augustana Campus, he received its teaching award and served as its head from 2004 to 2011. Under his leadership, Augustana became COPLAC's first Canadian member. As a public scholar his work includes

We Are All Treaty People: Prairie Essays (2008), a radio documentary on rural Canada, and articles in such diverse venues as *Inside Higher Ed*, the literary magazine *Geist*, the *Small Farmer's Journal*, and academic journals including the *Review of International Studies*.

As an associate professor of English at the University of Minnesota, Morris, **Janet Schrunk Ericksen** annually devotes time to teaching students that Shakespeare did not write in Old English and that medieval literature remains well worth reading. Her regular courses include first-year writing, early British literature, Old English and various other medieval literature courses, as well as the history of the English language and modern grammar. Her research focuses on Anglo-Saxon literature and culture, with emphasis on reading practices, religious poetry and narrative, and with additional work on Old Norse–Icelandic literature.

Kathleen S. Fine-Dare received her PhD at University of Illinois at Urbana-Champaign. She is professor of anthropology and gender/women's studies and affiliated professor of Native American and indigenous studies at Fort Lewis College in Durango, Colorado. She will serve as president of the Fort Lewis College Faculty Senate beginning in the fall 2014 term. In 2009 she received the Roger Peters Distinguished Professor award for excellence in teaching, scholarship, and service. She is the author of *Grave Injustice: The American Indian Repatriation Movement and NAGPRA* (2002) and co-editor/author of *Border Crossings: Transnational Americanist Anthropology* (2009). She is currently writing a book based on more than twenty years of research on performance and indigeneity in Quito, Ecuador.

Dylan Fischer is a faculty member at The Evergreen State College where he teaches Forest ecology and manages the Evergreen Field and Ecosystem Ecology Lab. He received his BS in environmental science and botany from Oregon State University. He received his MS and his PhD in forest science from Northern Arizona University. His research in ecosystem ecology addresses linkages between plant diversity, genetics, and ecosystem function.

Ellen Holmes Pearson is an associate professor of history at the University of North Carolina Asheville. She received a BA in history from Spring Hill College, an MA in history from the University of New Orleans, and a PhD in early American history from The Johns Hopkins University. She is the author of *Remaking Custom: Law and Identity in the Early American Republic* (2011) and numerous articles on early American legal culture. In her free time, she gardens and supports the arts and animals of Madison County.

Lee Rozelle is an associate professor of English at the University of Montevallo in central Alabama. He is the author of *Ecosublime: Environmental Awe and Terror from New World to Oddworld* (2006) as well as scholarly articles in journals such as *Twentieth-Century Literature* and *Studies in the Novel*. Currently, he co-coordinates the University of Montevallo's Environmental Studies Program and the University Sustainability Committee.

Milton Schlosser is professor of music at the University of Alberta's Augustana Campus located in Camrose, Alberta, Canada. He has resided in Camrose during his twenty-eight years of university employment where he has distinguished himself as a concert pianist, recording artist, lecturer, and researcher. He was awarded a McCalla Professorship in 2007 as universitywide recognition of his significant contributions to research, teaching, and learning. His most recent recording is *1890*, which includes a work composed by a former student, a Métis, to commemorate the nineteenth-century Blackfoot leader Crowfoot.

M. Therese Seibert joined Keene State College in 1998 with a PhD in sociology from the University of Texas in Austin. She is a strong advocate for community-based research; her students have produced numerous reports for local agencies, assisted with post-Katrina recovery in New Orleans, participated in Peace Building Institutes in Rwanda, and received undergraduate research grants. In 2007, she received the Distinguished Teacher Award. Her early research on race and gender inequality resulted in the monograph *Long Time Coming* co-authored with Mark Fossett and several academic articles. Her current research is on rescue during the Rwandan genocide.

Joel M. Sipress is a professor of history and chair of the interdisciplinary Department of Social Inquiry at the University of Wisconsin–Superior. He received his PhD in U.S. history from the University of North Carolina at Chapel Hill, where his studies emphasized the American South. He teaches broadly in U.S. and Latin American history and has published both on the history of the American South and on issues of teaching and learning within the discipline of history.

Bill Spellman is director of the Council of Public Liberal Arts Colleges and professor of history at the University of North Carolina Asheville, where he has also served as dean of Humanities. His most recent publications include *A Short History of Western Political Thought* (2011) and *Uncertain Identity: International Migration since 1945* (2008). He is also coauthor of a college textbook recently released in a third edition titled *The West: A Narrative History*, 2 vols. (2012).

Gary Towsley was born in western New York many years ago and has spent all but four years of his life in the region. His love of mathematics began in kindergarten. It led to a PhD in the subject and a long teaching career, thirty-nine years and counting, at the State University of New York at Geneseo. He is the recipient of the Mathematics Association of America's Haimo Award for Distinguished Teaching and has been named by the *Princeton Review* as one of America's 300 Best Professors.

Quan Tran has been an assistant professor of mathematics at the University of Science and Arts of Oklahoma since the fall of 2011. He received a bachelor's degree in computer science in 2002 and a doctorate degree in mathematics in 2011, both from the University of Oklahoma. His research interests lie in areas of geometry, particularly geometric group theory, geometric algorithms and computations, as well as areas of mathematics where mathematics intersects the visual arts.

Jeffrey Trawick-Smith is Phyllis Waite Endowed Chair and Distinguished Professsor of Early Childhood Education at Eastern Connecticut State University. He has authored or edited five books and over fifty articles— most related to young children's culture, play, and teacher-child classroom interactions. His most recent book, *Early Childhood Development: A Multicultural Perspective*, is published in numerous languages and is read throughout the world. He has conducted and presented the findings of eleven empirical studies with undergraduate students. He was a preschool and kindergarten teacher for many years.

Joseph Urgo is a senior fellow at the Association of American Colleges and Universities, in residence at the University of North Carolina Asheville. He has served in the public and private sectors, as president of St. Mary's College of Maryland (2010–2013), VPAA/dean of faculty at Hamilton College (2006–2010), and chair of the Department of English at University of

Mississippi (2000–2006). He came through the professorial ranks at Bryant University. He has published widely on the liberal arts, on humanities education, and most recently contributed a chapter in *Higher Education Leadership in Times of Crisis* (American Council on Education).

Jill Wicknick is associate professor of biology at University of Montevallo. She teaches ecology, behavior, and zoology, often while standing in a creek wearing waders. Her research focuses on the behavioral ecology, evolution, and conservation of salamanders, lizards, beetles, and spiders. She is faculty advisor for the Environmental Club and the Organic Community Garden, and co-coordinates the environmental studies minor and the Sustainability Committee.